W
FOR TODAY 1997
Notes on Bible Readings

Matthew's gospel

HBRA
INTERNATIONAL BIBLE READING ASSOCIATION

Cover photograph – The Image Bank
Easter Sunday in Jerusalem
Editor – Maureen Edwards

Published by:
The International Bible Reading Association
1020 Bristol Road
Selly Oak
Birmingham
B29 6LB

Charity No 211542

ISBN 0-7197-0866-4
ISSN 0140-8275

Typeset by Avonset, Midsomer Norton, Bath, Avon
Printed and bound in Great Britain by
BPC Paperbacks Ltd, Aylesbury, Bucks

CONTENTS

EDITORIAL

Introducing the Gospel of Matthew

Many of our themes this year are based on Matthew's Gospel. The author (most likely a second-generation Jewish Christian) has a strong pastoral concern for a Christian community (probably in Syria) which is facing some crucial questions about its calling and mission. Must they cut themselves off from their Jewish roots? What does discipleship mean apart from the physical presence of Jesus? How should they see their mission to the Gentiles in relation to their mission to their own people? Who was Jesus? What did he say about the place of the *Torah* (the Law) in their lives?

The author sets out to affirm his readers in this crisis of identity, and assures them from the words of Jesus, that no detail of the Law or Prophets – the heart of Judaism – is without significance (5.17-20). Jesus is the fulfilment of the promises made through their tradition. This Gospel carries far more Old Testament quotations than the other Gospels. The 'family tree' and story of Jesus' birth in chapters 1 and 2 emphasize his Jewish roots. In chapters 5 to 7, known as the 'Sermon on the Mount', Jesus is the new Moses delivering a new Law. But he is more than Moses, for the command to love our enemies – to break down the barriers that divide people – is central. And what he teaches, he also practises. Matthew encourages his readers to appreciate their Jewish roots but also to look beyond them to the universal nature of the Kingdom.

He tells of Gentiles who come to Jesus: the magi, the centurion ... The gospel will be preached to 'all nations' (24.14) and it is in Galilee (land inhabited by both Jews and Gentiles) where the Twelve are commanded to 'disciple' (not convert!) the nations (28.16-20).

The Kingdom in Matthew is often linked in the Greek text with *dikaiosyne* – translated 'righteousness' or 'justice' (6.33). We will not be happy unless we 'hunger and thirst' for it (5.6), see that justice is done, the hungry fed and the lonely cared for (25.31-46). To do this is an act of devotion to God, evidence of discipleship – 'following Christ'.

The writer strongly dislikes hypocrisy which he sees not merely as pretence, but an actual expression of evil (23.25-38). On the other hand, genuine disciples are challenged to bear good fruit (3.8; 7.16-20; 21.33-46); to be 'the salt of the earth', 'the light of the world' (5.13-16).

The Bible comes alive

What I enjoy most in my task as Editor of this book is the opportunity it provides to learn what the Word of God means to writers from places as far apart and different as Brazil, Fiji, Israel, India, the Philippines, Hong Kong, the Caribbean, the USA and many more. Each brings new facets of truth about God, that arise out of the amazing ways in which God is revealed through the variety of the world's cultures – all a part of God's creation. Coming from different social and political backgrounds means that we have much to share about how we experience God's presence in times of suffering and joy, despair and hope ...

This year, two writers from Hong Kong, Lee Ching Chee and Ralph Lee, reflect on God's Word in the context of their country's changing political scene. An Indian writer, Victor Premasagar, invites us to celebrate the 50th Anniversary of the Church of South India and to learn from his people how different Christian traditions can come together to serve God as one Church. Ebere Nze of Nigeria shares insights from African family life. Jean Vanier, well-known founder of L'Arche, shares insights that arise out of working with broken and marginalized people whose lives have been transformed by living in loving communities. Terrence Fernando speaks to us from a country torn apart by ethnic differences. Malcolm Weisman, a Rabbi of the Orthodox tradition, helps us to learn from insights that come from the many Jewish festivals as we prepare to celebrate Christmas. These are just a few examples. There are many more.

And so the Word of God springs to life in new and surprising ways as we open our minds and are excited by the breadth and magnificence of God's vision of the Kingdom which embraces the whole earth and its peoples. And in a world where so many of the innocent suffer, it must surely be God's design that we share one another's joy and sorrow – 'to rejoice with those who rejoice' and 'to weep with those who weep'. I hope above all that the coming together of these contributions is an expression of our solidarity and prayers for one another.

Kirsten Edwards

MORNING PRAYERS

Loving God, as a new day dawns,
the shadows of yesterday
and deep darkness of night disperse.
You did not forsake us;
you were in the loneliness,
uncertainty, separation, self-pity ...
You shared our brokenness,
pain and disappointment,
so that in despair we found hope
and were made whole by your love.
We praise you, for in the wilderness
you filled us with the peace of your presence.

Renew and deepen our trust in you.
Cleanse us of all evil
so that our love for you and one another may grow
and make us want to do your will today and everyday
for your Kingdom's sake. Amen   *Maureen Edwards*

Lord, if this day you have to correct us,
Put us right, not out of anger
But with a mother and father's love.
So may we, your children,
be kept free of falseness and foolishness.   *Mexico*

Lord! Give us weak eyes for things which are of no account and
clear eyes for all Thy truth.
                Soren Kierkegaard (1813-55) Denmark

O God, we pray you, fill your servants with your Holy
Spirit, that the works we undertake may be redemptive, our
words prophetic and our worship meaningful. Inspire us
with your love, challenge us with your truth and empower
us with your strength.
                Mercy A Oduyoye, Ghana and World Council of Churches
                – from Oceans of Prayer (NCEC)

EVENING PRAYERS

In me there is darkness,
But with thee there is light;
I am lonely, but thou leavest me not;
I am feeble in heart, but with thee there is help;
I am restless, but with thee there is peace.
In me there is bitterness, but with thee there is patience;
I do not understand thy ways,
But thou knowest the way for me.

Dietrich Bonhoeffer, Germany (1906-1944 – From Letters and Papers from Prison, The Enlarged Edition (SCM Press 1971)

Come, Lord Jesus, be our guest, stay with us,
    for the day is ending.
Bring to our house your poverty,
For then shall we be rich.
Bring to our house your pain,
That, sharing it, we may also share your joy.
Bring to our house your understanding of us,
That we may be freed to learn more of you.
Bring to our house all those who hurry or limp behind you,
That we may meet you as the Saviour of all.
With friend, with stranger,
With neighbour and the well known ones,
Be among us this night.
For the door of our house we open,
And the doors of our hearts we leave ajar.

Iona Community, Scotland – From 'A Wee Worship Book'
© 1989 WGRG. Used by permission

A blessing

The peace of God
keep us all.
He will confirm
Our hearts in goodness.

May the Son of God
and the Holy Spirit too
one God
Bless us all.
Traditional Maori hymn, New Zealand

Ways to read the Bible

Book by book   This year there are 17 weeks when we shall be studying a book of the Bible, or part of a book. The value of this is that it helps us to understand biblical writings in their original context. We need to know what the original readers of Old and New Testament books were experiencing, the problems they faced and questions they asked. Only then can we begin to explore their relevance to us. It is good to know some books in depth and discover afresh the challenges they make to us.

Look for 'golden threads'   It is also helpful to study the Bible thematically. This is not a matter of 'flitting from flower to flower' but of discovering (as one reader put it) 'golden threads' that run through the Bible and which speak to our day. So much of the New Testament developed out of the traditions, ideas and prophecies of the Old Testament, and these are explored as we look at themes. We can also take contemporary issues and slogans and see them strikingly reflected in the Bible.

Expect to be challenged   If we always read the Bible expecting to be comforted, we will be disappointed. Words of comfort are there, but they are intertwined with many more words and stories that challenge individuals and communities to show their commitment to God by trying new things, moving out in new directions, like Abraham, Moses, the prophets, Jesus, Paul ..., all of whom knew the costly nature of their actions.

Read with others   So many Christians worldwide are discovering the value of studying the Bible in community, especially in Latin America, India, the Middle East ... IBRA is an effective way of doing this. For if each person who meets in a weekly or fortnightly fellowship has read the set passages of scripture together with the notes provided, they will come well prepared to reflect together on the theme and discuss it further. IBRA provides a book to enable leaders to help their group to do this – *Finding our Way Together* (see page 16).

Find the right time   What time of day do we set aside to read the Bible and pray? Not so early that we are barely awake, or so late that we are too tired! Choose a time when you are alert and able to think about what you read and enter into a time of prayer to hear what God is saying.

GOD OF THE NATIONS

Notes based on the Good News Bible by
Lee Ching Chee

Lee Ching Chee, a Chinese, was the first woman minister in Hong Kong, ordained in 1966 by the Hong Kong Council for The Church of Christ in China (HKCCCC). Having been both teacher and chaplain, she responded in 1977 to an invitation from the Council for World Mission (UK) to serve as Secretary for Mission Education until 1981 when she returned to Hong Kong to serve as Associate General Secretary of the HKCCCC.

Many nations throughout history have suffered for various reasons, and many more nations suffer today. God who is loving and caring allows that to happen even to those who are innocent, and people down the ages have asked a thousand 'Why?'s'. There is no easy answer, but the Answerer, who is with the sufferers, is still God of the nations.

To start the year with passages of lamentation may seem inappropriate, but people in Hong Kong who will be facing changes this year – 1997 – may find in these readings words of comfort and a source of strength. So may other readers too.

Wednesday January 1   *Isaiah 49.13-23 **
New hope springs from God's promise

As we flick over the calendar to a new year, we come face to face with the fact that our days on earth are numbered. For the people of Hong Kong, such realization had never been so real until they started the countdown to 1997 some fifteen years ago. There will certainly be mixed feelings when they wish each other a 'Happy New Year' today.

On the surface, people in Hong Kong can hardly be described as a suffering people. The change of government (in 181 days' time!) will probably take place without tumult or bloodshed. But it is not so much a political crisis as a crisis of confidence. The feeling of being abandoned is so real.

Like the exiled people of Jerusalem in this passage, we easily lose faith in God in times of desolation. It is difficult to believe that

God cares and that his love never changes. In times of helplessness, let us remember his promise: 'No-one who waits for my help will be disappointed' (verse 23).

✳ *Without hope, we have no future.*
Without future, we perish.
We need to believe in a tomorrow.
Lord, grant us hope.

Thursday January 2   *Psalm 22.1-13*
God's presence in our despair
The lonely cry of anguish at the beginning of the Psalm was quoted by Jesus on the Cross when he experienced a similar desolation of the soul brought by suffering. Mockery makes suffering unbearable and tends to minimize the faith one has. This was what happened to the Psalmist, to Job (Job 12.4) and to Jesus (Matthew 27.41-44) when these mocking questions came from enemies or friends.

Faith has its ups and downs. At times, the faithful have doubts, especially when preoccupied with discomfort or despair. 'Trouble is near, and there is no-one to help' (verse 11). This feeling is not uncommon in Hong Kong today.

What made the Psalmist, Job, and Jesus hold on to their faith was their gratitude for God's help in the past, and their realization that God was with them in their suffering. Self-pity and self-centredness only magnify our anguish. We need to notice the suffering of others, for God is *our* God – the God of the nations.

✳ *Lord, help us to be strong and confident,*
trusting in you,
for you are with us at all times and in all places.

Friday January 3   *Psalm 22.14-24*
God's grace in our sorrow
The Psalmist's description in these verses might not be what literally happened to him; he uses vivid picture language to express feelings that are real and which could not be understood by anyone outside his experience. The situation facing Hong Kong this year is not as bad as some have described, but fear is there – very real fear.

The Psalmist's change of mood so suddenly (verse 22) is somewhat strange, but such a song of praise is from the heart too.

For after a good cry in utter desolation, the disappointment, doubt and anger – which block the vision of God's presence – are lifted, and the realization of God's faithfulness and mercy enables the Psalmist to sing this song of praise. The situation hasn't changed, but the Psalmist's mood has. It is like the prophet Habbakuk, who is able to say,

> 'Even though the fig-trees have no fruit
> and no grapes grow on the vines ...
> I will still be joyful and glad
> because the Lord God is my saviour' (Habbakuk 3.17,18).

✳ *Give us your grace, God,*
to accept sorrow and suffering when they come,
and may we know the fruit of joy from the seed of tears.

Saturday January 4   *Psalm 22.25-31*

God's greatness

There is an obvious change of tone in this latter part of the Psalm when desperate petition changes to confident assertion. The Psalmist sees God, not only as his personal Saviour or the God of his people, but as Lord of all nations, the King who rules the world.

Sometimes the way we think about God and pray to him suggests that the God we actually believe in is very small. We make it look as though he is only concerned about our petty welfare needs and personal safety, especially when we are in trouble. Surely our God is much greater than that!

We pay too much attention to people or nations with power, and feel helpless and hopeless unnecessarily. Our God is a great God, a loving and just God for all people, strong and weak, rich and poor. God does not only rule but has a divine plan for the salvation of all nations. Praise the Lord!

✳ *Lord, our finite minds cannot comprehend the magnitude*
of your greatness.
Help us to remember the power of your holy name.
Grant us grace to work for the realization of your reign
of peace and justice upon the earth.

TO THINK ABOUT

Recall when you prayed silently to God at a time of great anxiety. As you reflect on this time in your life, what part did prayer play in sustaining you and offering hope?

Ponder what Dag Hammarskjold says in his book *Markings:* 'For all that has been, thanks; for all that shall be ... yes!' Can that be your prayer?

2nd Sunday after Christmas, January 5   *Isaiah 11.1-9*

God's Kingdom

What a lovely picture of a peaceful Kingdom is described here! This is only possible if the King is one who has the power to love – not one who loves power – and rules with justice and integrity.

All through history, many nations including the Israelites and Chinese have longed for such a Kingdom. Every time there is a change of government, people hope to have an ideal ruler who will bring peace for all to enjoy.

People in Hong Kong had hoped that 'One country, two systems' would be actualized so that they could enjoy peace when Hong Kong is no longer a colony, but the reality seems to be 'Two countries, one victim'. Hong Kong is caught between the United Kingdom and the Middle Kingdom (China).

The prophet foretold the coming of a new King; Jesus described the way he was going to establish the peaceful Kingdom (Luke 4.18,19). Let all nations pray that his Kingdom may come.

✳ *Lord, help us to believe your promise,*
  to look for your blessing,
  and to live under your rule.

Epiphany, January 6   *Matthew 2.1-12* *

God's coming into humanity

It is strange to think that a vulnerable, helpless little baby could upset, not only a powerful king, but a whole city. On the other hand, the sight of this powerless baby caused the learned strangers to be full of joy and respect. To King Herod, the one in power, it was a threat; to the men from the east who came to worship, it was a promise fulfilled.

God comes, not with dazzling chariot and trumpet blast, but to live in human likeness so that we may come near without fear. He comes to us without the kind of status, wealth or political power we normally recognize. That is why he is often by-passed, neglected or even rejected.

Insecurity and fear make us anxious to please the one in power, to look for power and to hold on to power. So power not only corrupts; it can also dehumanize. True security can only be found in the promise of God who comes to dwell among us, not with power, but with love.

✴ *O God, help us to see you as you are,*
to worship you as you are,
and to come to you just as we are.

Tuesday January 7   *Matthew 2.13-15 **
God gives life

Ironically, the baby Jesus, a descendant of the Israelites who fled Egypt, had to be taken to Egypt for safety's sake! He had to experience the life of a refugee.

There are so many refugees in the world today, running away to 'a safer place'. They try to escape for their lives at all costs, uprooting, settling and re-settling, with the result that kinship links and friendship ties are broken. Tens of thousands of legal and illegal immigrants experience immense suffering. In the case of Hong Kong, many came from China in the past, and now many more are leaving for North America and other countries in the West because of '1997'. These are by no means poor, but they suffer just the same.

It is natural for people to want to escape from danger or suffering, but is the escape for life? Is it an escape for a greater purpose that will unfold later on? How and where do you see God involved in this process?

✴ *Deliver us from our fear, Lord,*
and give us strength willingly to embrace suffering
for your sake.

Wednesday January 8   *Matthew 2.16-18; Jeremiah 31.15-17 **
God's mercy in tribulation

When someone's power is threatened or his authority challenged, not only does he lose his temper but all sense as well. An order to kill is issued just to make sure his own position is secure. That has happened many times through the ages. Massacres have taken place which generation after generation don't want to remember, but can't forget!

For those who suffer the loss of loved ones, there seems to be

13

no cure for the pain and no way to stop the bitter weeping. It is difficult to see any light at the end of the tunnel. In such a time of tragedy we need to hold on to our faith that God does not turn a blind eye, nor a deaf ear, to our cry of dereliction. He is with us and his mercy endures forever.

God alone can take away our loneliness, conquer despair and impart hope. With him, suffering can be meaningful, survivable and transcend-able.

✳ *Help us, God, to develop that trust*
which will keep us faithful when trial and testing come
and when your presence is hidden from us.

Thursday January 9   *Matthew 2.19-23*

God's guiding hand

The whole episode of the holy family travelling from Judah to Egypt and back to Nazareth was under God guidance. Joseph, alert to God's leading, responded with utter obedience in making journeys which were by no means easy.

In the context of Hebrew culture, God's direction was given to Joseph in a dream. People of other cultures today might say that God offers guidance through something or someone else. But so often we only recognize it as God's guidance if it fits our own plans, and then we use God as an excuse for choices of our own liking.

Many people have left or are leaving Hong Kong 'under God's guidance', they claim. But God's guidance rarely leads us along an easy path. We need to surrender ourselves completely to God's will. This is better than any known way.

✳ *Lord, in the midst of confusion*
and when we have lost sight of life's direction,
create in us a deeper awareness of your presence
and a clearer vision of your guiding hand.

Friday January 10   *2 Corinthians 1.3-11* ✳

God – our help

In an earlier letter, Paul tried to help Christians in Corinth to take seriously the concept of the Church as 'one body' with many parts, all sharing each other's suffering and praise (1 Corinthians 12.26). In today's reading – an introduction to his next letter – he highlights two further insights:

- in gratitude for God's help or 'comfort' (RSV), we help others in a spirit of stewardship, and
- we rely on God and place our hope in him alone.

Some churches in Hong Kong have tried to learn that lesson of sharing in recent years, to share and support churches in need, not only in Hong Kong but also churches in China.

Hong Kong churches need to be reminded too that we should rely only on God, to place our hope in him, not in stocks and shares, or entry permits to migrate to other countries. We need to hold on to our faith in God, who is merciful and kind.

✻ *Help us to learn the depths of your love in our own hearts,*
  so that we can – with integrity and courage –
  act with love in your world.

Saturday January 11   *Romans 15.13-21* *

God – the source of courage

In Paul's time, it took great courage to proclaim the good news in places where Christ had not been heard of, to bring the Gentiles to God, and to speak the truth in love to a considerable Church like the one at Rome. Paul was able to do this because of his faith in God.

To speak boldly and honestly is not part of Chinese culture, especially when speaking to authorities, for fear of offending them or for the sake of saving their face. So people keep silent. The world is so full of injustice, not necessarily because of the number of bad people, but because too many good ones dare not speak up!

At times when things become politically complicated and ethically confused, the Church needs all the more to say boldly 'We must obey God, not men' (Acts 5.29). Such boldness comes from authentic faith. Soon, Hong Kong will no longer be a borrowed place living on borrowed time. May there be no more borrowed faith.

✻ *Lord, may your Church be humble enough*
  to play the servant role,
  and bold enough to raise the prophetic voice,
  and may we have the grace to be faithful.

TO THINK ABOUT

- Identify people, for whom you are concerned, who are enduring trials and hardships: in your family, your community, and throughout the world. Lift them up in your prayer.
- Who suffers in society today? In the Church? How is their suffering a way of restoration?

FOR ACTION

- List some ways in which your congregation can be encouraged to have more concern for the under-privileged and to participate in mission with marginal people.
- Write a prayer, or a letter of solidarity in Christ to:

The Hong Kong Christian Council
33 Granville Road
Tsimshatsui
Kowloon
Hong Kong

16

CALLED TO SERVE

Notes based on the New International Version by
Oliver Stevens

Oliver Stevens is a retired minister of the United Church of Canada, living in Beamsville, Ontario. He was also a teacher of English in High School near Montreal, and is the author of 'How Religious is God? and Other Irreverent Questions' (Wood Lake Books, 1991).

In each of these readings, someone is called to serve God and so to become part of God's everlasting life and purpose. We too are called to serve God in the way we live, the decisions and friendships we make, the hardships and disasters we may encounter, and the people we become through God's grace and help.

1st Sunday in Epiphany, January 12   *Matthew 3.13-17 **
Called to be the Christ

After the celebrations and pageantry of Christmas, it is easy to forget the obscurity in which Jesus lived for 30 years – presumably following the trade of a carpenter. But he must have been aware of the stories surrounding his birth and the birth of his cousin John.

John was called to be the forerunner of the Messiah. How was he to recognize him? The Fourth Gospel says he was given a sign (John 1.32-34). John may have shared the popular view of the Messiah as a 'Hebrew Alexander' who would drive out the Romans in a bloody revolution. Did John feel that his cousin didn't fit this expectation? See Matthew 11.2-3.

The sign that comes in verse 17, to both John and Jesus, echoes Isaiah 53, especially verses 11 and 12. Jesus was 'called', not to militarism but to call us to new life with God.

＊ *Jesus, who identified yourself with us in our sin,*
   fill us with your grace that we may always be identified
   with you in the life and love of God, for your name's
      sake.

17

Called to lead

This is one of the dramatic stories of the Bible and its sequel was a surprise to everyone, including David himself. Had we been there we would have been surprised too.

This pattern, by which God chooses to bless and use the humanly insignificant, the 'mustard seed' (cf. Mark 4.31-32) – is repeated time after time throughout Scripture, and is celebrated in the songs of Hannah (1 Samuel 2.1-10) and Mary (Luke 1.46-55). Like Jesus (in yesterday's reading) David was called from obscurity to the service of God.

As for ourselves, we may long to serve God in some *important* way, but if it is for God, then it *is* important, whether other people notice or not. For the LORD does not look at the things we look at. We look at the outward appearance, but the LORD looks at the heart (verse 7b).

✳ *Lord, create in each of us a heart like the heart of David,*
a person after your own heart,
serving you faithfully this and everyday, for Jesus' sake.

Tuesday January 14   *Matthew 4.12-17*

Called to take the stage

In moving from Nazareth to Capernaum, Jesus was to experience a radical change of lifestyle. Up to now he had been a private person; from henceforth he will be a public figure. Galilee was a strategic place to begin.

'The natural characteristics of the Galileans, and the preparation of history had made Galilee the one place in all Palestine where a new teacher and a new message had any real chance of being heard, and it was there that Jesus began His mission, and first announced His message.'
William Barclay, The Gospel of Matthew Volume 1 The Daily Bible series, Revised Edition (St Andrew Press)

Also strategic was Jesus' timing. Word came that John had been arrested. In dramatic terms, this seemed to be Jesus' cue to take John's place at centre-stage. And his message took up John's theme: 'Repent, for the Kingdom of heaven is near' (3.2). In the days to come, it was to become clear that the Kingdom is not just 'near': in Jesus, it is *present*.

* *Holy Spirit, lead us to the grace of a true repentance,*
  turning from our worldly values to the true service of
     Jesus,
  in whose name we pray.

Wednesday January 15   *Matthew 4.18-22 **
Called to follow

Sometimes I find myself in an argument with God – though I
never win! Recently, having read a heart-breaking story of
starvation and injustice, I threw down my newspaper, 'God, why
don't you do something about that?' *Silence.* 'You've made me
care, Lord? But what difference is that going to make?' And in the
silence, God said, 'Yes, that's what we're waiting to see!'

Our world, like that of the New Testament, abounds with
violent 'solutions' which generally make things worse. By
contrast, God comes in the person of Jesus and chooses to make
an impact through everyday person-to-person contacts; and to
help him do it, he calls – not an army – but fishermen. We know
from John 1.35-42 that this is not Jesus' first encounter with
Simon and Andrew. But now he comes to them and says, 'Come
lads – time to go fishing for people!' And they do. So also he
comes to you and me: to make a 'contagious difference' to the
people we are and the world we live in.

* *O God, amid the perplexities and doubts which torment*
  and divide us, open a plain path wherein we may walk
  with assurance and faith, and, despite the storms that
  may assail us, keep us strong in courage and loyal
  to Jesus Christ, our Lord.

                    Samuel Miller, Prayers for Daily Use
                    (Harper Collins, New York 1957)

Thursday January 16   *Joshua 1.1-9 (Martin Luther King Day)*
Called to journey with God

God makes no promise of a safe haven or an easy road; the
journey will be rough. What he does promise is that he will be with
us, as he was with Joshua (verse 5). Martin Luther King Jr.
discovered this too:

'Seek God and discover Him and make Him a power in your
life. Without Him all our efforts turn to ashes and our sunrises into
darkest nights. Without Him, life is a meaningless drama with the

decisive scenes missing. But with Him we are able to rise from the fatigue of despair to the buoyancy of hope. With Him, we are able to rise from the midnight of desperation to the daybreak of joy. St Augustine was right – we were made for God and we will be restless until we find our rest in Him. Love yourself if that means rational, healthy and moral self-interest. You are commanded to do that. That is the length of life. Love your neighbour as you love yourself. You are commanded to do that. That is the breadth of life. But never forget that there is a first and an even greater commandment, "Love the Lord thy God with all thy heart and all thy soul and all thy mind." This is the height of life. And when you do this you will live the complete life.'

The Words of Martin Luther
King Jr.,Coretta Scott King (Newmarket Press 1983)

✳ *We thank you God for leaders in every generation*
who have walked in the light, as you are in the light.
Give us grace to follow in their footsteps
for the sake, and by the power, of Jesus Christ our Lord.

Friday January 17   *Revelation 10.8-11 **
Called to speak for God
To think of prophecy as only fore-telling future events is to miss the point. The real prophet speaks the word God has given him which, more often than not, is a dangerous thing to do.

In this reading, the prisoner of Patmos receives the word from God, and finds it is as sweet as honey. But as it becomes part of his life, it is not *all* sweetness, which is why he is a prisoner. Yet he must speak this word clearly and compellingly to the world – its ordinary people, its nations and leaders.

We too are called to live and speak for Christ. Sometimes this will bring us comfort and reassurance. At other times it will bring pain and sacrifice. What is important is that God's word is heard.

✳ *Grant us thy peace, Lord:*
Peace in our hearts our evil thoughts assuaging,
Peace in Thy Church, where brothers are engaging
Peace when the world its busy war is waging:
    Calm Thy foes' raging.
Grant us Thy help till backward they are driven;
Grant them Thy truth, that they may be forgiven;
Grant peace on earth, and, after we have striven,
Peace in Thy heaven.   *Philip Pusey 1799-1855*

Called to freedom

'Freedom' is something we like to talk about, but few of us are good at achieving it for ourselves or others. Paul speaks of freedom as a quality of life – a quality we cannot achieve, but which we may receive as a gift from God.

Paul says, in effect: What do you want freedom for? If you want it so that you can dominate and possess the world you live in, tailoring your life and your world to your personal desires, then the more successful you are, the less free you will be. The road to real freedom is the way of surrender and service. JB Philips renders verse 23: 'Sin *pays* its servants: the wage is death. But God *gives* to those who serve him: His free gift is eternal life through Jesus Christ our Lord.'

✳ *Christ our companion,*
you came not to humiliate the sinner
but to disturb the righteous.
Welcome us when we are put to shame,
but challenge our smugness,
that we may truly turn from what is evil,
and be freed even from our virtues,
in your name, Amen.   *Janet Morley*
All Desires known (SPCK)

TO THINK ABOUT

1. Is there any situation to which God is calling you?
2. Identify the person or group with whom you feel the least inclined to relate. Write a short prayer seeking God's will and blessing for him, her, or them.

FOR ACTION

Look for a way of relating, in the name of Christ, to the person or group you have identified.

CALLED TO UNITY

Notes based on the Revised Standard Version by
P Victor Premasagar

Victor Premasagar – former Moderator of the Church of South India, writer and well-known teacher of theology – has served as pastor in rural and industrial congregations.

The Church of South India: a pilgrim Church moving towards greater unity

On 27 September 1997, the Church of South India celebrates its fiftieth anniversary. It was inaugurated in 1947, bringing together Anglicans, Methodists and members of the South India United Church (the Congregational and Presbyterian Union of 1912 and the Councils of the Basel Mission). It is not another denomination in the World Church, but a movement for the unity of all Churches in India and throughout the world.

Its emblem signals its vision and commitment to fulfil the high priestly prayer of Jesus 'That they all may be one' (John 17.20b). These words encircle the Cross and a burning bush, symbolizing a suffering and oppressed people who are assured of hope of liberation. The bush is not the wild thorny plant on the rugged Mount Sinai, but a lotus, in full bloom, opened up in all its radiance, beauty and splendour, burning and yet not consumed. The lotus, in the religious heritage of India, is the symbol of purity. It grows in muddy waters and yet is not stained or contaminated by them, like the disciples of Christ who are in the world and yet not of the world (John 17.11, 14, 16). The circle, an Indian religious symbol of completeness and righteousness, represents the fullness of life Jesus brings for all. The lotus has one further significance – God is often depicted standing on a fully open lotus flower. As the Church obeys the call of Jesus Christ to unity, it becomes the bearer of hope and life for the whole creation.

Unity as mystic bliss and for the prophetic task

While they are coming to the upper room, the disciples argue about who is the greatest among them. Jesus washes their feet and teaches them the new values of the Kingdom in which the greatest is the one who serves and not the one who sits at table (John 13.1-16). Then Jesus prays.

First, he prays that their union with God in Jesus Christ may bring them joy in all its fullness (verse 13). This mystic unity and joy remind us of the age long search of Indian religions for mystic union with the divine.

Secondly, he prays that God will protect them from the evil one, as they are sent out into the world on a prophetic mission. They will bring a prophetic critique to the dominant culture, proclaiming and working for the demands of the Kingdom of God. Conflict with evil is the inevitable result of prophetic obedience (verses 14 and 15). Both the union and the sending out reflect the relationship between the Father and the Son. This twofold emphasis is often affirmed in the saying: 'Unity and mission are two sides of the same coin.' This is a movement from being united to *doing* the mission of God.

✳ *Lord, we pray for Churches in every land,*
  that united they may engage in mission,
  sharing the good news of your love
  and working for the well being of all creation.

Unity in the name of God

Names in the biblical tradition reflect the character of the person named. Jesus makes God's name known to his disciples, so that they may unite, reflecting the nature of God in their life as the Church. Unity is for purposes that are in keeping with God's will and character. When we pray in the name of Jesus, we make sure that we do not ask for things that are contrary to his life and teaching. Unity should be for all that is positive and good, as we have come to know through the life, death and resurrection of Jesus Christ, and through the guidance of the Holy Spirit. Unity releases positive influences for peace and justice in the world.

Does your church reflect the character of Jesus Christ in its life and action? Do its programmes and priorities reflect the compassion of Jesus for the least and the lost? Does the budget of your church reflect its concern for the poor, the oppressed and the marginalized sections of the community?

✴ *Pray for the Anniversary of the Church of South India:*
  O God, who to an expectant and united Church did grant at The Pentecost the gift of the Holy Spirit and have wonderfully brought into one fold, those who now worship you here. Grant, we beseech you, the help of the same Spirit in all our life and worship, that we may expect great things from you, and attempt great things for you, and being one in you may show to the world that you did send Jesus Christ our Lord, to whom with you and the Holy Spirit, be all honour and glory, world without end. Amen. *From the Book of Common Worship of the Church of South India (© CSI)*

Tuesday January 21   *1 Corinthians 1.10-17*

Divisions in the Church – failure of leadership

Paul is appalled at the divisions in the Corinthian Church. He appeals to them not to perpetuate their differences but to be united. The divisions were probably based on the leaders of the Church as it sometimes happens in India. Paul, as a good leader, discourages sectarian groups, including those who had formed a party in his own name. Bad leaders encourage division for their own ends, though they may have worthy reasons for forming pressure groups:

● the Gentile group who claimed Paul's authority, upholding the rights and freedom of Gentile converts;
● a group following Apollos, emphasizing the baptism of John the Baptist as valid (cf. Acts 19.1-7);
● a Judaizing group perhaps emphasizing the Jewish religious and cultural heritage, and claiming Peter's authority;
● an ingenious messianic group using the very name of Christ.

Such divisions break the fellowship of the local church and are a bad witness to the gospel. Although they may have noble reasons, they often have hidden agendas to capture power and to use the resources of the church for themselves.

✴ *Lord, heal the divisions in your Church.*
  Grant that united we may witness to you,
  breaking down all barriers of caste, colour and creed.
  May our leaders foster unity and serve in all humility
  as servants of the servant Lord.

24

Signs of spiritual breakdown

Paul observes that the divisions in a Church indicate a lack of growth into a mature faith, a breakdown in the spirituality of its members. The Lord of the Church gives special tasks to the leaders who complete the tasks assigned to them, but it is God alone who effects growth. They are called to be co-workers with God, not to lead separate parties and create divisions within the Church. Members too should not allow themselves be led astray by self-seeking leaders. Each member has a responsibility to preserve unity in the local church community.

People often complain about Church leadership. Yet the level of spirituality among church members often determines the spirituality of their leaders. Christian nurture of the whole church should be given utmost importance, so that we prepare and raise committed and Spirit-filled leaders.

✳ *Deepen the spirituality of our congregations, O Lord,*
   that they may be a training ground for future leaders.
   Foster a spirit of unity that the Church may work for
   peace with justice and harmony in the world.

You are God's temple

New Testament images of the Church depict a house being built, a plant growing, or a living body increasing and growing every day as members are added to it. Here it is described as a temple being built by the leaders, called and appointed by Christ, the Lord of the Church. It is ever being built and always growing up. The Church is not static, but a living community, filled with the power of the Holy Spirit, sharing, caring for and serving one another. Leaders are to equip the faithful for service and not cause divisions and frustrate God's mission.

The Church of South India's programme **Vision for Equipping Local Congregations in Mission (VELCOM)** aims at such a focus for mission in every local congregation. There is a wealth of resources in every church – neighbourliness, accepted duties and obligations, the energy of the young, the wisdom and experience of the old, readiness to extend hospitality to newcomers, simplicity of lifestyle, the strengths of family ties. These truly Indian gifts are being developed and used.

Local congregations meet for a monthly communion service

and then sit down and take a look at the needs of every family in the village. Having identified the issues, they will ask, What is the cause and how can we help? It may be that a family does not have food because the father is out of work. They have borrowed money in previous crises and it is not possible to borrow any more. Once the church knows this, they can pray for them and give a few measures of rice. Sometimes the action required is political, to oppose an unscrupulous landlord who is exploiting a number of families in the village. Bible studies are used in these contexts to inspire and encourage local congregations to act.

When we pull together, we can be a strong Church, not in ability or riches, but in sharing what we have. That type of Church growth can bring change to our country and the world.

✳ *Grant, O Lord, that every believer may be a living stone built into a spiritual house upon Jesus the cornerstone, and in unity, serve and witness to the power of your love.*

Friday January 24   *Ephesians 4.1-16*

Gifts of our ascended Lord

Paul describes the diverse ministries of men and women as the gifts of the ascended Lord to his church – some as apostles, some as prophets, some as evangelists, pastors and teachers. These are gifts of the Holy Spirit for the work of the ministry, for the building up of the Church, and to foster unity in the local church. He gives different lists in Romans 12.6-8 and 1 Corinthians 12.4-11. These ministries probably differ in relation to the needs of the churches concerned. New contexts demand new ministries, but often the church continues to perpetuate the same old ministries even after the needs are no longer there.

The pattern of the threefold ministry, found in most churches under different titles, needs to be enlarged to include new ministries, to meet new needs in different countries and contexts. Ministries of development, social action, counselling and other relevant ministries need to be affirmed. In Acts 6.1-6, the writer tells how the apostles were willing to initiate a diaconal ministry to meet a local need in the Jerusalem Church. Many of the mission challenges of today go unaddressed, as there are no appropriate ministries with trained women and men to respond to them.

What new contexts do you perceive, and what new ministries would you suggest in your local church?

✳ *We praise you, O Lord, for sending down your Spirit*
upon your Church, giving diverse gifts
for strengthening your mission in every generation.

Saturday January 25   *John 15.1-17*
Abide in Christ

As we journey during the summer season in India, we see green mango groves with trees providing shade and their branches bent low to the ground by the weight of the fruits. There is often an odd tree that has only one or two fruits. It seems a waste that the tree has not borne fruit. Jesus wants his disciples to grow and develop their full potential, not just to bear one or two fruits.

The branches live and bear fruit because they are integrated parts of the vine. Once they are separated, they cannot live. The sap of the vine comes from its roots and flows into the branches giving life and sweetness to the fruit. A Christian lives and bears fruit only by being in Christ.

Fruit bearing branches are pruned so that they produce more fruit. They conserve the live sap flowing through the branch to maximize its energy and produce more fruit. Fruit is for others. The tree does not have the fruit for itself. Sadhu Sundar Singh told about the tree responding to children throwing stones at it by dropping fruit and not stones. The Christian life is one of sharing with others, even with those who hurt us.

✳ *Lord, let your life-giving power flow through me*
and bear much fruit. Let my life be a blessing to others
through abiding in you, day and night.
Prune me where you will.
Only let me overflow with your love for all.

TO THINK ABOUT and FOR ACTION

What can churches in your context learn from the experience and insights of the Church of South India? What challenges will you share with others in your congregation?

Ask your local church, through the appropriate meetings, to consider the basic principles of the CSI's VELCOM programme. Encourage Holy Communion and Bible study to become springboards for action in your church and community

---

JACOB – FLAWED YET BLESSED
Genesis 25-33

Notes based on the Hebrew text by
Jonathan Magonet

Jonathan Magonet is a Rabbi and for many years Head of the Department of Bible Studies at the Leo Baeck College, London, where he trained and where he is now Principal. He has organized for over twenty-five years an annual Jewish-Christian Bible Week in Bendorf, Germany and also a Jewish-Christian-Muslim Student Conference annually in the same location. He is the author of 'A Rabbi's Bible', 'Bible Lives' and 'A Rabbi Reads The Psalms' – all published by SCM Press, London.

The stories of Jacob are so rich in material, and the cycles of stories so cohesive, that it is difficult to extract individual passages and treat them in isolation. On one level we have the typical biblical emphasis on the journey of a flawed hero towards a kind of self-discovery. On another, like the cycle of Abraham stories, God's plan is interrupted by mistaken human initiatives (Abraham takes Hagar and has Ishmael, the wrong son who has to be sent away so that Isaac can inherit; Rebecca's misreading of Isaac's blessing sends Jacob away for twenty years into exile before he can return to the land). So the tension between human freedom and divine providence is magnificently expressed, and the awareness of how little we understand, at the time of our actions, of what is really at stake!

I have used the original Hebrew text of the Bible and made my own translations, though consulting a number of different versions. Unfortunately all translations lose the word-plays and interconnections of words that are present in the Hebrew text, so it is helpful to become aware of these.

FURTHER READING

For a thorough treatment of the cycle as a whole, see Jan Fokkelman's *Narrative Art in Genesis* (Reprinted by Sheffield Academic Press 1991).

---

a. I shall bring you back

Beneath the surface

There are enough themes in this section to keep a family therapist in business for months with the family of Mr and Mrs Isaac. Father Isaac, who submitted to his own father Abraham's attempt to sacrifice him, and who emerges from the Bible stories as a quiet contemplative figure, prefers his son Esau the hunter – though ostensibly for external reasons, the venison he provides. Rebecca's love for Jacob has no labels attached to it.

Rebecca has had a revelation from God about the respective fates of her two sons. But it is not clear whether she tells her husband about this. Certainly, by the time Isaac will wish to bless his eldest son, Rebecca only seems to know about it by eavesdropping on their conversation (27.5). Somehow, communications have broken down and disaster follows.

As the Rabbis expressed it: If love depends on some selfish cause, when the cause disappears, love disappears; but if love does not depend on a selfish cause it will never disappear.

✳ *As for me, let my prayer come before You at the proper time.*
Answer me God, in the greatness of Your love,
for Your deliverance is sure.   *Psalm 69.13*

Deception

The twists and turns of this family drama are uncomfortable. It is bad enough that Rebecca tells her beloved son Jacob to cheat his father – but his first response is not horror at the suggestion but fear at being caught.

What motivates Rebecca? Possibly a misunderstanding of what Isaac has in mind. It is always important to pick up small changes in language when something is repeated in the Bible. In verse 4 Isaac says to Esau: 'so that my soul may bless you before I die.' Rebecca tells Jacob that he said: 'I will bless you *before the Eternal* before my death.' The additional words suggest that Rebecca thinks that what Isaac has in mind is the Abrahamic blessing – to be fruitful and multiply and be a great nation. Instead (as verse 28 shows) Isaac merely gives him a conventional firstborn blessing for material prosperity. The special Abrahamic blessing is reserved for Jacob when he leaves home 28.3-4. Presumably Rebecca is influenced by the prophecy about the respective fates of her sons, but immoral acts have a tendency to backfire.

✳ *God, let us not come into the power of sin or wrong-*
    doing,
  temptation or disgrace. Let no evil within us control us,
  and keep us far from bad people and bad company.
                                      Jewish Daily Morning Service

Tuesday January 28   *Genesis 27.14-29*
Exiled
Does Isaac know what is going on? The voice is Jacob's even if the hands are hairy like Esau. Jacob's responses are also wrong. When Isaac asks how he got back from hunting so quickly he answers: 'because the Eternal your God made it happen.' Not the language of Esau. Isaac allows himself to be convinced. The smell of Esau's clothing is the decisive factor. Throughout, the sedentary Isaac has loved the hunter Esau; now that love has betrayed him.

The Rabbis tried to soften Jacob's betrayal by re-punctuating his remarks. Jacob's answer in verse 19, 'I am Esau your firstborn', can be read in the Hebrew, with a little imagination, as 'I am I! Esau is your firstborn!' Presumably they saw in Jacob's act a prophetic awareness of some higher destiny and felt justified in excusing him. The Bible is harder. Jacob has to go into exile for twenty years and Rebecca, who instigated the whole matter, will never see her beloved son again.

✳ *May we always be in awe of heaven in private*
  as well as in public.
  May we tell the truth
  and speak it in our heart.
                          Based on the Jewish Daily Morning Service

Wednesday January 29   *Genesis 27.30 to 28.2*
Every deed has its consequences
Esau's pain at this betrayal rises up to heaven: 'When Esau heard the words of his father, he cried a great and exceedingly bitter cry' (verse 34). Every deed has its consequences. The

Rabbis noticed that this same phraseology reappears in the Bible – presumably as the deliberate reminiscence of this event by a later writer. In the Book of Esther, when Haman plots to murder all the Jews, Mordechai tore his garments, put on sackcloth and ashes and went out through the city *'and he cried a great and bitter cry'* (Esther 4.1). Jacob's descendants pay the price for this action.

Nor does Jacob escape retribution. Isaac explains to Esau that his brother came with *mirmah,* 'deceit'. The same word will be used by Jacob about Laban who 'deceived' him by substituting Leah for Rachel (29.25). And Jacob's sons will use 'deceit' to defeat the Hivites who had dishonoured their sister Dinah (34.13). Jacob has established a pattern of behaviour that will return to haunt him.

✳ ***Blessed is God who has no fault and no forgetfulness, who shows no favour and takes no bribe.***
Righteous is God in all ways and loving in all deeds.
Based on the Jewish Daily Morning Service

Thursday January 30   *Genesis 28.10-22*

If God will be with me ...

Jacob is such a curious character. On the one hand he is someone with an eye for the main chance, even if it means cheating his brother and betraying his father. But on the other he can dream of a ladder reaching to heaven and recognize the importance of this encounter with God. It will be a long time till he is able to resolve these contradictions in his character. So his first response to this extraordinary experience is to turn his pious vow into a negotiation. 'If God will be with me, and will guard me on this way which I go and will give me bread to eat and clothing to wear and if I return in peace to the house of my father, *then* the Eternal will be for me God and this stone which I placed as a monument will be a house of God and whatever you give me I shall tithe a tenth for You.' If God looks after him, Jacob will return ten percent.

Most of us probably think of God in that way at some time or other.

✳ ***God, we do not rely on our own good deeds***
but on Your great mercy as we lay our needs before You.
Jewish Daily Morning Service

31

A choice encounter

There are any number of biblical stories of encounters beside
wells – usually leading to marriage. But what actually happens
here? It looks at first glance as if Jacob, utterly smitten with love
for Rachel, turns into Hercules. Perhaps it is true – the same
sentence (verse 10) speaks three times of people and things
belonging to Laban, 'the brother of his mother'. Such repetition is
unnecessary. Perhaps Jacob becomes infatuated with this vision
of a girl who so reminds him of his mother – the vulnerability of a
lonely exile.

But there is another way of reading the passage. The
shepherds are unable to roll away the stone, not because they
are physically incapable of doing it but because a matter of trust,
or the lack of it, motivates them. Only when all the shepherds of
the different families are gathered may the well be opened so that
all get their appropriate share. Jacob is his usual impatient self
and simply takes over.

✳ *God, what can we say before You? For in Your presence
    are*
   not the powerful as nothing, the famous as if they had
   never existed, the learned as if without knowledge and
   the intelligent as if without insight?

                                        Jewish Daily Morning Service

Poetic justice

There is a verse from our previous reading (verse 13) that offers
the Rabbis a chance to display their subtlety – and cynicism. It is
clear that Laban is a tricky customer, and a self-righteous one at
that. Having heard about Jacob from Rachel, he runs to meet him
'*and he hugged him and kissed him*'. In their view he remembers
the wealth brought by Abraham's servant who had taken
Rebecca to marry Isaac (Genesis 24). But this new visitor seems
to be without material possessions. So Laban hugs him, to feel in
his pockets – no luck! Then he kisses him, to see if there is a
diamond concealed in his teeth!

But even Laban can be an unconscious agent for requital.
Switching the daughters he points out: 'It is not the way things are
done here, to give the younger before the firstborn.' The
symmetry is precise and Jacob is punished for his actions. But

having two wives will condemn his household to a painful rivalry that will break out into conflict and further betrayal in the lives of his children.

✳ *God, everything is trivial except the pure soul which must*
  one day give its account and reckoning before the judgment seat of Your glory.

Jewish Daily Morning Service

TO THINK ABOUT

● How do we know when our motives, even those with a religious basis, are right?
● Where do we draw the line between duty to our parents and duty to ourselves?

FOR ACTION

Learn something about the ways in which families function and the nature of conflict.

b. Freedom and reconciliation

8th Sunday before Easter, February 2   *Genesis 30.25-36*

A battle of wills

Laban is revealed in all his trickiness – feigning willingness to pay Jacob and send him on his way, but at the same time cheating. But Jacob is his match. At first glance his ploy of asking for only the spotted and speckled sheep and goats seems a sensible way of ensuring that there can be no doubt about their ownership. And Laban is equally crafty in hiding such animals away. Jacob will do some mumbo jumbo with sticks in the following section thus ensuring that spotted and speckled animals are born – and will even subsequently explain that he learnt this in a dream from an angel. Actually Jacob's success can be shown to be the result of a careful analysis of the genetic constitution of the sheep and goats and some sensible selective breeding (see the *Encyclopaedia Judaica* Volume 4, 'Biology' 1024-1027 – Jerusalem 1972). Jacob was a competent shepherd and put his knowledge of breeding to good use in the six years he still had to serve Laban. Miracles are helpful, but technology can also go a long way.

* *In every generation we thank You and recount Your
    praise
    for our lives held in Your hand, for our souls that are in
    Your care, and for Your miracles that are with us every
    day.*   *Jewish Daily Service*

Monday February 3   *Genesis 31.1-18*

Signs of change

It is time to depart. Jacob recognizes that he has outstayed his
welcome with Laban and his sons. God's words reinforce his
decision that it is time to leave and to return home. Jacob is again
on the run. But this time he is on his way to face the ghosts of the
conflict he left behind those twenty years ago. But he returns as a
man of substance – with wives, concubines and children, and
vast flocks. In the urgency of this moment his task is to persuade
his wives to abandon their own home, their father's house, and
accompany him. So he reinforces his argument with the force of a
religious vision, at the same time justifying his behaviour towards
his father-in-law. His wives seemingly share his concern and the
decision to leave is endorsed. This is already a different Jacob
from the one who put his own self-interest first. Now he carries a
load of responsibilities and knows that he must consult and get
the agreement of his wives. Jacob has been humanized by his
own suffering and the long-term intimate relationship with his
family. But is he yet ready for the final test?

* *Our God and God of our ancestors,
    do not forsake us or reject us;
    do not shame us or set aside Your love for us.*
                                    Based on Jewish High Holyday Liturgy

Tuesday February 4   *Genesis 31.36-50*

God is witness between us

For once Jacob is in the right, and it is a curious thing to see him
protesting his innocence. He lists every part of his experience of
the past twenty years, and especially the difficult life of a
shepherd, burned in the sun by day and frozen by night. The
struggle with Laban seems to have given Jacob a perspective on
his own trickiness and from now on he will act in a more

34

honourable way than in his youth. No longer Jacob the runaway son, he is Jacob the patriarch.

What he does not know is the tragedy lurking in the background. Rachel has stolen Laban's household gods and hidden them. Jacob has cursed anyone who might have done so, not knowing that this will destroy Rachel. The family pattern of secrecy still seems to be operating between husband and wife. Ironically, had Jacob known he could not have stood up to Laban and discovered his own inner strength.

✳ *What are we? What is our life?*
   What is our love?
   What is our justice? What is our success?
   What is our endurance? What is our power?
   God hear! God pardon! God, listen and act!
                                   Based on Jewish Daily Morning Service

Wednesday February 5   *Genesis 32.3-21*

Approaching the real Esau

The moment approaches when Jacob must meet with his brother Esau. He sends ahead gifts, perhaps better described as bribes, to appease him. But is Esau the same person that Jacob remembers from twenty years ago? The first messengers return with the information that Esau is coming with four hundred men. Is this a guard of honour for the returning brother or a military group to destroy him? We know no more than Jacob, though clearly Jacob's guilt has made the figure of the irate, powerful Esau take on almost supernatural powers. His response is to try to buy his way out – not particularly noble, but practical – so he sends the gifts 'before his face' (verse 4). The literal meaning of that phrase is important, because this is Jacob's final ploy of hiding behind others. The text records that he was 'greatly afraid and distressed' (verse 8). The Rabbis saw here two elements: 'fear' that he would be killed, but also 'distress' that he might kill as well. Before Jacob can face the real Esau outside he has to deal with the 'demonized' Esau in his own conscience.

✳ *Here I stand before You, full of shame and confusion.*
   Because You command mercy and love, show me how
   to change myself so that I can serve You.
                                   Jewish High Holyday Liturgy

The pain of renewal

The opening verse of this section recalls Jacob's night at Beth El where he also 'stayed overnight' (32.22, compare 28.11 and 32.14). But that time he had a dream of the ladder and the reassuring vow to God. This time the text merely records that he slept there – no dream or message came to help or reassure him. So he sends his family on ahead, perhaps as hostages for his own safety. But then there appears the mysterious man who wrestles with him. Perhaps it is Esau, come secretly at night, or Esau's guardian angel – or even something from within Jacob, the final confrontation with his own sense of guilt at what he had done to his brother, that fantasy brother of whom he had been so afraid.

This is the fight that Jacob cannot run away from. And afterwards, given his new name, Israel, he steps out from behind his possessions and at a place to be called 'the face of God' (verse 31), he stands 'before the face of' his family and possessions (33.3) and literally 'faces up' to the approaching army of Esau.

✳ ***Turn us back to You, God, and we shall return.***
   Renew our lives as of old.   *Lamentations 5.21*

Coming full circle

The brothers meet and Esau falls on Jacob's neck – in friendship. How genuine it is, and how long it might last, is not certain. Jacob ensures that the two camps keep their distance so that nothing can go wrong in the future.

What actually takes place at this reconciliation? Throughout the narrative till now, the 'gifts' sent ahead by Jacob have been referred to by the Hebrew term *minchah* (32.19, 22; 33.10). But at the last moment he substitutes the word *b'rakhah*, 'blessing' (33.11), a change which is often ignored or misrepresented in English translations which retain the word 'gift'. This is to overlook Jacob's intent – to return to Esau the material 'blessing' that he had stolen from his brother. When Esau accepts it, the circle is closed and reconciliation, with material compensation, is effected. Jacob has stopped cheating and paid his debt.

* **Guard us when we go out and when we come in, to enjoy life**
  and peace both now and forever, and spread over us the shelter of Your peace.   *Jewish Daily Service*

Saturday February 8   *Genesis 47.27-31; 50.12-21*

Facing reality

The tragic game of betrayals has persisted into Jacob's children with the selling of Joseph into slavery. In fact this episode is only the last in a whole series of brotherly conflicts. Cain killed Abel; Ishmael was dispossessed by Isaac, Jacob cheated Esau; the brothers almost killed Joseph. Each generation has to cope as best they can with this all-too-human reality. The worst battles are not between strangers but between brothers. 'Brotherhood' is not a sentimental gift but a hard-earned achievement.

Jacob's name is evoked by Joseph's brothers to protect themselves from the revenge they fear he will bring upon them. Joseph too has grown up from the spoilt and selfish dreamer of his youth. But is his willingness to forgive the magnanimity that comes from having total power over them (the childhood dream fulfilled) or a genuine religious feeling? Joseph speaks of *Elohim* 'God', a general term that could almost mean 'fate' in the Egyptian context, rather than 'the Eternal', the name of Israel / Jacob's God. Perhaps it is something of both, as is usually the case in human motivations. From the first murder of brother by brother to a kind of complex but peaceful unity, Genesis has taken us through the journey humanity still has to make.

* **Soon let us witness the glory of Your power when all who inhabit this world shall meet in understanding and all shall accept the duty of building Your kingdom so that Your reign of goodness shall come soon and last forever.**
                                        Jewish Daily Service

Acknowledgment

All prayers in this section come from 'Forms of Prayers for Jewish Worship', Vols. I (Daily and Sabbath) and Vol. III (Days of Awe), published by the Reformed Synagogues of Great Britain, edit. Lionel Blue and Jonathan Magonet.

TO THINK ABOUT

● How do we learn to confront our own prejudices and fears about 'the other'?

● Is the rivalry between 'brothers' more bitter and destructive than other forms of conflict? If so why and how do we address it?

FOR ACTION

Seek out one context for an ongoing experience of dialogue – be it interfaith, inter cultural or interracial.

Useful addresses

Council for Christians and Jews
1 Dennington Park Road
London NW6 1AX

Calamus Foundation *(a Muslim organization which is involved in interfaith work)*
Flat J
18 Eaton Square
London SW1W 9DD

Leo Baeck College *(has an annual Jewish-Christian-Muslim student Conference and biennial Christian Theology Student Seminars)*
80 East End Road
London N3 2SY

LENT – LIFE OR DEATH?

Notes based on the New Revised Standard Version by
Alec Gilmore

Alec Gilmore is a Baptist minister with 20 years experience in pastorates in Northampton and West Worthing followed by a literature ministry for the benefit of developing countries including Eastern Europe as Director of Feed the Minds. He is presently Associate Baptist Chaplain in the Universities of Sussex and Brighton and lectures on the Old Testament.

Lent is traditionally a time for giving up something (like chocolate) and accepting a stringent form of discipline (like extra early morning prayer), or doing something distasteful and forcing yourself to enjoy it. Behind all this lies choice. Lent is therefore an ideal time to reflect on all the choices, major and minor, that we make every day, and to see them in relation to the supreme choice as to which way we are looking – towards life or towards death, hope or despair, a future or an end. And why?

7th Sunday before Easter, February 9   Matthew 4.1-11 *
The quick fix

In trying and painful situations we look for solutions. A road accident – how can we stop it happening again? Famine – how can we help? Always, there must be something we can do. Stones into bread. Why not?

When we feel misunderstood we want to explain ourselves. Products not selling need better marketing. Money, colour, flair and flash, and all that the media can offer will be called into play. We need a splash. More stones into bread. And if it is a straight choice between the easy way and the hard way, the line of least resistance is bound to be more attractive.

There are plenty of choices here. But every time the human says yes, the divine seems to say no. Why? Perhaps because there is more to life than the quick fix, the instantly impressive and the popularity that goes with it. Perhaps because we need to distinguish between 'the solution' which is often long-term and costly and the 'quick-fix' which gives immediate satisfaction.

Anyway, Jesus certainly knew why, and part of discipleship is travelling with him so that we can discover.

✳ *O Lord, you knew the difference.*
Help me daily to walk with you so that I can discover.

Monday February 10   *Matthew 6.16-21* ✳
Top show
The choice here is not between fasting and not fasting. But, having chosen to fast, there is a choice between finding personal satisfaction in it *or* making it such a miserable experience that everybody has to know about it and the price you are paying for it. In some circles it is known as 'collecting putty medals', and Jesus is not impressed by top show.

Nor is he impressed by 'treasures on earth'. The choice here is between real treasure and superficial possessions, and there is a simple test to see where we stand. Treasure on earth is when we are more interested in what a thing costs than in its worth, more worried by its price than its value. An inexpensive thoughtful gift, just at the right time, may be treasure in heaven. A luxury gift for someone who has no use for it, because it brings some return to the donor, is moth and rust.

✳ *Father, help me to resist the natural temptation*
to parade what I am doing,
and show me how I can offer treasure in heaven
to someone today.

Tuesday February 11   *Joel 2.12-18* ✳
Hearts not garments
These words were uttered in the context of disaster. The nature of the disaster is not clear, and it doesn't matter. But it does have a sense of urgency about it and it affects literally everybody. Even the bridegroom, normally exempt from military service, has to join in. We have no choice in how or when it comes, but we do have a choice in how we react to it: we can 'tear our hair' – 'rend our garments' – or we can take positive action.

Samuel Beckett, the playwright, had two women in his life. Suzanne was cool and practical and they were together for 40 years. Peggy, who was much more flighty and exciting, comments: 'She made curtains while I made scenes'. Joel says that that is our choice when we face the disasters and tragedies of life. Scenes or curtains? And if we are to make the right choice we need to know long before it happens which way we are likely to jump. Then we can start practising.

✳ *Reflect on times when you have faced tragedy and how you have behaved. Then pray for strength always to choose positive, caring and meaningful action.*

Ash Wednesday, February 12   *Deuteronomy 30.15-20*

Life and death

The starkness of the choice here is incontestable and sounds final. Life or death? Many English translations (following the Greek) make the choice of life dependent on keeping the commandments, but the opening words of verse 16 – 'If you obey the commandments of the Lord your God' – are not in the Hebrew text. Possibly they were inserted later to strengthen the idea of obedience.

It might therefore be better to focus attention on 'turning away' or not hearing' (verse 17) as being the touchstone. We can then read the whole passage in the light of much that has gone before. When we do the message seems to be, not that life comes as a reward for keeping a set list of commandments, but rather that if the heart is in the right place, and we are facing in the right direction, the life that flows from us is an expression of that choice. Keeping the commandments is the consequence, not the condition.

✳ *Lord, help me to keep my face turned towards you, that I may see my life and the world around as you see it. Then guide me to respond to it as you do.*

Thursday February 13   *Matthew 5.1-7*

Means and ends

The Old Testament Law suggests certain choices so as to achieve, gain or secure life. The Beatitudes, by contrast, encourage us to recognize certain attitudes to life, each of which brings its own reward. Whereas commandments are about 'means to an end' the Beatitudes are about ends, and leave God to worry about the rewards.

Choices here are of two kinds. First, there are those where we have little choice (such as mourning) so that we either 'choose' what we already have or decide to use a situation positively instead of rebelling against it. Secondly, there are those where we choose to go beyond what is inflicted on us, we make a sacrifice or go the second mile. Divide the Beatitudes into these two categories and choose one of which you have personal experience. Then reflect on the extent to which you can appreciate the force of the second half. How true was it for you? And in what ways?

✳ *Father, sometimes I can see what Jesus was driving at*
and sometimes I can't. When I can, thank you.
When I can't, help me to be honest enough to say so
and perhaps in the coming days
you can make it clear to me.

Friday February 14   Matthew 5.8-12
By-products

With so much conflict and tension everywhere (family, community, nation and world) there is always room for a peace-maker. Some people are very good at it, sometimes because they have just not been 'got at' by one party or the other, and so are able to see many sides of an issue. Often it is because their skill flows from the fact that they are very difficult people 'to own' or tie down. They are individuals with a strong independence of spirit. For this reason they suffer an uncommon degree of rejection or persecution. Peace-making and persecution are usually not far apart. Jesus was one of them, and so were many of the prophets. All of us know several people in this category, maybe a personal friend or someone in public life.

'Purity of heart' may be a quality we cannot 'choose' to possess, but peace-making is something we can all cultivate, and the persecution that goes with it is something we can learn to endure. Perhaps if we started there, a little practice and patience might make us good at it and perhaps purity of heart would be a by-product.

✳ *Think of a peacemaker and pray for him or her.*

Saturday February 15   Matthew 5.17-20
Law and prophets

By questioning the traditions Jesus was thought to be undermining the Law and destroying the work of the prophets. His defence is that far from destroying them, he is trying to fulfil

42

them. The choice here is between first principles and second-hand teaching. Jesus wants belief and behaviour that spring from within and not because someone has told us to 'believe this' or to 'do that'.

He therefore questions or rejects something not because it is wrong but because he wants us to discover the reality behind it. We are to remove the cover and appreciate the thing itself. Thus belief and behaviour become genuinely our own and not simply obedience to a third party. We love because we love – not because someone told us to love. We love in *our* way – not somebody else's. We love *when* we love – not when someone says we ought to love. And the same goes for forgiveness and a host of other things.

✳ *Father, show me your way.*
Help me to make it my way.
Give me grace to listen to others
and the courage to stay with what I hear
until I am really persuaded differently.

TO THINK ABOUT

● Make a list of the choices you have been called upon to make in the course of a day (or week). Which were real choices and which were not really choices at all? On what bases did you make your judgments? Was it reason or feelings? And was it a question of what suited you, what would please somebody else or what you believed to be fundamentally right? Where it was really no choice at all, how easy did you find it was to accept? Reflect on that again in the light of one of the week's readings.

● Think of a situation of conflict near to home but not one in which you are personally involved. Set down what you would have to do to play the role of peacemaker? What do you think it might cost you? And in what ways do you think it might make you a better person?

● Choose one or two of your favourite Bible characters who had to make choices. How did they do it and how differently might they have done it if they had read some of this week's passages?

43

LENT – Good or evil?

Notes based on the New International Version by
Joanildo Burity

Joanildo Burity, a Brazilian Presbyterian, is a political scientist who has worked for a number of years on the relation of religion and politics. This has more recently involved work on ethics and culture, to make sense of pluralism and to work for tolerance towards difference and change.

We live in an age when we need to develop greater powers of discernment. For a long time Western culture and religion believed it was easy to make judgments on the nature of things, people and situations. Trusting that there was one clear standard of interpretation, according to our culture and religion, we thought it was easy to tell the difference between good and evil. But the embarrassment which arises when we make wrong judgments calls increasingly for more discernment. Good acts may raise confusion, doubts and fears just as evil does, depending on how mature our faith is, and how open we are to the challenge they make.

I invite you to take these readings as moments of reflection on how we might find our way through the maze of contemporary cultural differences and ethical choices. We may discover at the end that we need not be extremist or stubborn to unpack this riddle.

1st Sunday in Lent, February 16   *Matthew 8.28-34*
Good that frightens
The first Christians were at home with the idea of spirits. They ascribed good and evil to distinct and incommunicable spheres. People who fell under the oppressive control of certain spirits were stigmatized, isolated, confined. Jesus often appears in the Gospels driving out evil spirits from 'possessed' people, restoring their sense of human dignity. These exorcisms struck deep into the patterns of discernment of good and evil in first century culture. And that stirred up fear, confusion and opposition. This passage, and the following four, will explore this problem.

We have here a double situation: first, the demons speak out and make a disguised confession: 'What do you want with us, Son of God?' Evil shudders before good and is forced to recognize its power. But that doesn't ensure that people are able to welcome the presence of the good. The second situation is that the whole town, in seeing Jesus, beg him to leave their region. How much does it take for us to lay down our fears before unexpected turns of events – just like these violent demon-possessed fellows who are suddenly healed by this strange man? What does it take to discern the work of God in unlikely situations, and to rejoice at other people's liberation? How much does it take to accept the presence of some good, wherever it may come from?

✳ *Lord, remove from us all fear that we may acknowledge the signs of goodness in your deeds.*

Monday February 17   *Matthew 12.22-29 **

Good that tricks?

Here, as in Matthew 8, there is a double situation: a few people hesitantly acknowledge some good in what they experience – 'Could this be the Son of David?' – while others call good evil and shut themselves up in their intolerance: 'It is only by the prince of demons that this fellow drives out demons.' This statement is not so naive as it seems. It is the paranoid argument of every orthodoxy. Behind all appearances, there is a secret agreement: the devil is tricking people into believing that this man can drive out demons in order to lead them astray from true religion. This kind of reasoning can surely be turned against anyone.

Jesus answers his opponents on three counts:

1. If the exorcism is authentic, then Satan is divided against himself and his kingdom will surely be ruined. If it is only a fake, it is dangerous still because there is no control once the game has started.
2. If the Pharisees are serious, then they have to explain by whom they drive out demons.
3. If God is really the power behind the exorcism, then orthodoxy is blind to the fact that the Kingdom of God has come, and evil is ultimately doomed.

What have been our patterns of judgment? How aware have we been of the double-edged nature of any event, its open possibilities of interpretation and the fragility of our criteria?

45

Tuesday February 18   *Matthew 12.30-32 ***

Calling good evil

Before the stubbornness of religious people in his time, Jesus
retorted uncompromisingly, raising a fourth point: 'He who is not
with me is against me'. But he did not seek simply to vindicate
himself. He meant that flatly refusing to discern God's action
amounted to cutting oneself from God's Kingdom. Taking good
for evil may be a natural reaction in the face of something new,
different or fearsome. But if Jesus drove out demons by the Spirit
of God, then accusing him of doing it by Beelzebub was
blasphemy.

We have a serious indictment here to be on our guard against
indifference, or plain rejection of the Holy Spirit's uncanny ways in
the world and history. We are called continuously to renew our
patterns of interpretation, so that we may freely follow the
direction of God's wind. And yet it is hard to balance ourselves on
this 'either/or' choice summoned by Jesus. How can we be sure
we are following the right trail? After all, things are turning ever
more complex and many-sided. That calls for prudence and
discernment once again.

✳ *Let us beware of any indifference
or rejection toward the work of the Spirit.*

Wednesday February 19   *Matthew 12.33-37*

Words: windows of the soul

Jesus' fifth rejoinder to the Pharisees follows the line of the
previous one: our words are evidence of our recognition of the
presence of God in the midst of our history. We will be judged by
them, not only being held accountable for what we said, but also
in the sense that by saying them we are already somehow
pronouncing judgment on ourselves. For, in this text, words are
seen as windows of the soul. Our lives and perspectives are
revealed through them. Let us not drift away from the context: it is
not a question of just *any* words. Rather these are words that
show how we read the struggle between right and wrong, justice
and injustice, good and evil and what kind of judgment we pass
on each situation. The warning goes against taking too lightly the

strenuous effort that it takes good to overcome evil. This struggle is going on inside ourselves as well as within social and historical contexts. The words that express our interpretation of events will be taken for their 'face value' – good words from a good heart, good fruit from a good tree, and *vice versa.*

✳ *Lord, help us to overcome evil in our judgments*
so that our words may reflect
an abundance of righteousness in our hearts.

Thursday February 20   *Matthew 21.12-17*

The Temple – a den of robbers?

Jesus could not tolerate evil. That was especially so when people's faith was exploited by the workings of a religious system that turned on money and power. And when those people gave in to the demands of the religious establishment, he held both responsible for the corruption of God's service and drove them out.

Religious leaders were outraged by what they had seen (Jesus' rage and healings) and heard (children shouting: 'Hosanna to the Son of David'). And though they expected Jesus to tell the children off, they did not seem to realize how insolent and disgraceful their own practices were. People tend to knock others' actions without considering their own wrong. Those in power in church or society are very inclined to play this game. That is why prophetic voices have often been so harsh with the authorities of their time.

✳ *Jesus, give us your courage to confront evil*
and guard us from pharisaic criticism of others.

Friday February 21   *Isaiah 57.14-21*

No one is exempt

The prophets always took pains to denounce the people's false assurance of God's unending patience. Religion involved ethical commitment, and there could be no excuse for wrongdoing. This text appears towards the end of one of these prophetic condemnations (cf. Isaiah 56.9 to 57.13). When misgovernment and corruption in society and religion seemed to leave no hope for them, the prophet announced: 'Prepare the road, remove the obstacles out of the way of my people.' For there was still that hope that peace, justice and comfort could be reached.

It is not just the leaders who must repent and be contrite. The text suggests links between the people and their corrupt leaders (cf. verses 16-17), so that even those who mourned, and were 'lowly in spirit', were implicated in God's indictments. Though directed towards them, the promise of peace demands repentance and humility. Can we ever pretend to be exempt from responsibilities on account of some privileged relation to God? The prophet is saying that, even though this was the case, a humble attitude of repentance and responsiveness toward God is the best way to mend our relationship with him.

✳ *Help us, God of the contrite and lowly in spirit,*
to recognize our share
in the evil of our community and time,
and to become more open to the Spirit's challenge
to change our attitudes towards peace and justice.

Saturday February 22   *1 John 3.1-10 ✳*
Who are children of God?
How can we distinguish, among hundreds of religions, groups and situations we come across, who are children of God and who are children of the devil? Is there a clear-cut way? It is easier when the contrast is obvious. But what about the bits and pieces of good and evil in each of us? The community of John could apparently make this judgment from an eschatological standpoint – they believed the End was near. Before the ultimate reality of God's salvation, in its consummation, there is no room for complacency: one is either on one side or the other.

However, the reasoning cannot be abstract. Being born of God is a matter of doing what is right and loving one's neighbours, brothers and sisters. Practice is the measure of being. Doing right is being righteous. Though we cannot claim to be without sin (cf. 1 John 1.8), we can rely on the fact that in Jesus the principle of sin has been overwhelmed. The question does not allow for complacency: if we cannot show in practice that we know God, and avoid the mastery of sin, we are under fire from this text.

✳ *May we be good children of God by doing what is right*
and loving our fellow human beings.

TO THINK ABOUT
● Jesus seems to be calling our attention toward the need for a strong commitment to God, so that we may open ourselves to

discern the good — the presence of the Kingdom — in history, and in our daily events. What do we need in order to give correct interpretations of those events?

● How can we be true to the 'either/or' tone in most of this week's passages, when we know that life is increasingly complex and every manifestation of the good in history is mixed with potentially, or actually bad, implications?

FOR ACTION

Work out the implications for some of our present commitments (professional, religious, ethical, political, and so on): our need to be at once uncompromising before evil and careful to assess permanently where we stand.

WHY DO THE INNOCENT SUFFER?
The book of Job

Notes based on the New Jerusalem Bible by
Sheila Cassidy

Sheila Cassidy is a specialist in Palliative Care at Plymouth General Hospital (UK). In her spare time she preaches, lectures, broadcasts and writes books. Her writing is deeply influenced by her involvement with suffering both in cancer wards and in her personal experience of imprisonment, torture and solitary confinement in Chile.

Why do the innocent suffer? This is a question which I have been asked so often that I want to scream, 'How should I know?' I'm not a theologian: all I do is work with the victims, the dying, the bereaved and those whose lives have been ruined by disaster or abuse. American writer Annie Dillard (in *Pilgrim at Tinker Creek* - Picador) describes it as one of the few questions worth asking and, after battering her head on God's closed door with the rest of us, gets a glimpse of the only answer possible: there *is* no answer, for 'we are created, *created,* sojourners in a land we did not make, 'Who,' she says, 'are we to demand explanations of God? (And what monsters of perfection should we be if we did not?)'.

The book of Job, a glorious poem (probably from the 5th century BC) is based upon a much older myth about the problem of innocent suffering. Job, the archetypal good man, wrestles with his own 'Why' until, driven to desperation, he confronts God as if in a court of law. Accustomed to hear nothing but the echo of his own voice, Job is poleaxed by God's reply ... Enough! Read on.

2nd Sunday in Lent, February 23   *Job 1.6 to 2.13*
Questions of good and evil
I think the best way to understand these first two chapters of Job is to imagine them as a very stylized piece of drama, or even opera. First, we meet Job who, to be truthful, is a bit of a 'goody, goody', a rather pompous church elder, or a member of some

pious guild of men which likes to dress up on holy days and process with the clergy. Then the scene changes and we find ourselves in the Court of Heaven, surrounded by angels and cherubs plucking their golden harps. And there, in a small but splendid ante-room off the main court, is God, deep in conversation with the Evil One.

What are we to make of this rather childish stuff? Should we meditate on it word by word, or just skip it until we find something more serious? The answer to that is: don't take it too seriously, but don't let yourself be fooled into dismissing it either. Instead, think about what the writer is *really* up to – asking himself (or could it be herself?) the eternal questions about good and evil: Is there really a God who controls what happens to us day by day? And if there is a Good Spirit, is there an Evil Spirit in conflict with it? And if there *is* an Evil Spirit, who is the stronger of the two? Sleep on it. Sweet dreams.

✳ *Holy God, Source of all good,*
protect us from the Evil One,
from the forces of greed and violence,
corruption and death.
And if we fall, pick us up again,
and hold us till we are strong enough
to walk on our own.

Monday February 24   *Job 3.1-11, 20-26*

God, why?

Before you go any further, go back to chapter 2 and note the behaviour of Job's friends Eliphaz, Bildad and Zophar when they first came to visit him: they sat and kept vigil with him. That's all. They just sat there, *doing* nothing, but in that very act *being* there for him. Later on, like all of us, they fell into the trap of feeling they must *say* something helpful. As you'll see later, they would have done better to stay silent.

In chapter 3, the stunning poetry begins, and we are drawn into Job's grief and desolation. As I read this passage, I remember one night when I was on duty in the hospital and we were told that there was a terrible fire. We waited while the firemen fought the blaze and struggled to rescue the family whose home was burning. Then, with a screech of sirens, the ambulances arrived and the victims were rushed in. There were nine of them – a man and his wife and their seven children. The children arrived first, the breathing apparatus obscuring their faces. I remember lifting the masks and seeing the blonde hair and the soot smudged faces, but mostly I remember the terrible grief that they were all dead, except for the childless mother. I never knew what happened to her, or how she bore her grief, but surely she must have cried in anguish, 'Perish the day on which I was born. Why did God not kill me too? What kind of monster is God to leave me like this, with my heart broken, to struggle on alone?'

✳ *O God, God, wild, terrible, all powerful God.*
  Why do you do it?
  Why do young mothers get cancer,
  little girls get raped and killed?
  What's going on Lord? What?

Tuesday February 25   *Job 4.1-17; 5.17*

Divine retribution?

In this first passage we listen, fuming, to Eliphaz of Teman as he pontificates so wisely. 'My dear chap,' he says, 'Surely you know that evil is God's retribution?' Surely you've read in the Bible that God rewards the good and punishes the evil doer? If you're suffering now, then you must have sinned. It's as simple as that!'

Eliphaz' speech reminds me of a friend who had breast cancer. One day, in desperation, she rang a 'healer', a woman who proclaimed that she had special secret powers and gifts. In a halting voice, my friend told the woman of her plight. The woman listened and when Mary had finished speaking she said, 'You must have been a very wicked woman!'

This story always makes my blood boil. If one thing is crystal clear, God does not protect the innocent, nor does he always punish evil doers. Torturers retire and go free, serial killers repeat their unspeakable acts twenty, thirty times over the years. The children of war torn Europe will carry the scars of violence to their graves, and their children and their children's children will inherit at least some of their pain. Sorry, Eliphaz, your argument doesn't convince me.

✳ *Why Lord, why?*
  Why don't you reward the good
  and punish the wicked?
  What have the children done to make you angry?
  O Lord, what's going on?
  Help us to understand.

Does God spurn the righteous?

Here we meet Job's friend Bildad of Shuah, another pious fool who is blind to the realities of the world. Believe me, Job, he says, God never spurns the righteous and he never helps the wicked. To which Job, had he not been so ill, might have answered, 'O yeah? What about all the dictators and bank robbers living in luxury, out of the reach of the law? And what about the people they killed? The students, the nurses, the human rights lawyers? What about Joan of Arc, and all the martyrs? Well? What about them?'

All this arguing with God's minister may seem disrespectful, even frankly vulgar. But if God is Truth, then surely he would not want us to pretend, to falsify the evidence? When I was an unhappy middle-aged novice, 'trying my vocation' in a convent, I had a poster which showed a rag doll being put through a mangle. The caption read, 'The Truth will set you free: but first it will make you miserable.' I think Job would have liked that poster, because he himself came to understand the freedom of truth through personal suffering.

✳ *Lord of freedom, Lord of truth,*
   put us through the mangle if you must,
   but please, please,
   set us free from the bondage of pious naiveté.

Determination to confront God

One of the themes that runs through the Job story is the growth of the spirit in adversity. At the beginning of his trials, Job wails in despair, wishing he'd never been born.

'If only my misery could be weighed,
    and all my ills put together on the scales! ...
The arrows of Shaddai stick fast in me,
    my spirit absorbs their poison ...' (6.1-4).

I love this image of the sick person's spirit poisoned: how else can we account for the anger, the bitterness and self absorption which so often overwhelms those who are ill? I see this spiritual malaise as an integral part of suffering, as is the sense of guilt and hopelessness that stem from depression. In today's passage, however, we meet a very different Job. His whinging self pity has been replaced by a determination to question his

Creator. God is all powerful, Job admits: he moves the mountains and commands the stars, and if, tiger-like, he snatches his prey, who ever is going to stop him, or dare to shout – Hey! You stop that! How dare you hurt that man?

And yet, Job determines to confront God, to challenge him and protest his innocence: 'Unafraid of him, I shall speak.' Well done Job!

> ✳ *All powerful, inscrutable God,*
> *you give us life and you take it away.*
> *We are afraid of you,*
> *and yet, confident of your love,*
> *we dare to ask why you let us suffer so.*

Friday February 28   *Job 11.1-16*

Integrity

I find it fascinating to contrast the attitude of Zophar, the pious comforter with that of Job. Zophar, with his clear sense of the transcendence, the 'otherness' of El Shaddai, the scary God of the mountain, counsels Job to hold his tongue and submit. Job, however, is rapidly regaining his sense of dignity and refuses to accept the time honoured doctrine that suffering is retribution for evil deeds. 'I am as good as you!' he shouts to Zophar. 'I won't admit to sins which I have never committed!'

I find a scary familiarity in Zophar's words, for he reminds me of those interrogators who set out to brainwash political prisoners. 'Come on now,' they cajole. 'Just admit that you plotted against the state, and we'll give you a drink of water, we'll untie you, let you go to the lavatory ...'

Perhaps Job is not just the archetype of the good man who has fallen on hard times, but also the man of integrity who would rather be tortured than lie.

> ✳ *God of Truth, hater of lies, give us the courage*
> *to witness to what is right, whatever the cost.*

Saturday March 1   *Job 13.1-5; 14.7-22*

Take God to court!

After rebuking Zophar, Job summons up all his courage and calls upon God to answer for his actions: 'My words are intended for Shaddai,' he says. 'I mean to remonstrate with God.' Job's courage is amazing. His God is not Christ, the Good Shepherd, the gentle Jesus, but El Shaddai, the God of the Mountain, the God whose theophanies are accompanied by thunder and lightening, hurricane and storm.

So what are we to make of all this, apart from acknowledging it as stunning poetry with unforgettable images? (Wouldn't you love your sins to be put in a bag, locked and sealed with tape marked 'Contaminated waste – to be incinerated'?)

I believe that Job's courage in taking God to court has a powerful message for us all. Instead of complaining *about* God when we feel unjustly treated, we should take our complaints straight to him. 'What the blazes are you doing, Lord?' is surely a more honest prayer than a tight-lipped acceptance that comes from a sense of politeness and fear. Surely we Christians, with our understanding of the Lord's compassion, should be able to summon up as much courage as Job. When my patients say to me, 'I've always led a good life. How could God do this to me?' I tell them that, since I have no answer, they should ask God himself (herself). After all, we have in the Psalms a long tradition of calling upon God in distress.

✳ *Lord My God,*
I cry out in my pain.
Why have you turned against me?
What have I done to deserve your wrath?
What have I done, O God?
What have I done?

TO THINK ABOUT

- What can we learn from the prologue in chapters 1 and 2 about disinterested religion?
- How would you answer a person who suggests that suffering is the result of sin?
- To what extent can we prepare ourselves to cope with suffering when it comes? What is good and what is bad about self-pity, and how do we recognize and deal with it?

3rd Sunday in Lent, March 2   *Job 19.13-27*

Rejection and faith

As I read Job's description of his alienation, estrangement from family and friends alike, I think of the terrible loneliness of those who have a mortal illness. It's not that people *want* to avoid the dying and the bereaved, but they feel ill at ease; they don't know what to say. After all, who feels comfortable trying to make conversation with a man with motor neurone disease, or a friend with AIDS. It's hard work; we're afraid of putting our foot in it, of saying something to upset them, so we persuade ourselves that they're too tired to receive visitors, that they only want to see close members of the family.

The truth is that we are scared. Being close to the dying reminds us that we too are mortal, we too could get cancer, or become paralysed, our voices distorted, or our faces a ghastly foetid cavity. It is this loneliness, this sense of being rejected, that is at the root of so much of the desolation of the dying. No wonder they often long for death, for release from the prison of their infirmity. It is in understanding the context, the world of the mortally ill, that we can best appreciate Job's powerful declaration of faith. 'Pity me,' he says, 'since I have been struck by the hand of God' (verse 21), and then in the next breath he affirms,

'I know that I have a living Defender' and when I die, 'after my awakening, he will set me close to him,
and from my flesh I shall look on God' (verses 25-26).

It's a powerful combination, isn't it: the courage to complain to God, and the certainty that he will be there to defend us at the end. This is faith at its naked best: the faith of the child in his or her parent.

✳ *Father God, loving Mother,*
despite all odds, we believe in you.
Everything seems against us, and even you;
and yet, blinded by fears, we trust in you,
for you alone are God,
and we know that God is good.

Monday March 3   *Job 21.1-15*
Bewilderment

Once again, Job struggles to hold in balance his experience of everyday realities and his faith in God. 'I am appalled at the thought of it!' he declares. Dictators live on, child abusers go undetected, drug barons sun themselves by their swimming pools. Why does God not punish them? How is it that their children go to the best schools, while the children of the favellas spend their days on the rubbish heap, desperately sifting other people's dirt for food to eat?

There is a certain repetitiveness in Job's speeches which could be tedious if we do not understand that the cry 'Why me?' is one which can never be silenced. The belief that God rewards the good and punishes the evil is deeply rooted in the human psyche. After all, this is the way we try to conduct our affairs: we reward those we admire with medals, titles and awards that make them feel good, if not superior (after all, what scientist does not harbour a secret longing to win the Nobel Prize?). And we delight in punishing the wrong doer. We build bigger, more secure prisons, to take revenge on the wrong doer. But God, it seems, is not like that. Disease and disasters are no respecters of persons, while the Mafia and Colombian drug barons laugh at those who pursue them.

So what's going on? What's God playing at? It's not fair! Of course it's not, but that, it seems, is how things are.

* *Perplexing, maddening, bewildering God.*
We do not understand your ways.
If you will not give us light,
then give us patience to wait for your justice. Amen

Tuesday March 4   *Job 29.1-25*

Loss of respect

(Before you read chapter 29, go back and read chapter 28. Although scholars think it really doesn't belong there, I find it wonderful, with its visions of wisdom being mined like a precious metal in the depths of the earth).

Poor Job. Not only has he lost his family, his money and his health, but he has lost the respect of those who used to revere him. I am moved to remember those priests who, after being held in high esteem for years, suddenly fall from grace because of sexually deviant behaviour. How easy it is to shout 'Shame!' 'Hypocrite!' 'Pervert!' forgetting the thirty, forty years of devoted service they have given to a community.

So what should we do? I have no doubt that it is wrong to cover up such transgressions, and it is now acknowledged that the Church's policy of protecting their own was both unjust and damaging. I believe we have to say clearly: this man did enormous good for thirty years, BUT he also did wrong and he must be both punished and helped to reform. Of course it doesn't make such a titillating story, but we should speak the truth, however unacceptable. After all, is it not time we all grew up and acknowledged that men and women are a complete amalgam of good and evil, of 'wheat and tares' which often cannot be separated?

> ✳ **Holy God, just and strong,**
> **teach us how to rebuke and how to forgive,**
> **and to love your prodigal sons and daughters**
> **as you yourself love them.**

Wednesday March 5   *Job 30.1-11*

Abandoned by all

In this chapter we have a terrifying description of the social isolation that has befallen Job as a consequence of his illness. I can imagine the scene portrayed by Breughel or Heironymous Bosch, artists whose canvases depict nightmare scenes of subhuman living. It brings to mind the very worst pictures of third world destitution, and refugees dying of starvation. One can hear too the mocking cries of street children, and feel Job's terror as suddenly he finds himself confronted by those he had dismissed as of no account. And in the so-called developed world there are the destitute on the streets of 'great' cities, their eyes pleading as shoppers hurry past, confused and guilty, not a little afraid, trying to convince themselves that these wretched people are impostors who return each night with their takings to a hot bath and a change of clothes.

> ✳ **Forgive us, Lord,**
> **when we close our eyes to poverty and hunger;**
> **teach us to be generous,**
> **to 'live simply that others may simply live'.**

Thursday March 6   *Job 36.1-12*

Put to the test?

Elihu, so sure of his own righteousness, is yet another to proclaim the accepted wisdom of the day: if you're suffering, then it's a sure sign that you've done something wicked, because God only punishes evil doers.

Of more interest is Elihu's theory that, by afflicting people, God is testing them, trying to make them repent of their wrong doing. This is a theme we hear again in the book of Wisdom (in the Apocrypha). In a discourse on the suffering of the just, we read:

> 'God was putting them to the test
> and proved them worthy to be with him;

he has tested them like gold in a furnace,
and accepted them as a perfect burnt offering.'

Wisdom 3.5b-6

There is a certain romantic attraction in the idea of life offered as a holocaust, and this notion persists to the present day. Jesus, however, was clear in his teaching. In Matthew 9.13, we hear him, exasperated, quote the prophet Hosea to his disciples: 'Go and learn the meaning of the words: *Mercy is what pleases me, not sacrifice.*' Again and again, the prophet tells us that God loves sinners, the humble, men and women whose hearts are tender and contrite:

'for faithful love is what pleases me, not sacrifice;
knowledge of God, not burnt offerings' (*Hosea 6.6*).

I find these passages immensely consoling, for like the prophet Micah I once stood trembling before the Lord, convinced that I must sacrifice my life, my possessions, my career, in order to win God's love. Having failed miserably to become an austere professional 'religious' person, I have taken for myself God's words to the prophet: This is what the Lord asks of you: only this,

'That you act justly,
Love tenderly and
walk humbly with your God' (*Micah 6.8*).

✳ *Lord our God,*
teach us the humility of the child
so that we may be small enough
to crawl on to your lap and hide there.

World Day of Prayer, March 7   *Job 38.1-18*

Look at creation

Chapters 38 and 39 are two of my most favourite passages. I love the notion of God replying from the heart of the tempest, for I have such a powerful sense of God in the wilderness of nature. These passages contain the secret and mysterious answer to Job's oft repeated question: but it's an answer which is hidden, which is not apparent at first reading. What God is saying is this: Job, my friend, you have no idea what you are talking about. Can you not understand that the world which I have made is infinitely more mysterious than you realize? Look up at the stars: do you know what holds them there? Do you know why they don't fall out of the sky on your head? No! Of course you don't. Nor do you understand why birds migrate, or how a mother penguin can recognize her chick among a thousand others. Job, Job! If I explained about suffering to you, you wouldn't understand. Can't you just accept that's the way my world is? From where *you* stand, my creation is flawed. Volcanoes erupt, babies die in their cots, wild youths beat up old ladies. One day you'll understand: that's the way things are!

✷ *Wild, scary God, speak to us through wind and storm,*
   through the kindness of others,
   in the depths of our prayer.
   Speak Lord: your servants are listening.

Saturday March 8   *Job 42.1-17*
The place of encounter
After yesterday's reading you might say, 'Well, what sort of answer is that? And you'd be right. What happened to Job was that *he met God face to face* (verse 5). That was what answered his questions. And that's the only way we'll be satisfied: by meeting God. That's the odd thing about suffering: so often it turns out to be a *place of encounter* with the Divine.

So now we come to the end of the story of Job. In dust and ashes, Job repents, not because of God's logic, but because of his theophany, his showing forth of his power. I think that's how faith is for most of us. Theology and logic are all very well, but there are as many wise and intelligent atheists as there are believers. Faith is a knowledge of things unseen, a leap in the dark, a hanging on to the pier with bleeding fingernails while the sea of doubt batters one's exhausted body. But somehow, somewhere, some of us catch a glimpse of the back parts of God (Exodus 33.18-23), and for this vision men and women have died on the gallows, at the stake and on a crucifix.

✷ *Lord God, we believe; help Thou our unbelief.*

TO THINK ABOUT and FOR ACTION

● To what extent do you see the cross reflected in the book of Job? And how do Job's experiences prefigure the cross?
● What light does the New Testament throw on Job's questions?
● Imagine you are a 20th century Jew reflecting on the bitter experiences of the Jewish Holocaust in the light of this book.
● Whose suffering will you share as a response to these readings? Remember the need for loyal friendship and sensitive listening.

LENT – Mountain top experiences

Notes based on the Revised English Bible by
Meg Chignell

Meg Chignell, daughter of an Anglican priest, is a Quaker by conviction, or 'convincement' as the Society of Friends describe. A teacher of Religious Studies, she has written many books, four of them for use in schools on biblical studies and ethics. She has visited the Holy Land and found its landscape, with its clear air and rocky precipices, truly awe inspiring.

I believe that the Bible asks us to learn from the lived experience of the past. It is useful to know, however, that the old writers associated mountains with an unspoilt and direct vision of God.

Mystical experience is more usual than one might suppose, either inside or outside Christianity, and individuals have even tried to induce vision, perhaps by drugs. The hallmark of such experience is that it changes life and that is our week's theme.

4th Sunday in Lent, March 9   *Matthew 17.1-13* *
Transfiguration

I believe Jesus was illuminated by prayer (Luke 9.29). We know from our own experience how people's faces can reveal their feelings. Love, joy and tenderness transfigure, just as the reverse emotions – of hatred and revenge – distort. So it is possible to visualize that Jesus' own relationship with God gave a kind of radiance to his face that was overwhelming to his three closest friends. As one would expect, the disciples interpreted their experience through scriptural ideas. Maybe it was their own shadows cast by the sun on the clouds below, each silhouette being surrounded by a halo of light.

Moses was the founder of the Jewish faith and the supreme law-giver. God promised him he would send another similar prophet to the Israelites (Deuteronomy 18.15-18) 'it is to him you must listen'. This is what Peter remembers when he hears the voice, and later this is repeated in a speech by Peter which is reported in Acts 3.22-26.

It was traditionally believed that Elijah had never died (2 Kings

2.11) and that he would return before the coming of the Messiah. Later Jesus identifies John Baptist with Elijah, probably because the ruling authority rejected him.

What do you think about this experience? Have you ever had one similar, even though you did not express it in these terms?

✳ **Dear God, may we be as translucent as was your Son Jesus**
in our devotion to you.

Monday March 10   *Exodus 24.3-11 **

Ratification

The text in this passage is difficult. The first part talks about a ratification of the Covenant which takes place employing animal sacrifice, a blood ritual and spoken commitment (verse 3). The second part considers an Israelite deputation on the mount consisting of Moses, four leaders and seventy elders. The juxtaposition of this story with the transfiguration is very challenging. It can be horrific for the modern reader, imagining the smell of blood, the fire and the incense, but on this occasion – such was the character of Moses as the God-filled man – that the deputation saw God.

Does the aspect of animal sacrifice and blood being splashed about offend you, as it does me? Have we any right to consider ourselves superior when we eat the products of factory farming?

✳ **God, the temptation is to reduce you**
to the size of our own plans and prejudices.
We praise you for your greatness.

Tuesday March 11   *I Kings 18.20-39*

Confrontation

Elijah was the epitome of courage. The great drought, in the background (I Kings 17.1-16), he interpreted as a sign of divine displeasure. Yahweh was punishing the interloping gods, which lay behind another and inferior way of life. By standing out and confronting the king, Elijah was insisting that the current way of living was put to the test.

The people saw God on this occasion in the coming down of the fire. The miracle however failed to make much impression, but Elijah's faith had been substantiated.

Perhaps each age needs uncomfortable people like this! Can you think of any? How far should we allow, and even encourage, opposition and confrontation when a serious principle is at stake?

✳ *Lord, give me courage at the right time,*
and charity all the time.

Wednesday March 12   *I Kings 19.1-18*
God in the silence

Jezebel was also courageous, but out of jealousy and frustration. Elijah fled far away to Beersheba in desperation and fury. His all-powerful God had failed to validate his role as a prophet. As it turned out, however, God was not to be found in the great wind, or the earthquake, or the fire. Miracles and spectacular acts have only a limited significance. It was in the silence that he was able to listen to that God-within-himself. As a Quaker, I believe that all human beings have access to the God within, although, sadly, in some it is unawakened.

Elijah was re-commissioned. He must return to work, anoint two new kings and, as his ministry was to continue, find a successor. This is like the experience of the disciples. They had to descend the mountain and go back to work (Mark 9.14-29).

Is it true in your experience that it is easier to rise to a crisis than to persevere with ordinary aggravations in daily life?

✳ *Lord give me the wisdom to find your will*
and strength to do it.

Thursday March 13   *Matthew 21.1-11*
Defiance

It is obvious from the arrangements Jesus made to procure a colt that he had friends in the neighbourhood. In the East the ass is held in high esteem, and symbolizes peace rather than war. Matthew elaborates his account by recalling a prophecy from Zechariah (9.9), which he feels Jesus fulfilled. He often does this to emphasize that Jesus is a fulfilment and perhaps a further interpretation of the old text. He also writes to strengthen persecuted Jewish Christians who needed to believe that Jesus was fully aware of what was to happen to his later followers.

The crowd's 'hosanna' echoes Psalm 118.25 – a psalm used at the Feast of Tabernacles when branches were waved, but Jesus was very careful to do nothing which would spark off violence.

Would you describe this incident, on the final part of his journey to the Passover on Mount Zion, as confrontational? Are you surprised by Jesus' tactics?

✴ *God, give me courage to speak truth to power whenever it is necessary.*

Friday March 14   Matthew 28.16-20

Commission

Jesus meets the disciples on a mountain in Galilee, reinstates them after their failure and sends them into the world to teach his way, promising to be with them always. For Matthew the significance of the mountain (perhaps where he visualizes Jesus' preaching his Sermon on the Mount – Matthew 5-7) is the Old Testament association with Mount Sinai and Moses. But here is one greater than Moses, as is indicated by the worshipful attitude of his disciples and the claim of universal lordship by Christ himself (verse 18).

Jesus' new law will supersede and fulfil the old Mosaic code and the new mission is universal. Jesus probably did not actually command his disciples to baptize in the name of the 'Father, Son and Holy Spirit', for in Acts the first converts were baptized into 'the name of our Lord Jesus Christ'. The phrase 'in the name of' really meant 'into the possession of', that is, into the new creation of Jesus Christ or into the Kingdom as envisaged by him, where the rule of Love is paramount (see Jesus' answer to the lawyer – Matthew 22.34-40 – and the Golden Rule – Matthew 7.12).

We need to consider carefully what we understand by the universal mission. Is it a matter of proselytizing, or converting from other faiths, claiming for baptism a special validity to change people's lives? As Quakers we would rather speak of recognizing the universal light of Christ, or the Inner Light, in everyone we meet, whatever their faith or creed. We would wish to be able to worship alongside those of different persuasions, rather than bar them from the Kingdom because they have not been baptized. We do not use baptism – or other sacraments – because we see the whole of life as sacramental and we look for the light in all.

In your thinking, how does Jesus' law and commission supersede the Old Testament? How do you feel about respecting the conscience and integrity of those with different beliefs?

✳ *God help me to be a reconciler*
in whatever situation I may be called upon to function.
This is not 'peace at any price',
but a genuine desire to be of use to you.

Saturday March 15   Psalm 121

Presence

This psalm is called 'a song of ascents' in the Bible, which means
it is a Pilgrim Song to be sung antiphonally and triumphantly on
the way to the Temple where the people hope to encounter God.

This psalm does *not* say, as so many people misinterpret, that
help comes from the high places. Although ancient peoples,
especially the Greeks, thought of mountains as the dwelling place
of the gods – and we have been studying how mountain top
experiences came to Moses, Elijah and Jesus – the psalmist is
quite clear that it is only from the Lord that help comes, wherever
you are.

What strength do you find in meeting with like-minded people?

In a Quaker Gathering where there are no set prayers and no
priest officiating, the silence enfolds one and people often do
speak, which in Quaker parlance is called 'ministry' if one is
inspired by the Spirit of God within.

✳ *God, let me joyfully find you in the events of today.*

TO THINK ABOUT
● Do these passages reflect my experience?
● What problems do I have with these texts?
● What new light do I see in them?

FOR ACTION
● What are the implications of these texts for my life?

IBRA International Appeal

Where does your money go?

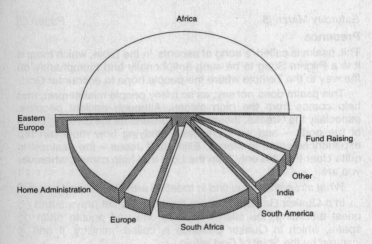

IBRA also supports work in many other countries where some Christians are not able to pay for their Bible Reading notes.

We need to respond to requests from former Eastern Europe, Romania and Estonia particularly, and provide extra help for the Gilbert Isles.

SO PLEASE HELP US AGAIN BY GIVING GENEROUSLY

Place your gift in the envelope provided and give it to your IBRA representative,

or send it direct to
The IBRA International Appeal,
1020 Bristol Road, Selly Oak,
Birmingham B29 6LB, Great Britain

THANK YOU FOR YOUR HELP

WERE YOU THERE?

Notes based on the New International Version by
John Hastings

John Hastings, a presbyter of the Church of North India and Church of Bangladesh, was a founder of community development organizations in Calcutta bustees, One World Week in the UK, and a people's movement for mass literacy in Bangladesh. He is well-known in many countries for his involvement in development, human rights, inter-faith co-operation, and literacy.

'Were you there when they crucified my Lord?' is not just a rhetorical question. To feel the force of what Jesus did and said, we need to place ourselves within the society of his time. Otherwise what we hear will be the words of a spiritualized Jesus, made more remote than Moses, David or Isaiah by the awe with which we approach 'the Son of God'. Young Christians in the Middle East Council of Churches have pioneered a method of 'materialistic Bible study' by which we avoid interpreting the Gospels to fit our society and the way we want to go, and instead try to experience what the first disciples of Jesus saw, heard, and felt. From the time he first preached in Nazareth, Jesus knew he was on a 'hit list' and must have been always looking over his shoulder for possible assassins (Luke 4.16-30; John 8.59; 10.31-39). Remember this as you study the Passion story. Ask yourself – *Am I there?*

5th Sunday in Lent, March 16   *Matthew 16.13-28 **
Can your leader rely on you?

No doubt the disciples had been dreading the day Jesus would ask them who he was. Saying he was the expected Messiah would be costly. They couldn't say they thought he was God's specially anointed servant without being prepared to follow him to death if necessary. The answer entailed commitment. So when Simon Peter said, 'You are the Christ, the Son of the Living God', he was laying his life on the line.

Peter would also have spoken with trepidation because he was aware that he was weak, impetuous and lacking in staying-power. Knowing this, Jesus immediately encouraged him – Don't worry, you're going to be as firm as a rock. Peter would never have forgotten Jesus' words of confidence in him. He was to deny Jesus, swear he didn't belong to his team and then weep in bitter remorse. But beneath the frail surface there was rock. He would come back ashamed and chastened to be a leader of the early Church in its struggles, and finally die for Jesus.

Are you there? Do you hear the Lord telling you that, whatever you might think about yourself, you are one of his rocks?

* *Son of the Living God, I am committed*
to follow you, to honour you and witness to you.
But I waver and falter. Like Peter,
I see the danger of drowning in overwhelming waves.
But then I see your smile and grasp your outstretched
* hand.*
And now I hear your assurance: 'You're a rock!'
It sounds absurd, impossible.
But if you say it, it will be true.
Say it, Lord, and make it true! Amen

Monday March 17   *Matthew 21.33-46*

Near the bone

All who heard this story knew that 'the vineyard' referred to Israel (Psalm 80.8-19; Isaiah 5.1-7): 'the landowner' was God and 'the landowner's son' was the promised Messiah. To the leaders of Israel, the implication – that they would criminally dispose of the Messiah when he came – was a smear on their right to be national leaders and guardians. Jesus suggested they would have to forfeit their God-given role to others – unclean Gentiles! Those who saw him as the anointed Servant-Son – perhaps only three or four disciples at that stage – would have got a different message: that Jesus was suggesting that one day he would not escape, as he had done before, a stoning to death or other form of execution. What then would happen to them? If the message was 'near the bone' for chief priests and Pharisees (verse 46), it was even more grimly uncomfortable for the disciples.

Are you there? Can you feel the impact? Do you wince at the thought of what Jesus demands of you?

The parable launches one more bolt – the world-shattering implication that the Kingdom of God is not to be one nation's prerogative, but the domain in which anyone, anywhere, can produce its fruit (verse 43).

* *Meditate on verse 42, and consider whether Jesus has become the 'Messiah' in your life. Has he become its cornerstone? Or have you put him on one side, and now find him putting pressure on you to change from your self-centred ways?*

Tuesday March 18   Matthew 22.41-46
Liberation by logic

Jesus was both expected and unexpected. The Jews knew God's anointed servant would come. In a world where hardly anything changes without violent action, rabbis, priests, lawyers, radicals and Zealots, all believed and taught that a strong leader would force the occupying Roman forces to leave. The warrior-king David was a good role-model. Only some pietist communities traced prophecies in the Scriptures that the Messiah's way would be patient (e.g. Isaiah 42.2-3 and 53.2-3).

Jesus found a verse that put the Pharisees on the spot. He was not merely aiming to get their holy, vaunted logic into a twist. He dented the David-model. Focusing on David would only produce a double tunnel-vision of the Kingdom: a belief that superior physical force would be needed to set it up, and that the Jews would be privileged beneficiaries (and rulers) of it. The centuries have revealed the unexpected Messiah – a very patient Prince of Peace. And the Kingdom is found to be shared by people of all races who learn to respond to God's fatherly-motherly love. Are you there?

* *Lord, we lumber along, chained by our worldly logic of trust in force and by our arrogant desire to be a latter-day 'chosen people'.*
  Save us from the weakness of relying on muscle, money and might, and give us the liberation of moving forward arm in arm with those we used to consider beyond the pale.

Wednesday March 19   Matthew 26.1-5, 14-25
Plot and crisis

Being on a hit-list changes your life, as I learned when a target of Naxalite terrorists in Calcutta in 1970. You learn to live on a knife-edge – literally. You watch out for anyone watching you. You go round every corner carefully. You let no one know where you're going next and you stop keeping a diary. You live for the task of the day, and at the end of each day thank God for having survived. Then you sleep, fitfully and eerily. Thousands upon thousands live like this today in many parts of the world – and they are by no means all Christians.

Jesus was a wanted man, and stoned more than once. He was sharply aware of the impending crisis. His disciples were not so aware. Although they couldn't expect to escape the wrath of crowds inflamed by the religious authorities and of death squads paid by them, they couldn't imagine their Messiah not being divinely protected.

The Gospels give more details of these last critical days than of any other part of Jesus' ministry. The betrayal is central. As so often, the crisis is precipitated by an inside job. A friend. Loyalty is difficult. Betrayal isn't. It's terribly, terribly easy. Are you there saying, 'Surely not I, Rabbi?'

✳ *We pray for all who live in mortal fear because they work*
  for peace and justice, whose lurking foes
  and one-time friends
  plot furtively against them.
  Give them confidence to carry on faithfully.
  Save us from any word, action or inaction
  by which we could betray them and Christ. Amen

Thursday March 20   *Matthew 26.26-35 ✳*

Solidarity

What Jesus said to the disciples at the Last Supper only made sense to them much later. We have to try to 'be there' to work it out for ourselves. We began the week with singing and dancing in the triumphal entry into Jerusalem. Then we met opposition and got wind of intrigue. Though we believe in Jesus' immunity to disaster, as Messiah, and we're sure that Palm Sunday must be the real model, we're afraid – those priests have power. Tension is high. It's hard to get into the spirit of a joyous Passover celebration.

Now, totally unaware of looming disaster, we find ourselves drawn into a covenant-contract of solidarity with Jesus. Our companionship (the Latin word means 'eating bread together') suddenly becomes very close indeed. Anyone not committed must get out. We're still sure victory is at hand, when Jesus stuns us by saying one of us is about to desert. Then, with Judas out, we close ranks even more tightly, and wine is passed round to seal our solidarity. We're a solid compacted company of committed people.

But it's not just a matter of one man's betrayal. Rock Simon (is that me?) will disown Jesus. Unthinkable! Mortally offended, he makes his most fervent declaration of allegiance.

✳ *Lord, I want your victory, your Kingdom to be*
   established.
   I shall never disown you. All I am I owe to you.
   You have called me a rock
   and given me a rock on which to stand.
   I would like to be stronger than Peter.
   Yet if, sadly, I prove to be just as shaky,
   I know you will have me back in solidarity. Amen

Friday March 21   *Matthew 26.36-46 ✳*

A willing spirit

Jesus prayed in Gethsemane. For our sakes and our salvation, he prayed for strength to drain the bitter cup. His very slight shift of emphasis from the prayer of verse 39 to that of 42 is an example of how we should pray when faced with a crisis or dreadful catastrophe. It was as though, with us, he was learning to pray. He was indeed praying *with* his disciples, though they were asleep in the warm, heavy evening air. Finding them so, he chided, but in the same breath spread his understanding forgiveness over them – an example of how we should forgive.

'The spirit is willing, but the body is weak.' You can say that again! How often it happens! But God gives full credit for real intentions. It happens the other way around too: when our spirit is weak and unwilling and our desires are selfish, then we have to turn to God and pray with the Psalmist, 'Grant me a willing spirit, to sustain me' (Psalm 51.12). Is this where you are?

✳ *Pray using the words of Psalm 51,*
   especially verses 1-4, 9-12 and 17.

Saturday March 22   *Matthew 26.47-56 ✳*

A shifty kiss

W H Vanstone in *The Stature of Waiting* puts a strong case for the view that the handing over of Jesus by Judas was a watershed of supreme importance. Up to that moment, he was

71

actively in charge of all he did. After it he was passive, at the receiving end of decisions taken by others. After receiving the barbed kiss, Jesus accepted this role reversal with a final active nudge: 'Friend, do what you came for' (verse 50).

He then confirmed his acceptance of passive helplessness, telling his impetuous sword-happy follower that he would not call on his Father for an army of liberating angels. After Jesus' choices in the wilderness, there was no chance of that (Matthew 4.1-11).

The ambiguous kiss opened the final Act of the drama. Jesus, who had always been doing, found the doing directed at him, and this was the most glorious part of his ministry!

You may be one of the millions who know the experience of becoming 'passive' and dread becoming helpless through some barbed fate – a terminal disease, caring for a bed-ridden loved one, imprisonment, mental duress, loss of a limb, rejected love, unemployment, or even 'normal' retirement. You enter the ministry of patient, painful waiting, having unwanted things happen to you. That ministry has the highest stature of all ministries. Are you there? Are you beside someone who is?

✳ *Meditate on the signs of friendship you give, and their meaning. Are there any double meanings? Then think of friendships which have soured, and pray for those you have come to suspect of ambivalence. Lastly, ask yourself if there is any selfish hope of gain in your love for God.*

TO THINK ABOUT

Was Jesus as much concerned about community spirituality and solidarity as about private, personal communion with God?

Go through the prayers of the past week and turn them into community-centred prayers.

Palm Sunday, March 23   *Matthew 26.57-68* *

Odd trial, odd law, odd verdict

Having a crime called 'blasphemy' can make mockery of justice in any country. It is a tool in the hands of extremist clerics. Touch any article of our belief and we'll hang you for it – even if our belief means a denial of human rights, exclusion of women, and suppression of honest opinion, education and science ...

The furtive trial at dead of night was a farce. The High Priest, lawyers and elders wanted a pretext for condemning Jesus to death. Even false witnesses could not provide the false evidence they wanted (verses 59-60)! Bringing true evidence (verse 61) didn't work either. Though the Temple was specially dear to them, what Jesus said about it was hardly a capital offence, and Caiaphas knew it. Many had claimed to be Messiah. That could be a delusion or a political threat, or both. It could not be blasphemy until tested – which is what Jesus was getting at in his reply to Caiaphas (verse 64). But Jesus had already been judged – on appearances. He was not a 'photo-fit' of what they expected the Messiah to be, a man loyal to national supremacy with a viable programme for establishing it. Peter, watching, was appalled. He was there to see justice done. Still the innocent suffer from bad law. Are you there?

* *Pray for those currently on trial because they have offended*
   the hierarchy, or are imprisoned under inhumane laws.
   Pray for law-makers, juries, judges and barristers.

Monday March 24   *Matthew 26.69-75* *

Wanted: super-human strength

At least it can be said of Peter that he was there. There was serious cause for alarm. Jesus had ruled out celestial military intervention. He could be facing execution. Perhaps he wasn't God's anointed one after all. The other disciples had fled. Peter decided to be there. Would you have been there? Are you there?

Things were even worse. The Sanhedrin trial had gone badly. There was so much Jesus could have said and didn't! Peter was disappointed with Jesus' self-defence. Maybe he had taken an unnecessary risk in coming to court? The risk was greater: after three years of looking out for assassins, he was in a cold sweat, close to panic. Who would have admitted allegiance in those circumstances? Peter remembered that he had sworn never to disown his Master. He knew how high were Jesus' expectations of him, and he wept. Are you there?

* *What am I afraid of?*
   Friends who jeer if I speak of my faith?
   Social penalties through holding on to Christian principles?
   The possibility that Christian faith is a delusion after all?

73

Discrimination and attack for belonging to a minority
community? Not enough strength of character ...?
Lord Jesus, as you appeared first to Peter
in your resurrection, and reinforced the rock of faith in
   him,
so come, forgive and affirm us when we fail.

(Corinthians 15.5)

Tuesday March 25   *Matthew 27.1-10*

Impatient!

What was in Judas' mind when he agreed to betray Jesus? Sheer
greed may have been the only motive (John 12.4-6). If he had
changed his mind about Jesus, his remorse shows that it was
only a temporary lapse of allegiance. A defence has been made
out for Judas that he was really hoping to hurry along the coming
of the new Kingdom. As a committed activist, it could have
seemed to him that Jesus was wasting time, not getting on with
the real work. Why not force his hand, and make a little profit at
the same time?

Judas' main failing may have been impatience. Jesus wasn't
to be hurried. He was bent on embracing the patient way – and
the root meaning of patience is 'suffering'. On the other hand, a
negative view of suffering can be self-destructive. Judas didn't
wait long enough for that message to sink in; he judged himself
too quickly, and destroyed himself.

Are we also inclined to get what income and comforts we can?
Are we impatient to get on and to encourage our friends to get on
too? Are we slow to understand the secrets of God's Kingdom? Is
it possible that we might act more like Judas than Peter? Are you
there?

✳ *Lord, teach me to be patient.*

Wednesday March 26   *Matthew 27.11-26*

Easily persuaded

Jesus, silent (though Mark and John record a few words), won
Pilate over. There was no crime. The accusation of blasphemy
cut no ice with a Roman governor. In the eyes of his accusers, the
Romans themselves were guilty of blasphemy many times over.
Yet Pilate did what the chief priests and elders wanted, and which
they then persuaded the people to demand.

When those with authority over life and death can be persuaded against their better judgment, society is in great danger. When a whole people can be so swayed, the world's stability is at risk. The twentieth century has shown us too many examples of this. Crucifixion has happened to millions upon millions of innocent people. Were you there in Pilate's hall? Everyone there, not just Pilate, was asked what should be done with Jesus. None could be neutral.

You are there, because you are part of the same world. You may not be able to do much to avert sorry judgments by corrupt leaders, but there are steps we can take to make it less likely that a whole people will bay like hounds for the blood of the guiltless.

❋ *Meditate on how religious extremism, racism and 'classism' have caused millions to suffer in our time, and pray to be shown how to take steps to combat these root evils.*

Maundy Thursday, March 27   Matthew 27.27-44

The peak of terror

Jesus had long been bracing himself for death. He must have expected it to happen by stoning (John 8.59; 10.31-33), and that could well have been in his mind when he said, 'my body is broken for you'. Such a death was a terrible prospect, but it could be quick. Suddenly Jesus found he was facing something far more terrifying, with the possibility of two days of lingering agony.

If something far more than your worse fears is happening to you, that will bring you here. But believers in Christ have to be here for two other reasons. First, at the cross we realize that he is dying for our sakes. Secondly, Jesus – stripped naked, spat on, mocked, beaten, lashed with thongs, forced to march with an unbearable load, then nailed hand and foot, dropped into the hole, then speared in the side for good measure – is one of millions who have done nothing worthy of execution but have been treated with comparable brutality. They belong, not just to the 'barbaric' past, but also to our 'civilized' age. They share Jesus' cross, and if we seek to be in 'solid' fellowship with Jesus, we are brought into solidarity with them too.

❋ *Bring to mind a few men and women or children, who are being brutally treated and are facing death in the world today. Come to the Cross and, with Jesus, pray for them.*

The peak of temptation

Jesus' last and hardest temptation was to prove that he was God's Son by coming down from the cross, tortured by the knowledge that in refusing to do so he would enable his accusers to say that this proved he was not God's Anointed One. His temptation in the wilderness (Matthew 4.6) was now more real than ever. You may be here because your temptation is reaching a peak too.

But Jesus, in excruciating pain and mental torture, did not yield. Are you here, crucified with Christ (Galatians 2.20), and by his strength uncompromised? Or you may feel you are utterly on your own, brought here, echoing Jesus' cry of being 'God-forsaken'. But feelings can deceive and that feeling is always false. The supremely active one had become passive from the time of his being 'handed over' by Judas, and now on the cross was absolutely helpless. But it was the moment of supreme victory. His bearing was extraordinary, just as it was before Caiaphas and Pilate. Dying from exhaustion and loss of blood, spiritual emptiness began to gnaw at him. He quoted Psalm 22. Perhaps he quietly recited the whole of it. Verses 6-8,11,13-16 and 18 were startlingly relevant. Read them if you have time (and refer back to the notes for January 8-10). His disciples had fled; he *felt* abandoned. But the women had not forsaken him (verse 55). And of course God hadn't either! God had simply 'let go' of him, to become one with us in death as well as life, completing his *gift* of his Son.

Are you there to receive him, God's gift to you for your life and death?

✳ *In the pain, misfortune, oppression,*
and death of the people,
God is silent.
God is silent on the cross,
in the crucified.
And this silence is God's word,
God's cry.
In solidarity,
God speaks the language of love. Jon Sobrino, El Salvador
From Theology of Christian Solidarity,
eds. Jon Sobrino and Juan Hernandez Pico
(Orbis, New York 1985)

Calvary woodcarving by Job Kekana, Petersburg
Used by permission of the
United Society of the Propagation of the Gospel (USPG)

When all is dark as the grave

Are you there in the grim aftermath?

Everyone had gone home, some in jeering jollity, others sick with horror, disgust, abject despair. Are you there with Joseph the Arimathean, who did not give way to dazed helplessness, but saw something practical needing to be done? He faced Pilate, tended the Lord's broken body, carried out the gruesome chore of cleaning up the wounds, and laid it out in the tomb which he had hewn out of the rock to receive his own body one day.

Joseph was a rich person. The rich tend to distance themselves from unsavoury chores and uncomfortable responsibilities and actions for which they risk criticism. They tend to opt out, protesting they are not rich, to excuse their failure to act in situations of darkness, despair or controversy. Doing nothing, they walk away.

And what of ourselves? Are you there with Joseph of Arimathea?

✳ *...Put me to what you will, rank me with whom you will; put me to doing, put me to suffering; let me be employed for you or laid aside for you ...*

From the Methodist Covenant Service © The Methodist Conference (by permission of the Methodist Publishing House)

TO THINK ABOUT

How far was the crucifixion of Jesus unique, in that it could only have happened to him, and how far was it typical, the automatic punishment coming to all who contradict dogmatic (or corrupt) religious or political authorities?

FOR ACTION

Think of one or two young people who are being 'crucified' in some way by family, church, or society. Try to empathize with them and, without being patronizing, plan some means of showing them love and understanding.

EASTER 1. We die and rise with Christ

Notes based on the New Revised Standard Version by
Lesley Husselbee

Lesley Husselbee is Secretary for Training in the United Reformed Church (UK) and is a past President of the National Christian Education Council. She has served churches in Coventry and Bourne End, Buckinghamshire.

For many, belief in the risen Christ is quite a struggle. How could it have happened? What does it mean? Has God sent a sign? What is heaven like? Isn't it a childish thing to believe in anyway? Why did Christ die and rise again? This week's readings may help you to wrestle with these difficulties, to know that Christ is alive, and that if we believe in him, we die and rise with Christ.

For further reading
Looking at Easter and Ascension, Brian Haymes (see page 248)

Easter Sunday March 30   *John 20.1-18 **
Jesus is alive! What does it mean?

This is the central and most important event for Christians – the resurrection of Jesus Christ from the dead – and yet most of the central characters were totally bewildered by it. At first, Simon Peter and the other disciple couldn't go into the tomb, and when they plucked up courage to do so, they saw, believed, and then – disappointingly – went back to their homes! Even Mary, the first to recognize the risen Jesus, initially thought he was the gardener. Although he had previously tried to explain it to them, they did not understand until he later appeared to them.

That is often true of us today. When we are given special and unexpected news, like the sudden death of a loved one, it often takes a long time to take it in. We find it difficult to accept truths from seemingly unimportant people, like Mary. Many of us are not happy to believe something unless we can work out a reason for it. No wonder so many today, especially in the West, find the idea of the resurrection of the Son of God incomprehensible and irrelevant. It may be difficult for us to understand fully the mechanics of the resurrection, but that does not matter. The important thing is to know, like Mary and the other disciples discovered, that Jesus is with us wherever we go.

✳ *'I believe; help my unbelief!' Help me to share*
the good news of your resurrection with others,
especially those who find it difficult to believe.

Monday March 31   *Matthew 12.38-42 **

Has God sent a sign?

After Jesus' resurrection, Thomas wanted proof that he was alive. 'Unless I see the mark of the nails in his hands ... I will not believe' (John 20.25). Do we, too, look for proof?

The scribes and Pharisees had difficulty in believing that Jesus was the Son of God. They wanted a sign. Jesus wanted them to realize the uselessness of looking for signs, so he used the Old Testament story of Jonah as a parable or coded message. The three days and nights that Jonah stayed in the belly of the sea monster, before being spewed onto the shore, symbolized the three days between Good Friday, when Jesus was crucified, and Easter Sunday morning when he rose from the dead – a spectacular sign after all! Jonah's message was believed immediately by the Gentile people of Nineveh, and Gentiles were more receptive than Scribes and Pharisees to Jesus' teaching.

Just as the story of Jonah is difficult for the worldly-wise Christian of today to interpret, so is Jesus' resurrection difficult to believe. We can't offer physical proof, but we can know God's presence around us. Think out how you could share your experience of the living Christ with others.

✳ *Loving God, show me your presence*
in everything that I do, and help me
to respond to life around me with this knowledge.

Tuesday April 1   *Matthew 28. 11-15 **

Resurrection cover-up

Throughout history, people have been offered bribes as hush money. Governments have covered-up things they did not want to be known, as the Watergate scandal in the USA showed. The guards at Jesus' tomb could have provided dangerous news of Christ's resurrection, which the priests needed to suppress at all costs. Spiritually bankrupt, they resorted to corrupt dealings to explain away what was to them an unacceptable event.

Today, we may be offered bribes in a variety of ways: 'If your number matches ours you may win a prize car – send it in with your order of goods.' 'If you buy a lottery ticket the 20 million dollar prize could be yours.' But the bribe might also be more subtle: 'You don't believe in Jesus Christ these days do you? That's just a myth for children.' Or more subtly still – many Christians in the West who admit to being Christian risk an awkward silence and ostracism from those around. It can take courage to tell others of Christ's resurrection, and to resist the attempts of others to ridicule such an idea. Sometimes, it is easier, like the guards, to accept the bribe of staying silent.

✳ *Courageous Christ, help me not to be swayed*
by others' opinions into denying you.

Wednesday April 2   *Revelation 1.12-18 *
What is heaven like?
Have you ever tried to imagine what heaven might be like? In one respect it is difficult to do because none of us has experienced life after death, but in another respect we know of it through our present experience of Jesus.

The Revelation to John shows a vision where heaven and earth are equally important – neither one is better or worse that the other, but they belong inseparably together. The seven gold lamps (like the seven-branched candlesticks celebrating the Jewish Festival of Lights), represent the seven churches of Asia; the seven stars represent heaven. And the risen Christ, the Son of Man, 'in the midst of the lamp stands' has not withdrawn from earth; he is no absentee who has withdrawn at his Ascension – he is there with his seven churches. The risen Christ is both with God and here with us on earth.

What a cause of celebration! The risen Christ is with us!

Hail the Lord of earth and heaven!
Praise to thee by both be given:
thee we greet triumphant now,
hail, the Resurrection Thou! Alleluia! Charles Wesley

Thursday April 3   Isaiah 12.1-6 *

Why did Christ die and rise again?

This passage from Isaiah reads like a Psalm of thanksgiving. Again and again it sings out that 'God is my salvation'. What do these words mean? The writer of this hymn in the eighth century BC probably had no idea of the full extent of God's saving power. He was aware of how God led his people out of Egypt, and saved them at the time of Passover, but he was writing at a time when Judah, the Southern kingdom, was threatened by a powerful neighbour, Assyria. Perhaps he saw God delivering his people from their enemies. He wrote, however, about 150 years before a second Isaiah wrote of the 'suffering servant', through whose death and resurrection we would be made whole (Isaiah 52.13 to 53.12). Today, our knowledge of God's salvation is much richer. We know how God sent his Son to live a human life, like ours, to suffer and die on a cross, and then to rise again so that we too can be forgiven our sins and be with God.

Notice that the Bible, especially this passage, is not at all concerned with asking what salvation consists of, or what we have to do to achieve it. Rather it proclaims, with joy, that salvation exists! Through Christ's death and rising again it is a gift to all of us.

✳ *Saviour God, help me to live secure in the knowledge and faith that you have died for me.*
May that joyful knowledge make a difference to my life.
Show me how I may respond to your loving gift.

Friday April 4   Acts 13.26-31 *

Telling it how it is

Have you noticed how people love stories? Small children love hearing the same stories told over and over again. Older children and adults read novels, and love to watch films. Stories help us to get alongside others and identify with them.

In Paul's one and only missionary sermon in Antioch, he simply retells the story of how Jesus was betrayed and killed. With excitement, he then retells how God raised him from death, and of those who saw him alive. He tells the story. One of the problems for Christians in the West is that we assume that everyone knows the story of Jesus, so we delve into many fascinating details, but fail to tell the story. Sadly, many people today have not heard the full story of Jesus.

82

Perhaps it is time that many of us recaptured the art of retelling the story. You notice here that witnesses were important to Paul. Those who saw the risen Christ and told of their experiences were vital; without Mary Magdalene, Peter and the others *we* would not have heard.

* **Storytelling God, help me to share the good news of your death and life with others.**

Saturday April 5   *Romans 6.3-11* *

We die and rise with Christ.

The river that ran through a Malawian rural missionary settlement was low and brown. Rain had not fallen for many months. But when sixty-two new Christians came to be baptized in the river, the dirty water powerfully symbolized for everyone there the way in which we are all baptized into Jesus' death – and rise again, washed from our sins, ready for a new life with the living Christ. The rite of Christian initiation introduces us into union with Christ's suffering and death – dead to sin.

Promising to follow Christ is a costly promise. We cannot any longer go on with our old way of doing things. Jesus' immense sacrifice on our behalf should make a difference to our lives too. Think of one or two ways in which you might change your life as a result of Christ's sacrifice.

* **Soar we now where Christ hath led,**
   following our exalted Head;
   made like him, like him we rise:
   ours the cross, the grave, the skies. Alleluia!
                                     Charles Wesley (1707-88)

TO THINK ABOUT

Read Matthew 28.11-15 again. Think of ways in which you try to cover-up the good news of Christ's resurrection.

FOR ACTION

Decide on one or two ways in which you might change your life as a result of Christ's dying and rising again.

EASTER 2. God's salvation unfolds

Notes based on the New Revised Standard Version by
Brian Haymes

Brian Haymes, Principal of the Bristol Baptist College, is the author of the 'Looking At' series published by IBRA. He has served as President of the Baptist Union of Great Britain.

Preachers often speak of what God has done in Jesus as 'finished work'. All that is necessary for the salvation of the world has been accomplished in the life, death and resurrection of Jesus Christ. The fight has been fought and the battle is won! There is nothing anyone can or has to add to 'Christ's finished work'.

But clearly God's work is not finished. What are the implications of the cross and resurrection of Christ for the future? What does it mean to say and live with Jesus as Lord? What can we expect as *God's salvation unfolds?* This week's readings challenge and comfort us with the good news of God's patience, persistence and transforming power.

Gracious God, you have never given up
on the world you have made.
We bless you for all you have done, are doing,
and will do for us in Christ.

1st Sunday after Easter, April 6   *Colossians 3.1-11* *
Lift up your hearts!
Something new has happened in God's work in Jesus. The victory over sin and death is to be celebrated every day. The Easter event is the basis for a whole new way of living, of being community.

The passage suggests Christian baptism. We are baptized into Christ and raised with Christ. Christians are no longer in the captive arms of their past or the present powers that challenge God's will. A whole new world is coming to be.

It does not happen automatically, as if God would deny our freedom and choice. But the new life is possible because of Christ. So, 'seek!' Do not allow the goods of this world to become gods. That is idolatry and the way back to slavery.

Live the new life where the old distinctions between people, that favoured the strong but hurt the weak, do not apply. Leave the past, live the new life in Christ. Enter into God's salvation! Each Sunday the Church proclaims this message. And each day Christians are called to live the reality of it in their lives.

✳ *Thank you, living God, for the gospel*
   and how you unfold its meaning in our lives day by day.

Monday April 7   *Genesis 1.1-5, 26-31 **
A very good beginning
God first saw a chaos, a mess, and into it he brought order and life. So the world came to be. And it was very good. From the first, God's intention was full and glorious life for all he made.

And that includes us. We were given a special place in God's purposes, to make creation work and flourish. In fact, at the moment, we have a problem. The natural world is under threat. Some lakes have become dead, poisoned by chemicals. Cutting down forest has led to deserts where once there was lush pasture. We have so subdued some animals that we have brought them to extinction, and have shut up others in batteries.

The Bible sees creation itself longing for God's full salvation (Romans 8.18-25). It will not know it while we look on creation as ours to do with as we wish. We are stewards, not owners. We have a part to play if God's creation is to know God's salvation. Matters of ecology are not just ethical. They have spiritual challenges for us. God has a purpose for us and for all that he has created.

✳ *Lord, help us to be good stewards*
   and never frustrate your gift of life.

Tuesday April 8   *Exodus 14.15-22 **
Forward march!
Imagine the Israelites standing there before the river, swirling water threatening death, declaring no way forward, and behind them the Egyptian cavalry thundering up, powered by Pharaoh's wrath. The people are trapped. Moses must have sounded mad when he said, 'Go forward!'

85

Entering into God's salvation requires faith, and faith sometimes calls for courage. Fear can freeze you to the spot. Without faith the Israelites would have been stuck ready for slaughter. To cross the sea meant having courage to step out in trust of God. There was no salvation in staying put.

Discipleship requires such courage. Jesus comes calling us to follow into new ways of life, new ways of loving, new kinds of relationships. And there is no knowing the salvation of God without stepping out into an unknown future.

Later in the story of Israel's liberation we read of the pillar of cloud and the fire going before the people. These symbolize the God who goes ahead of us. Living the life of those on the way to salvation involves following, trusting, journeying on with God, in confidence of God's utter faithfulness.

✳ *Give us courage, Lord,*
that we may walk on into your future today.

Wednesday April 9   *Ezekiel 36.16-28* ✳
God's commitment

Our patience can be very thin. At the first sign of difficulty some give in. All of us have our limit and cry, 'I give up!'

We could at least identify with God if that had been his attitude to Israel. He had set them free but they persisted in going their own way. God sent words of warning through the prophets. Disaster lay ahead if they persisted. And so it was. Into captivity went the people God had liberated.

Now what does God do? Abandon them and set off with another nation? No! God stays with his promises. His integrity is at stake. He will not give up or abandon these failures.

God's salvation is marked by endless patience. He works on and on like a potter working with clay that has a mind of its own and will not come right. God persists. This salvation is costly for God. We presume on God's goodness and faithfulness. We forget that it involves the kind of loving focused in the cross. God keeps faith. That is our hope.

✳ *Loving God, thank you that you never give up on us,*
that you are always working to fulfil your purposes.

New creation!

This is a stunning passage. Read it again and note the scope of God's saving work. It seems that God's intention goes way beyond redeeming a few souls for glory. Nothing less than a new heaven and a new earth is God's goal.

The signs of God's coming salvation are very down to earth. No child dies. The elderly reach their full term of years. There is housing, work and food for all. And before they even ask, God answers prayer. There is an end to harm and brutality even among the animals.

It is tempting to dismiss this as a wonderful but impossible dream. But at least it makes us realize that care for children and the elderly, housing and work provision, food for the hungry – all these are in keeping with the fullness of God's coming salvation. When Aid agencies, politicians and local churches engage in this work it is more than social care. Though they may not recognize it, they are sharing in the purposes of God for all.

✷ *Lord, thank you for visions of a new world*
   that disturb our present living
   and call us to greater responsibilities.

A new humanity

Imagine your life being so broken that repair was impossible. Much of the Bible sees humankind in these terms. Adam's 'fall' results in people being scattered all over the world and unable to communicate (see Genesis 11.1-9). Through the years we have seen the result of that in wars, racial prejudice, slavery and all the ways people get separated. In spite of visionary ideas like the United Nations we cannot find it in us to live as one human family.

Only God can do that in Christ. The great divide between Gentiles and Jews was overcome in Christ. People once separated were brought together. The walls they had made came down. Whenever we see people being reunited, seeking peace together – where once they were at enmity – there we see the unfolding of God's salvation. It underlines the Church's call to live and preach the gospel of reconciliation.

* **Bind us together, Lord, in the love of Christ,
and make us one.**

Saturday April 12   Hebrews 12.18-29

Awe-ful comfort

The first readers of the letter to the Hebrews were people who knew discouragement because of persecution and misunderstanding. Was this what being a Christian amounted to? What have they come to in Christ?

Not to the old covenant with its terrifying signs, fire, earthquake, tempests such as scared even Moses. These 'natural' happenings are far from being the whole story of God.

The writer reminds the Church that we have drawn near to the living God, to angels throwing a party, to the saints. All this is heaven, and so the writer stresses Jesus and his sacrifice, bringer of the new covenant with whom there is no heaven. And our coming near to heaven is possible because of God's coming to us in Christ.

This is the comfort of the gospel. Here is affirmation of what cannot be shaken in a sometimes frightening world. But this is not to be taken for granted, as if such a work of salvation is easy and cheap for God. Faithful trust marks the Christian life, but so does reverence and awe.

* **God our Saviour, what you have done for us is amazing.
We bow in wonder, gratitude and adoration.**

TO THINK ABOUT

● Where do you see God in his saving purposes at work in the world, and your own life, today?
● This week's readings suggest a broad vision of God's salvation, including the natural world. How have you responded to this? Should this affect how we treat animals?

FOR ACTION

This week's readings also have a theme of hope. Can you think of people in hopeless situations? Why not do something: write a letter, or make a visit, give a gift, or get people together to plan and work to convey a sense of hope in despairing and broken situations.

EASTER 3. Salvation work is costly

Notes based on the Revised Standard Version by
J Maunglat

J Maunglat is pastor of the Sinai Baptist Church in East Gyogone, Insein, Myanmar (formerly known as Burma), and he teaches Church History at the Myanmar Institute of Theology.

Christ offered himself on the cross, fully and with love. This was the price of salvation for all people, for all times. What is our response to this and to the long line of faithful martyrs? What costly service are we called to offer in the community? In what situations might we be challenged to face unpopularity and even death?

2nd Sunday after Easter, April 13   Nehemiah 2.1-18 *
Courage

Wine tasting was regarded as a pleasant occupation, so the cup-bearer was expected to look happy, or he might be suspected of treachery. Nehemiah, a Jewish captive, served as cup-bearer to King Artaxerxes of Persia, but his heart was saddened by news that his people in Jerusalem were in 'great trouble and shame'; their walls and gates were broken down and destroyed by fire. His face reflected his feelings and caused the King to ask the reason. Nehemiah prayed to God to give him a suitable reply and was given courage to ask the King for help in rebuilding Jerusalem. The King might have thought that Nehemiah was planning a rebellion against him, but Nehemiah's faith in God and honest answers were plain to see. Had Nehemiah evaded the king's question, the course of Jewish history might have changed in ways beyond recognition. Salvation work is costly. It takes courage, honesty and a deep faith in God to accomplish. Nehemiah had a vision of a rebuilt Jerusalem and a mighty people.

It took courage, and a great vision of the Kingdom of the redeemed, for our Lord Jesus Christ to face and endure the cross. We are indeed thankful that he did so.

✳ *Jesus, our Lord and Saviour,*
help us to be more like you each day,
and to realize what it cost you to save us.
We pray for those who witness to their faith
in countries where it is not safe to do so.

Monday April 14   *Nehemiah 7.73b to 8.3; 9-12*

Obedience

The Jews loved and venerated the Law. During the feast of Tabernacles, they came together to hear the words of Scripture read to them by Ezra the priest and scribe. As the books were read, they showed their repentance by their weeping (verse 9) and made booths and lived in them to remind them of the Exodus (verse 16-17). Before the time of Ezra and Nehemiah, ordinary Jews did not have access to the Law. Now they were overwhelmed by its goodness and readily obeyed its instructions. Obedience was the price of the life to which God called them.

In his work of salvation, Jesus fulfilled the Law and the words of the prophets. Those who desire to be partners with Christ in the work of salvation will help others to live pure and holy lives under the guidance of the Holy Spirit.

For some, salvation means separation from family and loved ones. When Ko Than Myint, a Buddhist, became a Christian, he was isolated from his family and ostracized by his friends. This was the price he had to pay. Throughout the world many others pay a heavy price for theirs' and others' salvation.

✳ *Dear Lord, you died upon the cross at Calvary*
to save and redeem the world.
Make us – co-workers with you – upright in word and
deed
that we may glorify your holy name in our lives.

Tuesday April 15   *Luke 14.25-33*

No compromise

In any major undertaking, before the work begins, one must carefully consider the possibilities, probabilities and impossibilities. After all these have been taken into account, one must step out in faith, put oneself on the line, ready to triumph or face defeat. A king with an army of 10,000 men thinks twice before he sets out to conquer an army of 20,000. He has to negotiate for peace or a truce before the battle commences. In the same way, if we are to follow Christ, we need to be aware of the cost.

Following Christ is not easy. It is like learning to hate one's parents and relatives and even one's own life. In its biblical context, the word 'hate' is a strong word: the opposite of 'love'. If we really love Jesus, we cannot compromise this love with anything else.

✷ *Dear Father, help us always to be true to you.*
In times of problems and difficulties,
help us to make good and wise choices.
Teach us to know how and when to go forward
and when to stop.

Wednesday April 16   Revelation 2.1-7
Love one another
The church at Ephesus had a reputation for patient endurance in the face of adversity. And they were discerning in choosing and admitting evangelists and apostles.

In Myanmar, most of our Baptist churches, unlike the community at Ephesus, permit a variety of preachers to use our pulpits, providing they are good speakers. If the preacher keeps to traditional theology, there is no problem. But sectarian issues sometimes cause misunderstanding, and some churches have split as a result. One group teaches, for example, that unless a believer can speak in tongues, he cannot be said to be filled with the Holy Spirit. But we know from the Bible that those who have the Spirit of God will also bear the 'fruits of the Spirit' (Galatians 5.22-23). The risen and glorified Christ praised the Ephesians for their endurance in time of persecution, but also warned them not to forget to practise love, the first fruit of the Spirit.

Sometimes we are so busy with church work that we forget to care for those who need our help. A pastor and minister can be so involved in church administration that he is liable to forget that he has a family needing his love and encouragement.

✷ *Dear God our heavenly Father,*
help us to make the judgments we have to make
with wisdom and grace,
that we may be judged to do right by you.
Teach us to love one another, to be kind and gentle.
Give us the power of endurance to overcome all evil.

91

Carry one another's burdens

It is easy to commit sin, but difficult to counsel a sinner and mediate forgiveness. Paul asks the Galatians to help those who need to be gently restored to the right way. But he reminds them that the counsellor must watch his or her own life (verse 3). Honest self-criticism is needed before anyone can carry his own burden, let alone help to shoulder the burdens of others. 'God is not to be fooled; everyone reaps what he sows' (verses 7 and 8).

What we do during our temporary life on earth has eternal consequences. Read the story of the rich man and Lazarus in Luke 16.19-31, and see what Jesus has to say on this subject.

We have such a short span of life in which to carry out God's will. Each decision we make and put into practice has its consequences in the rest of our lives and in eternity. So let us live one day at a time, trusting our Lord and Saviour Jesus Christ to lead us and guide us by his Holy Spirit.

✳ *Heavenly Father,*
   help us not to squander our time on things that do not
      last,
   but to spend our time wisely, caring for others,
   that we may glorify your name. Amen

Faithful to the last

For the early Church, following Christ was like running a race before a crowd of faithful witnesses, from Abraham to the present time. Each person's actions were not forgotten; they were recorded. Some were tortured and some were killed. Some had nowhere to live. Each one ran the race of life to its conclusion and won through faith in God. That is the kind of witness we should emulate. Early Christians suffered all manner of persecution, though it is not the manner of our death but how we live and die which is the crucial issue. There is a saying that 'a brave man dies but once and a coward many times'.

The first notable martyr in Myanmar was King Natshin Naung, the King of Toungoo. He was a famous warrior, politician, musician and poet whose poems are still taught in schools and sung by the people. King Natshin Naung was beheaded by the orders of a rival king in 1613. The value of a person's death lies in the fact that he died for the truth.

* *Father, help us to live as noble subjects of your*
    Kingdom.
  May we be worthy of the price you paid to save us from
    evil.
  Bless all Christians who are suffering persecution
  for the good of others, and for your noble cause. Amen

Saturday April 19   Romans 15.1-13

Hope – a gift of God

The life of a Christian is of great worth, for God accepts us the
way we are and not because of what we do. We strive to lead
good and holy lives, to be strong in the faith and morally sound
before others, yet those with lesser faith easily fall into
temptation. Paul includes himself here as one whose faith is
strong. We are not to judge or condemn the failure of the weak.
God is their judge. We must be patient and understanding,
sensitive to their feelings, support them and guide them into a
stronger faith in our Lord.

At the time this letter was written, while most Roman subjects
worshipped the state and its traditional gods, Christians
recognized only Christ as Lord and Saviour. Paul holds before us
the example of Christ whose righteousness is seen in his
obedience to God, despite the derision and suffering he endured.
Encouragement to endure like this comes from God, and this
gives us hope (verse 4).

* *Jesus our Lord and Saviour,*
  it is so easy to despise and condemn those who go
    astray.
  It is so easy to be puffed up with pride
  in our own spiritual strength and moral achievement.
  Please forgive us our sins and lead us to your truth,
  that we may cultivate patience
  and show forgiveness to those whose faith is weak.
    Amen

TO THINK ABOUT

We talk about giving ALL that we have to Christ's service. What
do we mean? Find the hymn 'Take my life, and let it be ...'. Read
it and reflect on the meaning of each verse.

EASTER 4. Power to change

Notes based on the New English Bible by
Ralph Lee

Ralph Lee is a minister and secondary school chaplain of the Methodist Church in Hong Kong. He served in the Cardiff circuit (UK) from 1990 to 1995 with the World Church in Britain Partnership. Before coming to Britain, he was also the chaplain of the United Christian Hospital in Hong Kong and on the staff of the Hong Kong Christian Council.

A historical event to come in Hong Kong is less than three months away, when China reclaims her sovereignty after 155 years of colonial rule. Since the Sino – British Agreement in 1984, people in Hong Kong have lived with anxiety and fears about this uncertain future. What are the options to ensure the continuing development of the quality of life in this city? In times of both despair and hope, what strength and faith can we rely on to meet the greatest crises yet in the history of this 'Barren Rock'? What does the gospel offer to ordinary people – wherever they are in the world – in their feeling of helplessness?

3rd Sunday after Easter, April 20   *John 11.17-27 **

The power of hope

The incredible thing is that Lazarus had been dead for days and yet Jesus was able to raise him to life. Jesus repeatedly refused to accept death as the end of life. People, who thought they knew best, accepted the inevitable outcome. Martha, resigned to circumstances, even took Jesus' words to mean 'at the resurrection on the last day'.

Yet one who has faith will not give up trying. By faith and with God's power, one might just change that which by ordinary thought is impossible. On Sunday 17 September 1995, people in Hong Kong had their first and probably last general election of the Legislative Council before the change of sovereignty in July this year. After 153 years of colonial rule from an appointed government we changed to an elected legislature. History was made. Only hours after the start of the poll, China reiterated that she would dismantle the whole political reform after taking over

Hong Kong in July this year. Yet, amazingly 920,567 citizens cast their votes in support of the democratic election. More than this, only one candidate backed by China succeeded in gaining a seat in the Legislature. What a clear and loud voice for democracy. The people of Hong Kong refused to accept the pronouncement of 'death' before the election. We believe that nothing is final. There is always hope for change if we believe in ourselves. On Sunday, the Lord's day, much more can happen!

How much more this can be realized if we have Jesus coming into our midst! If we dare not hope, then, nothing can happen.

✳ *In our helplessness, Lord,*
  give us faith to be aware that Jesus is present.
  In our despair, help us believe
  that nothing is impossible in your strength.
  Give us faith to trust in you and feel your power of
      change.

Monday April 21   *1 Corinthians 2.1-8*

The power of faith

When does one not need to display his or her importance and authority by status, qualification, appearance and claim to long standing traditions? Can one be more acceptable – and more influential – simply by belief in the power of love?

Over a year ago, on the Hong Kong Methodist Church Education Day, tribute was paid to the Church's former education secretary who had died of cancer. A book was published in her memory, and three hundred copies sold in one morning. Betsy Lee, in her love of children and of God, displayed gentleness with warmth, and a strong conviction and power. She had given up a prestigious position as principal of a secondary school and devoted herself to the education of young children. For thirty years she steered the Church's education work to a high standard and was well loved and respected. A Chinese expression – 'the naked heart of a child' – aptly describes her. That presentation of self – not boasting of human authority – is the more memorable and sets a model for others to follow.

Paul and Jesus displayed that humble gentleness and carried strong convictions and influence. There is an invisible strength behind what may seem like weakness.

Love is gentle, love is never boastful. Love does not need force and authority. True love is spiritual power.

✳ *God, help us to follow Jesu's example and not the
world's.
Strength and respect comes from giving of oneself
and not from acquiring more.
By dying to self, may we gain life and your name be
glorified.*

Tuesday April 22   *1 Corinthians 12.4-11*

The power of community

A major difference between Western and Eastern culture is that
one emphasizes the individual and the other community. Both
has advantages and disadvantages. In the first case, one person
excels while neglecting the majority, and in the second, the
individual sacrifices but the whole benefits. Both are incomplete.

We live in an age of individual excellence. We tend to go
deeper and further into our own speciality so that we become
experts. The church is no exception to these trends. We might
admire someone who can preach powerfully or someone who
has the power of healing and dream that one day we could be
that somebody. By seeking personal advancement, we
consciously or unconsciously ignore the power which comes from
the whole people of God. The more powerful one person is, the
weaker the majority becomes. Lasting strength comes by working
together, everyone contributing according to the gifts God has
given each person. Combined and multiplied the force is
unimaginable.

We are gifted in a variety of ways by the Holy Spirit. Let them
not be buried by any individual leader or charismatic person. We
can all contribute to the advancement of God's Kingdom in our
own areas. It is corporately and with God as our head, that we
can expect change, not simply by relying on one leader.

✳ *Teach us, Lord, how to sacrifice
that we may complete your will for each person.
Move us also, Lord, that we might join together
to hasten the momentum.*

Wednesday April 23   *Philippians 3.10-17*

Resurrection power

It is almost incredible that a great number of people in Hong Kong
would do something totally against the predictable opposition of

force to come – in the belief that democracy will win at the end of the day. This wishful thinking may bring further suppression of the people, but it may also bring hope and harmony in the long run to the six million people of Hong Kong.

Jesus had a mission and experienced suffering on the cross. Yet through it life came from resurrection. He also encouraged believers to follow him. At the heart of our Christian belief is life from death. The power of change is that we can face death squarely with courage, for Jesus has gone through it for us. If the ultimate fear of being human is no longer the threat of death, then what emerges is powerful courage. Behind all this is our faith in God, that he walks with us.

For the second time of democratic election (from partial to general election in 1995 of the Hong Kong political legislature), people decidedly and stubbornly elected many that the sovereign to come will not accept at all. I believe that the power of change comes from the people as well as from God. There must be a purpose in all these happenings. People are constantly making their stand clear, regardless of the threats of those in power.

To seize the present, in order to secure a future according to the people, may require taking risks. But if that is the goal of life, as Paul said, we shall strive forward without fear. For God is with those who take risks.

✳ *God, give us the courage to stand by our belief,*
even willingly prepare ourselves to suffer,
for the power of resurrection enables us
to meet all challenges in life – here and now and in the
    future.

Thursday April 24   *Ephesians 1.15-23*

The power of God's presence

Paul points to seeing a vision with inward eyes, that we may be illumined to see the hope that is in us. What makes people able to see beyond today? Even if they are not certain about the present, any knowledge of the future is beyond them. Could such a dream of seeing the future be confined mainly to those who are more capable of effecting change – the educated, middle/higher classes or the visionary? And if they could start to dream, where would the power to change come from?

I have been teaching some senior secondary school students in a housing estate. Many of them come from the lower stratas of society, with difficult family situations and low self esteem. My difficulty at first was how to motivate them to realize that within themselves they have the potential to grow. Then secondly, if they would welcome it, there is a 'power to change' in the universe. God is around if they want to be closer to him.

Sometimes we close our eyes and say to ourselves, 'I am blind. I cannot see.' But we are not. In fact, there is that 'inward eye' that connects our weak, low self to the wider vision of God.

Only when we turn to God, we have hope in the present and power to face our future with confidence. God has given us the 'inward eye'. Let us not waste it.

✳ *Be thou my vision, O Lord of my heart,*
Be all else but naught to me, save that thou art;
Be thou my best thought in the day and the night,
Both waking and sleeping, thy presence my light.

Irish c. 8th century

Friday April 25   Acts 20.16-27
Unshakeable power

How courageous and at the same time at peace Paul was in spite of what lay ahead of him – 'imprisonment and hardships'. Yet the impending suffering was no deterrent to him when it came to completing the mission God had given to him. He knew the direction of his life's journey.

How important it is to have a goal, a purpose for everyday life, so precious that we embrace it whole-heartedly and are willing to sacrifice our own future for its sake. We might be called naive and unworldly. Yet, so often, the world is shaped by the idealistic few. Fearless until the finishing line, not for our own interest but for the good of others. Since my return to Hong Kong from Cardiff, I have been impressed and encouraged by some of Hong Kong's leaders who, for the sake of a better Hong Kong after 1997, dare to speak up and be counted, in spite of being labelled as 'subversive'. We thank God for giving courage and power to that small group of people who dare stand up for whatever cause it might be. The challenge is whether I can take the gospel seriously into myself, forgetting my own security and possessions for Jesu's sake!

✳ *Jesus, for our sake, you came and gave us all you had.*
Move us to keep back nothing for ourselves
so that others may have all that you have shared with us.

God's power sustains

Can we remain calm when facing imminent danger? Where can we gather power to defend ourselves? It may seem that we have strength, but can we really have enough confidence?

We tend to think that defence lies in material and human strength. In the past decade or two Hong Kong people have accumulated wealth and resources and, with it, possibly a false hope of strength and power in facing the 1997 issue. Many – the young, the professionals, the wealthy – can emigrate and start a new life, to avoid the change. Would life be better, or at least equally good, by not taking on the challenges? Is happiness really built on human possessions and security?

Paul cites two alternatives in dealing with crises: empowerment from God and the happiness that comes from giving oneself. This is the centre of our Christian belief; life from death and faith from a mustard seed which could become the Kingdom of God. Life becomes meaningful by meeting the challenges. It is by giving to others that we obtain life.

In 65 more days, the sovereignty of Hong Kong will revert to China. Many have equipped themselves by personal wealth to secure a better future. Yet, a significant number have, with faith and courage, committed their lives to their people by staying with the majority who lack resources to leave Hong Kong.

✳ *God, it is you who have given us the ideals of hope*
   and the example of Jesus, your Son.
   Give us the strength and love to live not for ourselves
   only.
   Move us forward with your mighty power
   for you are the Lord of history always in the making.

TO THINK ABOUT and FOR ACTION

- What challenges does this testimony of faith from Hong Kong make to your situation?
- When has God's 'power to change' been most active in your life and community, and how can you share this experience with others?
- Follow the news about Hong Kong and remember its people in your prayers. Pray for the leaders of China that they may use their power with true wisdom and for the benefit of world peace.

WORK OF THE SPIRIT
1. A renewed community

Meditations based on the Revised Standard Version by
Jean Vanier

Jean Vanier is a Canadian who founded the first community of L'Arche. In 1964 he welcomed Raphael Simi and Philippe Seux, two men with mental handicaps, into a small house in Trosly-Breuil, a village in northern France. This first community has grown into twenty homes and different workshops in Trosly and adjacent villages. From this first community, over one hundred others have grown around the world (seven in the UK, thirty-four in North America and three in Australia). Each community is composed of a number of family-type homes and frequently workshops; each one brings together men and women with mental handicaps and those who come to befriend them in a new form of Christian community. At the heart of each community is the belief that people with mental handicaps, so often rejected by society, are important to God, 'chosen' by God (see 1 Corinthians 1.27-29). One of the founding texts of L'Arche is Luke 14.12-15.

---

*This section is offered by the writer as a series of **meditations** (in place of the usual notes on the text). Each day, read the passage of Scripture together with the meditation. Take time to absorb the thoughts and reflect on the challenge they make to the way you relate to your local community, your church community and the wider community of the world.*

We live in a world of much 'ethnic cleansing'. People are frightened of difference. Walls go up between people and groups. Jesus sent his Holy Spirit on the day of Pentecost, and continues to send the Paraclete (from the Greek *Paracletos)* into the hearts of those who call out from their needs and poverty. Little by little the Holy Spirit transforms hearts. This transformation takes place in community. The new commandment of Jesus, to love one another as he loves us, is a call to community. Community is the place where we grow in love, in the knowledge of Jesus, and where we learn to accept difference. Community is a place of celebration and forgiveness. Today the Holy Spirit is calling the disciples of Jesus into community, and to renew community.

The promise of a new force

The risen Jesus is about to leave. The disciples will no longer see him physically, or be dependent on his visible presence. Jesus says they are going to receive a new force, the force of the Holy Spirit, who will descend upon them. This new force will make them witnesses to Jesus throughout the world. Each one will be in direct relationship with God, in and through the Holy Spirit who will guide and inspire them, strengthen and illuminate them, and change their hearts of stone into loving hearts of flesh, like the heart of Jesus. Here at last the prophecies of Joel 3.1-2 and of Ezekiel 36.27 are about to be fulfilled. The night before he died, Jesus had already said that it was good for the disciples that he leave, 'because if I do not leave, the Counsellor will not come upon you; but if I leave, I will send her' (John 16.7). Now the hour has come. Within a few days, this new force will descend upon them, transforming them so that they may accomplish things that humanly speaking they could never accomplish on their own.

So today, we call upon the Holy Spirit to come into our hearts, to transform us so that we too may be witnesses to the risen Christ, to his good news of love.

✳ *Come Holy Spirit.*
Come into our hearts.
Transform our hardness into gentleness, openness and love.
Come and guide us, lead us,
so that we may accomplish the work of God.

Waiting and praying for the Holy Spirit

The first Christian community, men and women chosen by Jesus, are together, full of hope, waiting for the gift of the Spirit. They are praying fervently, reciting the psalms, singing hymns and praying in silence. They are convinced that they have been called together by God to live and to announce Jesus' new, beautiful vision of love and of peace. They have been called together to do the work of God, and to give glory to the Father and to Jesus, not to seek their own glory. They are listening to each other and to the signs of the Spirit.

Is this not the way we are called to be today as we embark upon our projects? We are called to pray together for the Holy

Spirit to come upon us so that we may build communities of love, so that the work of the Holy Spirit may be accomplished in us and through us. This means that each of us needs to be open, without any fixed ideas or prejudices, open to what the Paraclete is going to teach, to show and give us together as a body.

✳ *Come Holy Spirit.*
  Come into our hearts.
  Liberate us from selfishness
  and from the need to prove our own worth.
  Give us listening and open hearts and minds
  so that we may welcome you together in love
  and that together, as a community,
  we may be a sign of the risen Jesus.

Tuesday April 29   *Acts 2.1-13*

Signs of the Spirit

And then the marvellous thing happens: there is a terrific blast of wind, and tongues of fire come upon each one. Each one is renewed, transformed; hearts are burning; each one feels a new strength flowing through their bodies. Each one begins to speak in a language they have never heard of or learnt. People are amazed. Something new, totally new, is happening. Is this the work of God? Or are these people drunk, hysterical, caught up in some spiritual and irrational illusion?

I wonder how we would have reacted if we had been in that crowd? Would we have been open and believing, or critical and cynical? It is important that we learn how to discern the ways of the Spirit, not to judge too quickly in a negative way. God can manifest his presence through amazing spectacular events, or through a gentle breeze. He can reveal himself through miraculous healing, through dreams or an inner voice, through speaking in strange tongues and prophetic utterances, through simple gestures of love and of compassion. It is important to be open to the ways of God, which are not always our ways; to be open to the God of surprises, the God of love who comes to make all things new.

✳ *Come Holy Spirit.*
  Come into our hearts.
  Teach us your ways.
  Help us to be open to your amazing work.
  Heal us from being closed up
  in prisons of certitude and security.

102

Teach us to listen to each other
and to discover in each person and in each community,
in all Christians, in all churches,
your presence of faith and love.

Wednesday April 30   Acts 2.14-21

Open to others

Peter gets up to explain what is happening: These people are not hysterical nor drunk. It is the fulfilment of the prophecy. The Holy Spirit is being given to all people today, not just to me or to my community, or to my church! The Holy Spirit is given to other people in other communities, in other churches and in other faiths. Hearts are changing; people are becoming more open; they are listening to one another, praying together, yearning together to meet the God of love, the God of unity, the God of peace.

It is no longer the time for believers to fight against each other, trying to prove that they are right, that they have the truth. It is time to stand up against the powers of evil, of hate, of corruption, of oppression, of division, and of death. It is now the time given by the Holy Spirit for all those who believe in love, and in the dignity of each human being, to work together for the Kingdom of love and for God who is love.

✳ *Come Holy Spirit.*
Come into our hearts.
Break down all that is closed up in us
so that we may love one another,
work with each other,
and be united with others
for the work of the God of love.

Thursday May 1   Acts 2.22-35

Announcing Jesus

Peter continues to announce Jesus. All those listening have probably seen Jesus. At least they have heard about him. 'This Jesus whom you have killed, well he is risen from the dead. We can testify to this and it is the risen Jesus who has sent the Holy Spirit upon these people.' This is the first Christian sermon announcing Jesus. Those listening are amazed by these people speaking in so many different languages. Peter explains that this is the work of the Spirit.

How do we announce Jesus today? Where are those extraordinary works of love, of compassion, of truth, of peace and of reconciliation that we can point to and which can announce: This is the work of God! This is the message of Jesus! This is the good news! Jesus wants to reveal his loving power through the Holy Spirit, and thus he can be known as a messenger of good news.

* *Come Holy Spirit.*
Come into our hearts.
Give us the strength and wisdom to build loving
*   communities,*
to create places of love and of compassion
which may touch people's hearts,
so we can then announce
that this is the work of Jesus,
this is the good news!

Friday May 2   *Acts 2.36-42*

The Word of God that penetrates hearts

Peter's words, spoken with authority, enter into people's hearts like a lance; their hearts burn with light, truth and love. The word of God spoken with authority and with love touches and opens hearts. Peter's faith is grounded in reality. It is not just ideas. He himself has suffered. He denied Jesus. He was not present at the cross. Peter was humiliated by his own inner poverty. Then he had an experience of the risen Jesus who forgave him, loved him and affirmed him in his mission. Peter's words spring from the reality of his own poverty, sinfulness and transformation.

Have we experienced preachers who speak with conviction of Jesus out of their own experience of transformation, whose words have touched and opened our hearts? Have we experienced our own words as life-giving? Do we trust that we can also announce the good news? What prevents us from announcing Jesus and the good news?

* *Come Holy Spirit.*
Come into our hearts.
We humbly ask you to help us
to welcome our own poverty and brokenness
so that we may experience the healing power of Jesus,
so that we may announce his love and presence.

The first Christian communities

These first Christians are transformed by the gift of the Spirit.
Together they create a community built on fidelity: fidelity to the
word of the apostles, fidelity in their love for one another, fidelity
in prayer and in the breaking of bread together. They agree that
everything they possess shall be held 'in common': they share
their lives and their goods, each one according to his or her
needs. There is no longer any distinction between classes and
races, the 'haves' and the 'have nots', the strong and the weak,
the healthy and the handicapped. All belong to one body, the
body of Christ which is the Church. And these communities
radiate a simplicity of life, of love, peace and joy. Many others are
attracted to this way of life.

How have we experienced this form of community? Have we
met families and friends who are living this love, welcome and
openness that spring from the Spirit of God? Are we truly
convinced that this sort of life – that radiates love – is possible?

Do we believe that the Holy Spirit is calling the Church to build
communities of love? How can we stimulate this belief and start
building such communities?

✴ *Come Holy Spirit.*
Come into our hearts.
Bring us together in love
so that we may fulfil the new commandment of Jesus:
'Love one another as I love you,'
so that we may be a sign
that the message of Jesus is truly good news.
Through love may we change our world
and bring unity and peace where there is division and
    conflict.

TO THINK ABOUT

● How can we deepen our faith in the Holy Spirit who has been
  promised to us and who comes to renew our communities?
● What are the most important elements in community life?

Healing of hearts

My experience in L'Arche is that many people with mental handicaps are healed by love, love which is commitment and fidelity; love which is respect for each person just as he or she is; love which is creative and intelligent in order to help others to progress and to live more fully; love which is caring. People close up when they feel lonely and unwanted. They open up when they feel respected, loved and appreciated.

People with mental handicaps need good doctors and psychologists, but above all they need friends who appreciate them and who reveal to them that they are precious, important and loveable. Then they have a reason to live. People who have no friends fall into a pit of despair and anguish. They lose trust in themselves and do not want to live.

We are all called to be healers, though maybe not in a spectacular way like Peter and John. We are called to heal others through love and caring, by the way we listen attentively to them; by our joy in being with them; by our fidelity. Perhaps this is the miracle of love to which Jesus is calling us.

Can we open our hearts today to someone in need who feels lonely? Can we look at such people with kindness and offer them our friendship? Perhaps this will enable them to walk on the path of life again.

＊ *Come Holy Spirit.*
Come into our hearts.
Open us to love.
Teach me to become a friend
to someone in need, someone who is lonely.

Ruach, a gentle teacher of love

Yes, there are truly miracles born from love and friendship. The lonely feel wanted, the rejected find a place, the weak and the poor discover they have gifts to bring to others. Jesus came not to enforce law but to heal our broken and fearful hearts, and to teach us how to love. We are all so deeply wounded in our affectivity, our capacity to relate to others. So quickly we seek those who are like us, who flatter us. We try to avoid those who are different, those who disturb and annoy us, those who perhaps threaten us because of their different ways and ideas. But Jesus came to free us from fear, to break down the barriers that separate people from one another.

The Spirit, the *Ruach* (the Hebrew word for Spirit is feminine), has been given to us precisely that we may learn to love others just as they are. She is a gentle teacher of love, like a mother who teaches her children. She is the womb in which we were conceived, and given life. Like Peter, we can announce that Jesus is our gentle Lord. We need Jesus because without him and his Holy Spirit sent into our hearts, we could never love.

* ***Come Holy Spirit.***
  Come into our hearts.
  So we shall be able to announce
  that Jesus is our Lord, our healer, our lover,
  our Good Shepherd
  who leads us to the waters that refresh and give us life.

Tuesday May 6   *Acts 4.1-22*

The danger of being closed up

The High Priest and the elders are embarrassed. Peter and John have obviously healed this man who was paralyzed and they affirm that they did this 'in the name of Jesus' whom the High Priest and elders condemned to death a few weeks earlier.

How stubborn and blind people can be! Jesus was surely a prophet. He performed miracles but people did not want to believe in him. They were closed up in their own ideas, theories and certitudes. Jesus did not fit into their theories. He disturbed people because he called them to truth and to change, to a new vision of the world. They wanted to remain with their own power and prestige. They dared not let go and trust Jesus. Instead they got rid of him. They did not want to change. They were closed up in themselves.

We might be believers, yet there are parts of us that are closed up. We do not want to surrender ourselves completely to Jesus and his message of love. We hold on to our prejudices and certitudes. We are controlled by fear. There are things we do not want to give up: our need for money, prestige, certain habits and friends, which hold us back from following Jesus.

* *Come Holy Spirit.*
  Come into our hearts.
  Lead us to greater belief
  and a total trust in Jesus and in his message.
  Heal our blindness and our paralysis of fear
  so that we may truly be disciples of Jesus.

Wednesday May 7   *Acts 4.23-31*

Pray for hearts that are closed

Many people today are arrogant and refuse the message of Jesus. They do not want to believe because it is too demanding. Jesus calls them to change and to leave their selfishness and self-centredness, to be open to others, to leave their projects for power, success and admiration to work for God. Many people are closed up. Perhaps many are waiting to receive the good news. Perhaps the real problem is with us, disciples of Jesus. Are we really living, radiating and announcing the good news of Jesus? To many people the message of Jesus appears to be bad news. They have not seen Jesus as a messenger of love who comes to bring peace, hope and reconciliation.

This passage calls us to prayer. Let us pray that God will send signs so that people can believe. Let us pray that our communities become the signs of the risen Jesus and of his message of love.

* *Come Holy Spirit.*
  Come into our hearts.
  We ask you to bring faith to our society and to our world,
  that Jesus may be known and loved
  particularly by the poor, the suffering and the rejected.

Ascension Day, May 8   *Philippians 2.1-11*

Our ascended Lord

Paul wrote this letter probably from a prison in Rome to the first community that he had founded in Europe, in the city of Philippi. He loved this city dearly and the Christians of Philippi clearly loved Paul. This letter is filled with love and emotion. It is perhaps a good-bye, for Paul may soon be killed by the Romans. Like Jesus the night before he died, Paul begs his disciples to work for unity: 'Be of the same heart and mind ... Don't seek your own interests but the interests of others.' And Paul ends by showing the road to unity: humility. He says: be like Jesus, take the downward path of humility and service. Take the last place. And because Jesus took the downward path and identified himself with the poor, God raised him high – exalted him – and now all creation kneels before him and proclaims that he is Lord.

This is the Ascension Day message, and it is the Holy Spirit's message to us in our communities and in our families: Work towards unity; become one. Do not struggle for power. Seek not to prove that you are right or best. Be there to serve others, to help them to grow. Do everything you can to bring peace and oneness to your community through service and humility. This is the path we are all called to take. If we take it, the Father will raise us up in the glory of Jesus in the Kingdom.

✳ *Come Holy Spirit.*
Come into our hearts.
Give us humble and serving hearts
so that we may be instruments of peace and unity
in our communities.

Friday May 9 ⠀⠀⠀⠀⠀⠀⠀⠀⠀⠀⠀⠀⠀⠀⠀⠀⠀⠀⠀⠀⠀⠀⠀⠀⠀⠀⠀*Acts 5.1-16*

Truthfulness at the heart of community

This text about Ananias and Sapphira is rather horrifying. But it tells us something important. This couple did not have to sell their land. They did, but then instead of truthfully saying how much they had sold it for, they gave only part of their money and hid the rest from Peter. Truthfulness is at the basis of community life. We are not obliged to be part of it, but if we do agree to be members of a community, then we must abide by its principles and rules. If our motives are wrong, and we join a Christian community, not because we feel called by Jesus and want to follow him, but because we want to belong to a group and to feel esteemed, then within we will die. We are refusing something. We are hiding something. We are cutting ourselves off from the grace of community and of Jesus. Community can only be renewed if all the members grow in truth. That implies that we accept all that is broken and twisted in us. Jesus does not call us because we are perfect, but because he wants us to grow in love and in truth.

✳ *Come Holy Spirit.*
Come into our hearts.
Purify us, cleanse us, heal us.
Send your light into our darkness
so that we may become light and shine truth.

Follow Jesus

If we truly want to follow Jesus and live his word, we may be rejected, mocked, and looked down upon by some people. Some may even be angry with us. In a world where the values of truth, of faith, of love and of fidelity are frequently rejected, where morality is seen as out-dated, Christians may be pushed into ghettos and their voices stifled. That is what the religious leaders of Jerusalem tried to do with Peter and the other disciples.

Let us not be concerned about what people think of us. Maybe we will be counter culture; maybe we will be seen as 'old fogies' and laughed at. What is important is not to obey the crowd, but to obey Jesus and his word and Spirit. Let us stand up for Jesus, for his message and his truth. And, as Gamaliel says, a community that is really founded on the love of God, and not upon our own needs to do things our way, will stand the test of time. If a community is of God, no one will be able to destroy it.

✳ *Come Holy Spirit.*
Come into our hearts.
Give us new strength and courage
to love Jesus, to live and announce his message
even when we are pushed aside.
Help us not to be angry and defensive,
but give us loving hearts
so that our witness may be a witness of love for others
and not of condemnation.

TO THINK ABOUT

● Is there a danger for Christians, for us, to compromise with the values of our society and to be fearful to announce the truth of Jesus?
● How can we as individuals and as a community grow in truth so that we may be renewed?

FOR ACTION

Meet with a community that appears to be full of life. Ask the members how they have grown together as a community. Let us be inspired by others.

WORK OF THE SPIRIT
2. Challenging injustice

Notes based on the New English Bible by
Gillian Weeks

Since 1990 Gillian Weeks has been Christian Aid Area Co-ordinator for West Yorkshire, based in Leeds (UK). She taught for eleven years in Kenya where she lived with her husband and three children.

In the United Kingdom this is Christian Aid Week when over a quarter of a million volunteers visit homes to collect money. Most of the income is spent on support for struggling communities in developing countries – health, adult literacy, clean water ... but ten per cent goes on education and campaigning about the causes of poverty and injustice.

Why are people poor? It is small use putting sticking plaster on the wounds caused by poverty and injustice, unless at the same time we begin to look at what is causing them. Challenging and changing systems and structures is what Christian Aid is increasingly about – standing alongside the poor in their struggles against injustice. This is not new. The Bible tells us of the same struggles several thousand years ago.

6th Sunday after Easter, May 11   Acts 4.31-37
To each according to need
Many small groups and larger communities over the centuries have lived communally, in the same spirit as is shown in this story, working and praying for a better world, sharing all they had, no-one in need, of one heart and mind ...

'Yes, but ...' the cynical can say, 'Those people were expecting the end of the world at any time and they were sharing only with like-minded believers.' 'Communism was based on such an ideal and we know it doesn't work.' 'It is not practical for today's society.' So – what can we learn from this passage?

Filled with the Holy Spirit, their instinct was to love and to share. Many Christians today have that same compulsion, an instinctive generosity when faced with human need – giving and giving again of themselves, their time and their money. I see it so much in my work. Christians of every nationality, denomination, age and background challenging injustice, not just by words and actions, but by their lifestyle, their attitudes, their sharing. Filled with the Holy Spirit (though they might not put it that way), recognizable to those like themselves. A Holy club. 'A righteous remnant' in today's materialistic world. Present in every society.

✳ **Pray to see the world through God's eyes and for the power of the Spirit to know what to do about it.**

Monday May 12   *Leviticus 25.8-22*
Distribute resources fairly
What revolutionary talk this is! What attitude is implicit in these laws? The fiftieth year was when debts were to be written off, pawned possessions returned, land restored to original owners, freedom to those in bonded labour. What an amazing dream of justice and hope!

These economic rules of behaviour recognize a limit to the right of the rich to make profit from their land, property or loans. Land must be prevented from falling into the hands of fewer and fewer people. The poorest must be protected. How different this is from today's thinking! How different from the policies of today's financial institutions. Have our 'modern', 'advanced' societies progressed at all? Gandhi said, 'There is enough for everyone's need but not enough for everyone's greed.' Jesus said he had come 'to bring good news to the poor.' Following Jesus involves campaigning for the rights of the poor, working for change in economic systems and structures, praying with our newspaper in one hand and our Bible in the other.

✳ **Pray for guidance in what you can do or say or write, however small, to change unfair systems.**

Tuesday May 13   *Leviticus 25.23-34*
A place of one's own
Everyone needs a place that is their own, where they belong. For rural people this is their farm, in towns it is the house and garden. This passage gives rules concerning three sorts of houses – those in the country, which were considered part of the land, those in the towns, and those belonging to the Levites, the church

ministers of their time who relied on the whole population for their food and other needs, and had no land in the country.

Recently we have seen the handing over of vast tracts of land to multinationals. We see people becoming waged workers on land which used to be theirs, often housed in accommodation that is no longer their own. Others have had to move into towns, increasing the numbers of the urban poor. In Britain some people who once began to buy their homes are losing them because of unemployment.

What is our modern equivalent to the year of Jubilee which returns to rural people the land they once farmed, and gives to urban people the security of home ownership? How do we, in our time, deal with these problems?

✳ *Pray for guidance to ask the right questions in the right places – and the courage to do so.*

Wednesday May 14   *Leviticus 25.35-38*
Stop exploiting the poor
In the 1970s, many developing countries borrowed money from commercial banks in the UK, when interest rates were 4 per cent, to cover the cost of education, health care, road building and so on. Then in the early 1980s world interest rates soared to approximately twenty one per cent and the price received from export crops like coffee and sugar dropped dramatically. Many governments were faced with the terrible choice of repaying their debts or running their hospitals. Debt repayment, we are told, is killing more of the world's children than any other factor.

Yet here we read, written thousands of years ago, 'When somebody is reduced to poverty, do not charge him interest on a loan'!

Should Christians get involved with the problems created by international, financial institutions? Is it our business? I believe it is. Christian Aid is owned by the Churches, and works on their behalf. We can support Christian Aid by joining their current campaign. Simple actions like writing letters to MPs *do* work if enough people take part.

Helder Camara wrote, 'The rich will accept talk of aid, but it's not done to talk too much about justice, rights, structural changes ...' That is not always so; thousands are working for change.

✳ *Lord, give us your urgent longing for a just world and show us how to turn that longing into action.*

We need leaders of integrity
Following yesterday's discussion about debt, here we read of
Nehemiah saying, 'Cancel the debts, stop oppressing the poor.'

The Jews were returning from exile and were struggling to
reconstruct their society. There was a famine as there often is
when people have been forced from their land, and have been
unable to plant. Some people were financially secure, but there
were many who were so poor they had to mortgage their land and
sell their children into bondage. The wealthy were taking
advantage of the poor in this situation. Nehemiah, who had been
appointed governor, called together a big, popular assembly and
accused the rich and powerful of exploiting the poor.

Nehemiah must have been a charismatic leader for everyone
present to reply, 'We'll do as you say.' It's interesting that he did
not claim his allowances (verse 18). He practised what he
preached – maybe the reason for his influence with the people.

Countries need leaders of integrity. An American political
leader once said, 'It's often easier to fight for one's principles than
to live up to them.' That has always been true.

✳ *Pray for God to raise up leaders of integrity in the world,
in your country, in your town or village. Pray for yourself
that you may have integrity in your sphere of influence.*

We must challenge injustice.
On Wednesday, we were thinking about the massive debt owed
by some countries and the pressure to bring about their
cancellation. Now we read this parable of debts that were
cancelled and those that were not. Notice the people who
challenged the injustice in this story (verse 31). They saw what
was going on, knew it was not right, and reported all that had
taken place. They saw the situation and, not having the power to
change it themselves, put pressure on the King.

Often we see injustice and feel powerless to change it
ourselves – but we know some person or some group who can.
Letter writing is one of the powerful tools of campaigning.
Sometimes people tell me they don't feel knowledgeable enough
to write to people such as MPs or bank managers. All that is
needed is time, a genuine concern and the ability to ask
questions. Those who work with Amnesty International or with

Christian Aid's campaigns can tell of the enormous successes brought about by letter writing.

* *For the healing of the nations,*
Lord, we pray with one accord;
For a just and equal sharing
Of the things that earth affords.
To a life of love in action
Help us rise and pledge our word.   *Fred Kaan*
        © Stainer and Bell Ltd, London, England

Saturday May 17   *Matthew 25.31-46*

Care for those in need

This is a parable of judgment – God's judgment upon his world. Some were in big trouble, not because they did bad things, but because they ignored the good things they could do to improve the lives of others. Indifference doesn't kill but it allows people to die. Those who are blessed in this story are those who went out of their way to relate to those who were disadvantaged.

A research study carried out for Christian Aid called *The Gospel, the Poor and the Churches* says that some Christians have an active response to poverty, showing anger at unfairness and a desire to help. They convert their anger into action. Others take a passive stance. They are angry but they respond by avoiding the issue, believing that responsibility lies elsewhere and leaving it 'in God's hands'.

If only they could see the effects of an active response. A whole community transformed by a well being dug, bringing fresh, clean water to the village. The joy of a newly literate adult with a new world opening up to her, saying with real joy, 'I was blind but now I see.' We *can* have hope. So much is being done.

* *Pray for the work of Christian Aid – staff, overseas partners and volunteers.*

TO THINK ABOUT and FOR ACTION

● How far is it necessary for Christians to work politically?
● What can I do to challenge unfair systems?

If you live in the UK, join Christian Aid's campaigning network. Write to: Christian Aid Campaigns Group, P O Box 100, London SE1 7RT.

THE WORK OF THE SPIRIT
3. Dreams come true

Notes based on the New Revised Standard Version by
Desmond van der Water

Desmond van der Water is a minister of the United Congregational Church of Southern Africa (UCCSA). He served as pastor of a local church in Cape Town from 1982 to 1989, before taking up a post as lecturer at the Federal Theological Seminary of Southern Africa (Fedsem). He is currently working full time, as the Mission Enabler of the UCCSA.

Since biblical times dreamers and dreams have been viewed with scorn and scepticism. 'Here comes this dreamer', Joseph's older brothers said, 'Come now, let us kill him ...'(Genesis 37.19ff). Of course, Joseph's dreams came true, to the benefit of all concerned.

But dreams do not always come true, and some dreams are downright dangerous when wrongly interpreted and acted upon. In some instances, one person's dream is another's nightmare, for example, when the dream of the poor and oppressed for liberation is the nightmare of the rich and powerful.

In African religious traditions, dreams are of special significance and as Christians, we affirm that our dreams are indeed one of the important ways in which God speaks to us, and to others.

Pentecost Sunday, May 18   *Joel 2.23-29 **
Turning things upside-down
Conventional wisdom in ancient Israel had it that the *young* dreamed dreams, and the *old* saw visions. Joel's prophecy turned conventional wisdom on its head; '... your old men shall dream dreams and your young men shall see visions' (2.28c). Surely we could infer that, with the outpouring of the Spirit the young shall be given wisdom previously only associated with the aged, *and* the aged will be endowed with new vigour and enthusiasm only associated with the young!

The account of the fulfilment of this prophecy in Acts 2.17-18 certainly suggests that the old order of exclusivity has been replaced. The Spirit is poured out '... upon all flesh'(2.17b). God's blessing and empowerment through the Spirit is given to all, to awaken faith in Jesus Christ, and for witnessing to Christ's resurrection from the dead.

Many of our churches have become so preoccupied with themselves. We are maintenance oriented rather than mission driven. It should not surprise us that those outside of the Church looking in may conclude that God is not at large and working in the world.

✳ *O Pentecostal Spirit,*
blow through us afresh,
breath in us anew,
blaze across us again
that the dying embers of Christ's mission
be revived among us, to the glory of God.

Monday May 19   *John 16.5-15*
Into all truth
The Holy Spirit is here characterized as the 'Spirit of truth', who will 'guide you into all truth' (16.13). This statement says something about the *dynamic* nature of the Christian faith.

There have always been those people within history, and there will always be, who think they know it all, and have nothing much more to learn. But God has a way of confounding our carefully worked theories and our grandest schemes. Even in our life-time, for example, we have witnessed kingdoms fall, tyrants vanquished, ideologies shattered and oppressors overthrown, especially when least expected. The swift transition from a racist autocracy to a non-racial democracy in South Africa illustrates the point.

As Christians we should always remember that we have *not arrived*. Of this St. Paul was clear, stating, 'Not that I have already obtained ...' (Philippians 3.12). All of us, young and old, are *en route* as God's pilgrim people, with more of God's truth to learn and to share with others, and much to hope for in Jesus Christ.

✳ *O Spirit of Truth,*
lead us today, tomorrow, and always
into all truth, through Jesus Christ
who is the way, the truth and the life.

117

Into the image of Christ

The African Independent Churches in South Africa are known, among other things, for their non-formal style of worship, and for not being tied down to church buildings and property. Often one would see them worshipping out in the open, and clothed in their distinctive colourful uniforms, they would always be *walking* from one given point to another. They seem to be constantly on the move!

In verse 4 St. Paul describes Christians as those who '... walk not according to the flesh, but according to the Spirit'. Clearly the apostle is here contrasting life lived under the guidance of the Holy Spirit over against a life without reference to God or regard for God's commands. And the essence of living in the Spirit is that our lives are dynamic and not static, always moving away from sin and towards God.

The Christian life is lived in constant openness to Christ, in a readiness to *move* with the *movement* of the Holy Spirit – the Spirit which is always transforming us personally and communally '... from one degree of glory to another ...'(2 Corinthians 3.18c) into the image of Jesus Christ.

✳ *O Spirit of Movement,*
   open us up, and keep open our hearts and minds
   to the infinite depths and richness
   of being transformed into the image of Jesus Christ.

Free to be

The experience of slavery is one most intensely encountered by people from the continent of Africa. In South Africa, the policies and practices of Apartheid were seen and experienced by most black people as a modern form of slavery. Today, even though the policy of Apartheid is consigned to the scrap heap of history, its cruel legacies remain.

Africans and African Americans, therefore, could more readily relate to the metaphor St. Paul uses when stating that Christians '... did not receive a spirit of slavery to fall back into fear, but you have received a spirit of adoption' (verse 15a). For God is no slave-owner, or slave-driver. We do not fear God as slaves would fear their master. We are free of dread and fear – free to be God's children, 'adopted' in and through Jesus Christ.

To this amazing truth the Holy Spirit bears witness, and works patiently and lovingly to free us from bondage to anything or anyone, and to confirm our adoption as sons and daughters of the living God.

✳ *O Spirit of Liberation,*
  increase in us an awareness
  of our freedom from bondage to sin and evil,
  empower us to help others to be free
  through Jesus Christ our Liberator Lord.

Thursday May 22   Romans 8.18-25

In union with creation

It is significant that the Pentecostal symbols for the Holy Spirit – wind, fire and the dove – are all symbols of creation as well as symbols of new life, of renewal and hope. Pentecost, therefore, represents the crucial link between creation and redemption.

In our Scripture passage for today, St. Paul draws attention to our unity as human beings with the entire created order, within the scheme and process of redemption. Again, the coming of the Holy Spirit at Pentecost gave momentum to the process whereby we, together with creation, await in joyful anticipation the final act of redemption through Jesus Christ.

Growing worldwide concern about the environment is to be welcomed. But this is not simply a major issue *out there*. It is a matter that permeates the very core of our spirituality, and should be part of our daily prayers and action. In a very profound sense all things in heaven and on earth are integrated and shall be finally consummated in Jesus Christ, through the working of the Holy Spirit.

✳ *O Spirit of Unity,*
  hold us together when things fall apart.
  Empower us to create the oneness of all things
  that is to be found in Jesus Christ our only Lord.

Friday May 23   Romans 12.1-21

Being transformed

The Pastoral Plan for Transformation in Church and Society - this is the name of a programme adopted by the United Congregational Church of Southern Africa (UCCSA). It was adopted in response to the challenge of the *Kairos Document* (published in 1985 by the South Africa Council of Churches). This programme, which is currently in full swing, has steered the UCCSA in the direction of transforming itself – its structures, ministry and mission – to be more effective as God's agent of transformation in society.

Transformation is God's business. And this is not a process that happens outside of our personal selves. St. Paul makes it clear in 12.2 that transformation is something very close to home, and has to happen to us in a very personal way. But for the Holy Spirit to work meaningfully within our hearts and our minds, we have to be receptive and responsive to Jesus Christ at all times.

✳ *O Spirit of Transformation,*
cleanse our hearts and our minds
that we may see a clearer vision of God's Kingdom,
and work and pray for its fulfilment.

Saturday May 24   *Revelation 21.1-8*
The eternal spring
Drought is an ever present threat to life itself in Africa. Many people in this continent daily experience the ravages of famine, as a result of no water. They literally go hungry and thirsty.

In contrast to a water-source that dries up, St. John the divine speaks about a 'spring' in verse 6, which suggests that the supply of the 'water of life' is that which does not dry up. Significantly, this 'water of life' is offered as a 'gift'. A gift only truly becomes a gift, when it is received.

In the context of our Scripture reading, there is an essential condition for receiving this gift, namely that we be 'thirsty'.

It is true that we often try to satisfy our God-given thirst for God by 'drinking' from the wells of materialism or from the springs of sensualism. But our deep inner thirst remains, for only God can satisfy! And God does not give us *of himself*, but gives *himself* to us as Father, Son and Holy Spirit.

✳ *O Spirit of Renewal,*
create within us a deep thirst for God
and a desire to provide for the needs of others
who are hungry and thirsty,
through Jesus Christ. Amen

TO THINK ABOUT

- **Dreams** What is the significance of *dreams* in your life? Recall some of your recent dreams. To what extent have they come true?
- **Mission** How do you understand and define mission? In which way is your Church / Christian grouping engaged in mission?
- **Witness** In which way is your personal life a witness to the resurrection power of Jesus Christ?

FOR ACTION

- **Dreams** Take some time to 'dream'. Dream of how you would like to see yourself in five or ten years time. Ask yourself what you can do to make your dreams come true. Then do some basic planning.
- **Mission** Do a simple exercise of calculating how much time, money and effort your church / Christian group spends on *maintaining itself*, and how much of the same it spends on mission (e.g. evangelism, social justice, healing, etc.). Think of how you can begin a process of moving your church / group more in the direction of mission, to be less governed by maintaining itself.
- **Witness** Think of the ways you can be more vocal and active as a witness to Christ, at work / school / home, etc. Then pray for the Holy Spirit to create the opportunities to witness, and be prepared to act!

THREADS OF CREATION

Notes based on the New English Bible by
Donald Hilton

Donald Hilton, now Moderator of the Yorkshire Province of the United Reformed Church, was Moderator of the General Assembly of the United Reformed Church (UK) in 1993/4. Previously he served in three pastorates in the UK. He has written and compiled a number of books published by the NCEC.

How can we best understand the vast creation in which we live? The poet Thomas Traherne had two answers.

First, look for God within his creative work:

'You will never enjoy the world aright, till you see how a (grain of) sand exhibits the wisdom and power of God; and prize in every thing the service which they do you, by manifesting his glory and goodness to your soul.'

Secondly, recognize that although we have the ability to stand back and observe creation, we are ourselves a part of it:

'You will never enjoy the world aright, till the sea itself flows in your veins, till you are clothed with the heavens, and crowned with the stars.'

The Bible adds another comment: our experience of creation provides us with symbols and images through which we can better understand God: e.g. the Spirit is like wind, and faith is like a growing plant within us. Our study for the next two weeks will emphasize these three factors.

1st Sunday after Pentecost, May 25   *Ephesians 1.3-14 ***
One creation
In the earlier verses Paul reminds his readers of their Christian experience. They have received Christ's blessing and been called into his fellowship. Sins have been forgiven; God's free grace lavished on them. In the later verses Paul shows two important consequences of this:

● It has given them a sense of belonging. They have a share in Christ's heritage and are incorporated into his Body.
● It has given them a purpose and a mission. They responded to

Paul's preaching. Others will hear the good news from them, till all believe.

Between these two assertions lies verse 10 which is the pivot of the passage: all the universe, all in heaven and on earth, will be brought into a unity in Christ. The purposes of God are not slap-dash. His is not a broken or disorderly creation. There is purpose behind it. It holds together in a unity which includes tiny flowers and tall trees, hard rock and the alluvial mud out of which creation first emerged. Flesh and spirit are ultimately united. Faith and works have a common purpose, and all creation is shot through with the coursing gift of God's love, best revealed in Christ.

✳ *Hold a flower in your hand. So much else in creation has affected it – soil, water, wind, minerals. Such unity of purpose! In imagination hold your own life in your hands. Are you not like the flower?*

Monday May 26   *Genesis 1.14-19*
Order out of chaos
No journalist was present at the birth of creation to write down all that happened! The opening chapter of Genesis is one thoughtful writer's reflection on what most likely happened. The 'Big Bang' theory is a twentieth century attempt. This biblical explanation, written from a priestly background, was completed about 300 years before Christ. It enshrines a clear belief in a planned universe which emerges out of chaos to be systematically arranged by an orderly God. Earth and water are separated; each plant yields a distinctive seed.

The author knows from experience that day follows night follows day. It could have been different. An untidy god could have made a random universe in which three nights followed four days followed two more nights – followed by goodness knows what. No diaries, calendars, tide-tables or clocks would have made sense. There would have been no seasons and no pattern of sowing, planting and harvesting.

Notice the priest's own agenda. He sees the sun and moon marking not only the passing days, so that everyone knows when to work and when to sleep, but also marking the religious festivals. Here is a writer who believes a God of reason produced an orderly universe and invites a patterned response of worship and prayer.

✳ *This is the day the Lord has made;*

He calls the hours His own.
Let heaven rejoice, let earth be glad!

Isaac Watts (1674-1748)

Tuesday May 27   Numbers 9.15-23

Knowing God's presence

The journey of the Hebrews from captive Egypt to the Promised
Land was a formative period. It led to their becoming an
independent nation and, for a period, a major power in the Middle
East. As they looked back on that time their conviction grew that
God was present with them in that desert journey. Threads of
creation have always been used to express convictions about
faith and for these travellers fire and cloud became the symbols
of the presence of God.

In the dark days of bombing and death in Northern Ireland a
young child went on holiday to Corrymeela, a community centre
on the coast dedicated to peace and reconciliation. It was a
marvellous week of quietness, friendship and peace. As she was
about to leave Corrymeela she looked at the sea and said, 'Good-
bye, sea'. Then she looked at the sky and said, 'Good-bye sky'.
Finally, she looked at all the friends and helpers she had met
during the week and said, 'Good-bye, God'.

Sun, sea, friendship, peacefulness, and love had become
symbols of the presence of God.

✱ *Lord, let me be the kind of person*
  through whom others see God.

Wednesday May 28   Nehemiah 9.9-21

A steadfast God

But symbols of God can be corrupted. God is not a cloud or a fire;
neither is he 'Corrymeela friendship'. He is bigger than any
symbol we might imagine. The threads of creation may point to
God, but they are not God. Biblical authors are fierce in their
criticism whenever a symbol of God is treated as though it
actually is God. When the wilderness travellers made a metal
bull-calf and said, 'This is your God who brought you up from
Egypt', their leaders had to condemn it. They reminded them of
God's true nature (read verse 6), and told the ancient stories of
God's action in their lives.

Verses 19-21 get close to a gospel truth: even when we are

124

unfaithful to God, he remains faithful to us. This orderly God is no more random in his affection than he is in the ordering of day and night. The steadfast pattern of God's creation reflects the steadfast pattern of his love.

✻ *Father, do not let me be false to you,*
   But if I am, do not be false to me.

Thursday May 29   Jeremiah 23.23-32

God's fire scorches

If the people can go astray, so can their leaders. Jeremiah identified false prophets who had peddled their own fanciful dreams as the word of God. But no inner fancy can proclaim the God who is both 'near and far', and who 'fills heaven and earth'.

Jeremiah lived when the Israelite nation was under attack by Babylon. He was a sufficiently astute politician to realize Israel would be defeated. No nation likes to hear such a message – even if it is true. Jeremiah was persecuted; the people preferred to listen to the false prophets' simplistic dreams of political success.

Don't expect the word of God always to be comfortable. God's fire scorches! His hammer splinters!

Oscar Romero, archbishop of El Salvador openly criticized the right-wing government of his country for its oppression of the poor. He was no less critical of his church in its complacency. He said, 'A church that doesn't provoke any crises, a gospel that doesn't unsettle, a word of God that doesn't get under anyone's skin – what gospel is that?'

Such a message burns like fire and splinters the rock-like hearts of oppressors. It is also dangerous for those who preach it. Romero was assassinated.

✻ *What uncomfortable word should the Church be*
   speaking in this nation?

Friday May 30   Acts 17.23-34 ✻

Unknown?

In Athens Paul noticed many religious shrines including one 'to an Unknown God'. He seized his opportunity. Beginning with their experience of creation he argued that belief in God belongs to all ages and races. Read Romans 1.19-21 where he refines that argument. In Athens he went on to say that no shrine can contain him but the God of creation has been revealed in a person – Jesus Christ.

Angela was just nine. She wrote in her diary: 'I used to think that God lived behind the curtain behind the minister, but I looked one day and there was only bricks.' It must have been a devastating spiritual experience as she realized that her 'shrine' was empty. Later in her life God became real for her in the person of Jesus Christ.

✱ *O God, glimpsed in creation,*
declared in worship,
seen only by faith, we worship you.

Saturday May 31   *Psalm 33*

A creator – and much more besides

Why should we praise God? The psalmist calls us to worship (verses 1-5) and then offers at least three reasons why 'it is meet and right so to do':

He is Creator of all things (verses 6-9)

Lord of the boundless curves of space
and time's deep mystery,
to your creative might we trace
all nature's energy.

He is ruler of the nations and their history (verses 10-14)

Your mind conceived the galaxy,
each atom's secret planned,
and every age of history
your purpose, Lord has spanned.

He cares for every individual person (verses 15-19)

Yours is the image humans bear,
though marred by human sin;
and yours the liberating care
again our souls to win.

The verses used above to affirm the psalmist's belief are from a modern hymn by A F Bayly. He also knew of God's ultimate creative act:

✱ *... Christ ... is your wisdom's perfect word,*
your mercy's crowning deed.   A F Bayly (1901-84)

TO THINK ABOUT

- The child who visited Corrymeela became aware of God in the people there. How would you have helped to retain the awareness on her return to Belfast?
- Oscar Romero was not afraid to get involved in politics. What arguments can you think of for the church a) to avoid political issues, and b) to be actively involved in politics?

2nd Sunday after Pentecost, June 1   *Ezekiel 1.4-28*

Indescribable God

This passage needs much time even to begin to understand. Read these notes first and then slowly read the passage. Don't try to understand every word; get the feel of it as the writer seeks to portray God's greatness and majesty. He uses images from creation to communicate God's wonder:

Natural creation – storm, wind, lightning – suggest power and grandeur.

Animal creation – lion, ox and eagle – suggest strength and nobility.

Precious minerals – brass, topaz and sapphire – suggest brilliance.

The human face and human likeness suggest intimacy and approachability. The winged creatures are on a moving platform with universal wheels allowing movement in all directions. The creatures face in four directions, the wheels have eyes to see everything.

On the platform is a sapphire throne. Ezekiel hints that God was on the throne but he dare not be explicit. No-one should describe the wonder, beauty, majesty, and glory of the Creator-Redeemer. Ezekiel drops into similes – The Mysterious One is like brass, like fire, like rainbow.

The message is clear. Think of the most radiant threads of creation imaginable. Multiply their glory a thousandfold and you might just have one fleeting glimpse of our wonderful God.

✳ ***God, we have no words, save to adore.***

Dry bones – live!

Imagine a nation dragged from their homeland and exiled in a foreign land. Older people think they will never see their homes again; young people know nothing but exile. The nation's bones have been picked bare. Can these bones live? Of course not!

'But God is still God,' said Ezekiel. 'His promises remain.' He tells his parable. History proved his confidence in God to be realistic. Like the wind of creation, the breath of God restored the people. It has happened since. Nations held by colonialism found independence. Walls came down in Germany. Borders were opened to Albania.

On Christmas Eve 1990 a carol service was held in an Albanian cemetery. It was the first in forty years; Albania had been an atheist state; all worship of God forbidden. The minister who led the service had been in prison 28 years. Ten thousand people crowded into the cemetery. But no-one knew any carols! Then a few 70 year-old women began to sing the carols they had learned as children and had locked in their minds during persecution. The others picked up the words. The breath of God swept through the cemetery. Dry bones received the living flesh of faith.

✷ *Spirit of the living God, fall afresh on me.*

Wind of the Spirit

'New life for old' links yesterday's ideas in Ezekiel with those in John. God brought new life to the dry bones; the Spirit brings re-birth into God's Kingdom. John exploits the fact that the Greek language uses the same word *pneuma* for breath, wind and spirit.

Nicodemus probably expected some revised Jewish teaching from Jesus. He had to learn that what was needed was a totally new start leading to people so changed that it was like a new birth, due to the direct action of God in their lives.

The Spirit is like wind. We cannot control either. Wind may come as gentle breeze or mighty whirlwind. It can sweep a whole community or blow into the life of an individual. To be caught in the breath / wind / Spirit of God is to be whirled around and changed.

A baby has no say about its birth. Parents determine its birth and behind them lies the providence of God. We cannot tell what the child will become. Similarly, we have no control over the wind or its effect. It is the same with our birth into faith. It is an act of God and only he knows where it will lead.

✳ **Reflect on whirlwind changes and gentle movements in your life.**

Wednesday June 4   Matthew 3.1-12 *
Sign of the new start
When rivers dry up and reservoirs are reduced to a puddle, we learn afresh the value of water. It is crucial to our health; without it we quickly die. It provides our food since neither beast nor vegetable can survive without it. It has cleansing power to wash away dirt and reduce disease. Little wonder, therefore, that this thread of life running through creation has become an important religious symbol, and especially in baptism, the rite that marks a new beginning in faith.

John the Baptist issued a call to renewal. It was both spiritual and social. Calling for spiritual repentance, he urged the people to get ready for God's action. But this spiritual renewal was to be matched by a new way of life which bore fruit. The other Gospel-writers are more specific. Read Luke 3.10-14 and the specific commands. Give a shirt away! Don't bully! Share your food!

Baptism has little significance as a mere rite; it calls for spiritual renewal of the person, of the parents when a child is baptized, and of the community of the church. And the sign of the spiritual renewal is social justice.

✳ **Lord, cleanse your church and your world with the flowing waters of baptism.**

Thursday June 5   John 4.5-15
Living water
In this account Jesus is crossing bridges. There was a gap between Jews and Samaritans based on an ancient feud. Jesus crossed it. There was strong prejudice against a rabbi such as Jesus giving instruction to a woman. Jesus ignores the prejudice. These aspects of the story are reason enough for John to include it in his Gospel.

An even deeper reason lies in the conversation between them. Jesus uses her surprise that a Jewish teacher should ask a Samaritan woman for a drink, by offering her 'living water'. The phrase is ambiguous. It also means 'running water'. Some Rabbis referred to the Jewish Law as 'an inner spring welling up to eternal life' and Jesus, going further, is offering her a relationship with God which will bring her, not merely the daily life which well-water provides, but the eternal life which only he can give.

Joy Cowley, a New Zealand author has written: 'There is within each of us a quiet clear pool of living water fed by the one deep Source.'

✳ *Living water, run through my life*
   with renewing, cleansing power.

Friday June 6   *Psalm 104.1-18*

God – Creator and Provider

This psalm we read today and tomorrow is the testimony of one who has examined creation and is confident that he can see the hand of God in it.

Read verses 1-10. Remember that ancient people believed in a three-decker universe with waters both beneath and above the earth. God is here portrayed as the great landscape gardener who has decided exactly where everything should go. The earth has been fixed on unshakeable foundations, the heavens are like a tent above them, water has its allocated place, and God sits in splendour above all things. He uses wind and fire as his messengers to tell of his pleasure or anger. This earth is like a well-ordered country estate. Thus the psalmist has explained even the natural disasters that befall the normally peaceful creation.

Read verses 10-18. This estate has become populated. It provides a home for beasts, birds, vegetation and human beings. Everything interlocks. Cattle need grass, badgers need rocks, birds need trees and people need bread and wine. This Creator God is also a Provider; his creatures lack nothing.

✳ *What God's almighty power has made*
   that will he ever cherish.   *Johann J Schutz (1640-90)*

130

God – Planner and Foundation

Read verses 19-23. Life needs rhythm and purpose. This a twenty-four-hour God. He has planned his vast estate to operate day and night. Nocturnal animals have the night to themselves, leaving men and women to live and work in peace during the light. Again, creation is all of a piece.

Read verses 24-30. The psalmist has only been able to mention a section of creation but the inhabitants of the earth are countless. They depend utterly on God. When God is present all is well; if he should be absent creation is restless. 'He's got the whole world in his hands.'

Read verses 31-35. This is not only the conclusion of the psalm, it is the purpose in writing it. The threads of creation are finely drawn. With God's interlocking, providential, ordered world so described, how can you fail to fall on your knees in praise and adoration.

✳ *I will sing to the Lord as long as I live!*

TO THINK ABOUT

● Make a list of the images used to describe God in this week's notes. Decide which appeal to you most, and which you find unhelpful.

● Friday and Saturday's notes revealed an idyllic picture of God's creation in which everything fitted together in an orderly way, all needs provided. How do you think this psalmist would explain human starvation?

FOR ACTION

Choose one of the threads of creation, e.g. earth, fire, wind, water and explore it in greater detail. For example, you might visit a fire station to see how society copes with the damaging aspects of fire, or produce a large collage showing both the many practical ways in which we use water and how biblical authors have used it as a symbol of spiritual truth.

CRIES FOR HELP

Notes based on the New Revised Standard Version by
Jane Montenegro

Jane Montenegro, a Filipino, was gripped by Christ's liberating gospel in the Martial Law period. She moved into Christian Education within and outside the Church, working in both urban and rural areas. Today she facilitates workshops on liturgical renewal, children's work, and the empowerment of women. She is presently pastor of a mountain church while studying Asian feminist theology.

The Psalmist's cries for help arose out of experiences of injustice, violence and pain. If they have been deeply reflected and acted upon by thousands of Bible readers in their own space and particular time, why have they not lessened the miseries of the world today? Why haven't sufferings abated, even among so-called Christian groups and countries?

This week's true stories and testimonies from the Philippines echo the Psalmist's cries. Reflect on them together, and enter into the suffering of others. They are for spiritual inspiration and a call to action as we are touched by the groaning of the Spirit of God. And, having been touched, we pray that we may be converted to participate in God's work – to offer our lives for the transformation of a world so sadly wanting in justice, love and peace.

So help us, tender-hearted God! Amen.

3rd Sunday after Pentecost, June 8   *Psalm 10*
Sighing of the poor

My grandmother came home in tears when the store owner refused to lend her a *ganta* of rice to make porridge for her sick children. Five of them were lying on their mats, getting weaker and restless. She had promised payment as soon as the coconut meats were dried, just three days away. But the store owner would not believe that a peasant woman who tilled the land with her bare hands could readily pay. On bended knee, she lit a candle and sobbed,

'O God of life, why do you withhold food from my sick and
    starving children?
Let them know the gnawing pains of hunger!
Let them know the shame of rejection!
But let me offer you my sincere promise.
Take the strength of my hands, take my life – if need be ...
Just let my children live!'

Such sighing by the poor and oppressed is common in the
Philippines where most people live below the poverty line. Yet,
like the oppressed Israelites of old, they know God is listening –
amid the tragedies and crises.

✳ *We sigh, O God, from the depths of our suffering*
   because we know you are listening.
   Grant that our neighbours and government leaders listen
   as well. Amen

Monday June 9   *Psalm 25*

Waiting for God

Zinnia, a single mother who works for the US navy personnel in
Olongapo City, never knew who her father was. Her mother died
in childbirth. Her alcoholic uncle forces her to make money by any
means. Confused and battered, Zinnia bares her soul and cries
out,

'Have mercy, O God. I have sinned again.
If it were not a sin – I could kill ...
Or better yet – that I kill myself!
But who would take care of my child?
Who would protect her from further abuse?
Who would save her from further violence?
Have mercy, O Lord, have mercy on us!'

There are hundreds and thousands of Zinnias all over Asia
and the world. Complex socio-economic, political conditions have
made them vulnerable to a maelstrom of war-oriented, pleasure
seeking cultures. Women's crises centres, sister-bonding,
mediation centres and some churches have become their
sanctuaries and hope shelters.

✳ *Cause us to weep, O tender-hearted God,*
   with all the Zinnias of Asia and in other parts of the
      world,
   that our tears may cleanse and our hands may redeem
      them

from their shame and their enemies. Amen

Tuesday June 10 Psalm 42

Feeding with tears day and night

Despite modern mechanization, human slavery is still at its height today in the United Arab Emirates. Global economic imbalance has caused 100,000 foreign domestic helpers to leave their poverty-stricken home countries to work for these oil-rich nations. Such migration has meant heart-breaking miseries, ranging from the separation of family ties to forced labour with hardly any sleep or food, brutal beatings, rape, murder, imprisonment and summary execution. Loved ones are hardly informed or are the last ones to know what these migrant workers are suffering.

One case is Sarah who is only sixteen and who killed her employer in self-defence. Hundreds more Filipino Sarahs, Elenas and Marias plead,

'Why must we suffer so from the oppression of the rich?
We long for God every moment of the day.
Our tears have been our food, day and night ...'

Hundreds of years ago, the same cry was uttered by a slave-Israelite while in captivity.

✴ *O living God, move me to offer one cupful of justice*
that my neighbour's thirst may be quenched,
and she can praise you once again! Amen

Wednesday June 11 Psalm 57

Taking refuge under God's wings

Her lips trembled in anger, 'I will not allow them to take over the land ... they can only do that over my dead body and my children's bodies!' In church, the congregation sings and cries with Raquel:

'Under his wings, O what precious enjoyment!
There will I hide till life's trials are o'er.
Sheltered, protected, no evil can harm me.
Resting in Jesus, I'm safe evermore!'

Raquel – 55 years old – a frail-looking widow was threatened by para-military men that her brains would be blown to pieces if she did not leave her farm. If she stayed on, it meant that she was feeding rebels. But she could not be fooled. She refused to let them take away her family's subsistence of poultry and corn. 'We

134

will stay, God will protect us,' she declared to them.

Today, Raquel beams gently at the para-military, knowing that her courageous stand stopped them in their tracks. 'It is God's gift! And God has always kept us safe under her wings ...'

✳ **Thank you, O God, for the Psalmist and Raquel**
who inspire us with courage to stand against evil and
wrong
today. Amen

Thursday June 12   *Psalm 63*

My soul clings to you

At 46, a preacher went deep into the hinterlands to experience God's love. In pain, he left church politics, finding it false and immoral. The simple tribal community respected his deep love of farming. He would lift up his hands with rice seedlings for God's blessings. At dawn, he joined the birds with hymns of praise. At sundown, he clucked with his chickens with petitions to God. The valleys of corn sang with him in hymns of thanksgiving. But still he condemned the church leaders: 'The liars will end in destruction!'

On the tenth year of 'feasting with the marrow and fat of the land', he had a strange dream. His old father who had died was holding him tenderly in his right hand, saying brightly to him, 'It is true what you said, God has a place for me!'

That same day, he turned over the farm to his sons, went back to his preaching for the rest of his life, with a passion no one could stop. I know, for he was my father, and Psalm 63 was a psalm that expressed the very heart and soul of his life.

✳ **In all life's tragedies and joys,**
let me cling to you, O God! Amen

Friday June 13   *Psalm 107.1-22*

God, deliver us ...

They were a hard-working group of farmers who came to the city to improve their parents' lot. They welcomed any job: laundering, baby-sitting, food vending, singing, dancing at discos, anything just to make a little money. Being innocent, they easily flowed with the city tide: hard drinks, Mc Donald's, X-rated films ... In a few months, one of them began coughing hard; one became pregnant, one was recruited to be a dancing entertainer in Japan, and another was locked behind doors by her master. They longed for native chicken soup and the warmth of joyful worship at home.

One day, while sharing their concerns, some blurted out, 'I am going back to the farm. I don't care for city life any more. I hate its food, its glitter, its pollution! I'm sick of it! God is so far away here! I want to go home!'

Today, five of them have set up a youth centre for tree-planting. They have accepted responsibilities in the community, in church, in school and home. The older people remark, 'God has delivered them!'

✳ *O God, use us that we may heal the earth,*
  and work with you to deliver the vulnerable
  from further destruction. Amen

Saturday June 14   Psalm 107.23-43
'God, raise us up ...'

For so long, the Filipino population hungered for food, the farmers longed for land reform, the students demanded academic freedom and human rights advocates marched in street rallies for justice, truth and freedom. The Marcos regime had no respect for priests, ministers or lay church members who opposed government corruption. They were jailed, tortured, raped or killed. Internal war in the countryside broke up family ties as relatives suspected each other of being rebels or informers. Tribal communities killed their own kinsfolk while those in power enjoyed profits from the sale of arms. The presidential family and their cronies were amassing wealth from multi-nationals and from the sweat and blood of the poor.

The faithful continued to pray and fast, pouring out to God the social indignities they suffered. They persevered, receiving Holy Communion in all kinds of settings as a constant reminder that God in Jesus Christ suffered with them, and promised resurrection and liberation.

In February 1986, God heard our cries. Our prayers, roses and bread toppled the mighty. The Marcoses and their supporters fled the palace forever.

✳ *O God of history, thank you for making us part of your*
   miracle,
   raising us up out of our affliction. Amen

136

PSALMS FOR TODAY FROM THE PHILIPPINES

I

My heart weeps with pain and grief,
but my eyes will shed no tears.
No, God, don't let the enemies see my tears.
Don't let the soldiers feel my quivering voice.
Let me speak clearly words of truth;
and boldly speak words of freedom.
Let me ask them, 'Where is my daughter?
Where is the child of my womb?
Was she still in chains when you buried her
with eight others in a shallow hole?'
O God, let me dare to ask these questions -
Let me look straight into their eyes!
And let me not weep in pain and grief before them!

II

We vigil in the night
with candles and prayers for justice and truth.
Once we were in deep darkness and silence,
but now we want to be free!
We shall shout!
We shall dance, and sing, and march!
We shall laugh!
We shall cry our freedom songs together.

TO THINK ABOUT

1. Who are 'the afflicted' in your country? What are their cries?
   What is the Church doing about them and with them?
2. What other biblical passages or stories support the saying,
   'Personal is political'?
3. Do you see a relationship between the extravagance of the
   affluent and the hunger of the poor? If so, trace the causes
   biblically and globally.

FOR ACTION

- Make a list of words, phrases, statements and actions that are
  related or linked with your own personal or social experience
  of domestic violence.
- Start a project or link with a group that works to minimize
  social violence in your neighbourhood.

137

STANDARDS FOR TODAY

Notes based on the New Jerusalem Bible by
Joseph G Donders

Joseph Donders, a Dutch priest of the Society of Missionaries of Africa, is Professor of Mission and Cross-cultural Studies at Washington Theological Union. He was formerly Head of the Department of Philosophy and Religious Studies and Chaplain to Catholic students at the State University of Nairobi, Kenya.

The word 'standard' is an old Anglo-Norman term. It originally meant 'an unfurled banner on a battlefield'. Later on it stood for the point from which all authority came – the norm or a criterion. In Holy Scripture we find many of those standards. Jesus unfurled them, giving them a new and wider meaning, while Paul in his letters drew further conclusions. They all set standards that remain and to which we should refer, in order not to lose the battle of our life.

4th Sunday after Pentecost, June 15　　　　　　　*Matthew 5.21-26 **
Neither thing nor fool

A boy was kicking a doll. At first I could not see it was a doll; it seemed just a piece of dark wood. A small African girl was trying to get at the doll, shouting: 'Don't kick her! It is my doll! It is Lucy.' The boy kept on kicking, 'It is not Lucy! It is only a thing!' and he kicked, while she screamed.

It made me think of what happens to people when they are not considered as human beings, let alone as sisters and brothers. It also made me think about that norm Jesus asked us to maintain: 'You shall not kill ... but I say this to you, anyone who calls a brother "Fool" will answer for it.' The West Indian psychiatrist Franz Fanon once wrote that no one ever abuses a fellow human being without first calling her or him a fool, an animal, or a thing. Jesus warned us never to call others names like that. The outcome would be disastrous.

* ***Source of our human life,***
let us never be disrespected by others,
and let us never disrespect them.

Let us be true to ourselves and to you.

Monday June 16   *Matthew 5.33-37*

Nothing but the truth

Yesterday we considered how Jesus asks us to treat a human being as a human being. He warns us that we will end up in disaster if we don't. Today Jesus extends his warning. He repeats a warning from Proverbs 12.22:

'Lying lips are abhorrent to Yahweh,
dear to him those who make truth their way of life.'

Neither the book of Proverbs nor Jesus explains these standards. 'All you need say is "Yes" if you mean yes, and "No" if you mean no; anything more than this comes from the Evil One.' Jesus revealed to us the truth about God, about ourselves and about the world. Those who twist facts are cheats and deceivers. They are a danger to society and the world.

'The Son of God, Jesus Christ, who was proclaimed to you by us, that is, by me and by Silvanus and Timothy, was never Yes-and-No; his nature is all Yes' (2 Corinthians 1.19). His *Yes* is the one fixed point in our moral universe.

✴ *Almighty God, open our hearts and minds*
to the reality about ourselves,
our world
and about You, the principle of our being.

Tuesday June 17   *1 Corinthians 6.1-11; Matthew 18.15-17*

Mediation instead of litigation

Paul is writing to a young church, a church of people who came together around Jesus Christ, forming a new type of community based on their shared experience of the Holy Spirit. It is in this context that Paul writes: 'Can it really be that it is impossible to find in the community one sensible person capable of deciding questions between brothers?' (verse 5). He considers it a scandal that they take lawsuits outside the community (6.1). It would even be better to suffer injustice!

In a society where litigation has become like a disease that tears individuals and families apart, Paul's words offer a new challenge. In many parishes Mediation Councils are being formed to settle issues that otherwise would cost a lot, take a long time, and cause plenty of bitterness. People who engage themselves in this kind of work are real peacemakers. They are the kind of persons our world badly needs at all levels. Why not take the initiative in your community?

✳ *Almighty God, let our good sense be obvious to everybody,*
so that they may know that you are very near

(Philippians 4.5)

Wednesday June 18   *Matthew 5.27-32 **
Infidelity and society

Even people who do not take the biblical prohibition of adultery as their personal way of life often get very upset when a royal, political, ecclesial or other celebrity is caught in that act, or admits to it. It is not necessary to mention any names. Examples of this consternation abound. It is an interesting reaction that seems to point at a moral insight in this matter – the intuition that the structure of our society would not be able to survive if adultery became the accepted norm. The greater the role model the person in question is supposed to play, the greater the threat, the fear and indignation. Tabloids and television stations profit on this resentment!

Jesus speaks about another danger when he says that the ones who look lustfully at others commit adultery in their hearts. That lust runs the risk of reducing the other to a mere object, a thing. This attitude does not do justice to someone created in the image of God and alive with the divine breath.

✳ *Ever-loving God, help our families with an abundance of grace*
as they are the woof and warp of our church and society.

Thursday June 19   *Matthew 19.1-12*
Becoming one flesh

Before the schism of 1045, the Eastern and Western Churches' decrees on divorce had already divided the two. The East decided that Jesus' words in Matthew 19.9 (and 5.32) permitted the injured party to remarry after divorce resulting from adultery. The Western Church decided differently.

Jesus' words 'and the two become one flesh' are also interpreted differently. Is Jesus speaking of the act of marital intercourse, or about a process by which the two gradually become one flesh? In the latter case, the two who 'married' might grow into 'one', or they might not. Churches are divided over what to do in the latter case. One church community might allow a divorce, another might not; and a third might declare an annulment, reasoning that the two were incompatible from the very beginning and never 'married'.

In all cases the demands of marriage are not only the business of the two who marry: they are also God's business and that of the community. It is the whole church community that has to act towards its members who are facing issues our forebears never faced.

✳ *Pour out your Spirit*
and make us sincere in our love for each other.

Friday June 20 1 *Corinthians 5.1-13*
Shunning
Paul complains that the Corinthians had misunderstood him. He had written to them that they should have nothing to with people living immoral lives and worshipping false gods. He now writes that he had only been speaking of members of the community. He had been trying to point out how believers should deal with believers. The calling of a Christian is to be light in the darkness. 'Our calling is to be a society within a society, committed to dealing with any hint of sexual, social, or economic scandal within our own ranks' *(Martin de Haen, Times of Discovery, May 1993).*

Paul had not been writing about others. Shunning everyone in this present world who is immoral would mean to cut yourself off from humanity. We have to relate to others, but not in a way, that says: 'It is the only game in town! What else am I supposed to do?' The Christian answer to that question is: 'Something other than the only game in town!' *(Gerard S. Sloyan, Catholic Morality Revisited, 1990).*

✳ *Almighty God, let us be part of the little new yeast*
that will leaven the whole batch of dough
with the Spirit of your Son.

Saturday June 21 1 *Corinthians 6.12-20*
Our body and the glory of God
How many do realize that our bodies are the temples of the Holy Spirit? Julius Nyerere, the former President of Tanzania, once remarked: 'If a human being is really the temple of God, we have

to do something about the flies in the eyes of a child, as those flies are ruining God's temple.'

Paul draws his conclusions in relation to our bodies. Paul's context in his Corinthians' letter is illicit sex, but to keep our bodies a fitting place for our divine Guest is about more than that. Drunkenness, gluttony, drug-taking, careless driving, and even workaholism, are all offences against the body in which the Holy Spirit dwells.

There is a further consequence to draw. It is our Guest we should worship and not our body. Though we have to take good care of it – honouring our body – its muscle tone, a flat stomach, a redone face should not become our main concern. 'You are not your own property!'

✱ *Holy Spirit, assist me to favour you*
   as the Partner of my heart,
   and the Guest of the bodies of all whom I meet.

TO THINK ABOUT

● Discuss with your children, your grandchildren or some friends why disobeying any of the ten commandments would lead to the dissolution of society.
● Remember when taking the next shower or bath how your body (and that of others) is the temple of God's Spirit.

5th Sunday after Pentecost, June 22   *Exodus 20.1-17*
Breathing space
The story tells how Gentiles visiting the Temple in Jerusalem were amazed that they did not find any idol. There were only two golden Cherubim covered by their wings and the Ark of the Covenant, containing the ten commandments. The ten precepts stated: I am Yahweh, your God. Do not bend to any other god, and do not abuse my name. As for the rest, they were about human life, even the one that commands us to take time off on the seventh day. This command was not only meant 'to honour Yahweh'. It was   meant to give us a rest: 'On the seventh day you will rest, so that your ox and your donkey may rest, and the child of your slave girl have a breathing space, and the alien too' (Exodus 23.12).

Recently some atheistic countries tried to undo this seventh day. They introduced a tenth day of rest, or tried another formula

– schemes that failed. We seem to need the seven-day cycle, a rhythm that is under attack by a world whose behaviour is determined by market forces that disregard our human needs.

✳ *God, our Creator,*
help us to take the rest we need
in honour of you,
and of ourselves.

Monday June 23   *Exodus 23.1-9*

A fallen donkey

It was in a deserted place in the Great Rift Valley in Kenya. Suddenly my car spluttered and stopped. No petrol. I had misunderstood the attendant of the rental firm. I saw far away some smoke above a bush. It was a long walk. Some people were drinking a cup of tea. A van was parked in their compound. I told my story and they helped me, driving me in their car to a petrol station.

Reading the text of today: 'If you see the donkey of someone who hates you fallen under its load, do not stand back; you must go and help him with it' (verse 5), I thought of that incident. The person who helped me did not hate me. We had never met before. He did not feel attracted to me in a special way either, for the same reason. Why did he help me? I asked him. He answered: 'I am a Christian, you are my brother.' An answer as simple and explicit as those decrees in the Book of Exodus.

✳ *Lord Jesus,*
help me to be the comfort, the support and the joy
you want me to be for others.

Tuesday June 24   *Matthew 23.1-12*

Pluralism

Pierre Teilhard de Chardin, the famous palaeontologist and theologian, thought that humanity had spread out over the world from somewhere in Oldevai Valley in Tanzania. They spread out on a globe, getting further and further away from each other until they would meet one day again. Looking around in our cities you can see that this is happening now.

More and more countries are facing a plurality of people and cultures, causing all kinds of problems in our communities, churches and nation states. Issues like cross-culturalism, racism, inculturation and the difficulty of organizing our worship in a way that does justice to all. How can you be faithful to yourself and to others?

Jesus told the Jews of his time to listen carefully to the interpreters of their culture – though they should not follow a hypocritical way of life. Besides that, being faithful to their tradition, they should have God as their Father and Christ as their teacher, implying that they should be helpful sisters and brothers of all. This guidance was given to all of us.

✳ *O God, be gracious and bless us,*
let your face shed its light upon us,
and let all nations learn your saving help.

Wednesday June 25   *Matthew 15.1-9*
Widows and senior citizens
Everyone knows the story of the widow's mite (Mark 12.41-44). Everyone also knows how Jesus praised her. Not everyone knows the rest of that story. After having said that the widow had given 'all she had to live on', Mark makes it clear that Jesus is indignant about a religious institution that makes people do a thing like that. Mark uses for Jesus' departure (Mark 13.1) a Greek word that indicates that he left the Temple angrily, never to return there again!

Jesus praised the widow, who did not have a cent left to live on. Jesus blamed the Temple authorities who allowed, and maybe even provoked her, to overlook herself in honour of God, like he blames them for letting others neglect their indigent parents in view of their 'help' to the Temple.

All those involved in getting money for charitable funds and trusts have to remain aware of the widow's story. They should not ask in such a way that they almost force poor and elderly people to do what they really cannot do without harm to themselves.

✳ *Loving God, known as the protector of widows and*
*   orphans,*
let them find their friends and protectors among us,
your children.

Thursday June 26   *Matthew 15.10-20*
Hygiene of the heart
A recent study in the United States concluded that the television broadcasts 65,000 sexual references a year in prime afternoon

and evening hours. The same statistics show that television exposes children to thousands of acts of violence before they are of school age. We have no idea what all those scenes do to our minds and hearts. We do know that they are – in a mysterious way – permanently stored up in them. And television is only one type of media that bombards us day and night if we are not careful.

Jesus does not speak about television, of course. Yet in a way he does. He asks us to keep our hearts hygienically clean, so that what comes out of them will be unblemished, a pastoral counsel that helps us to prevent personal crises. It is at the same time a spiritual advice, helping us to relate well to God, keeping our hearts for God's indwelling. It is the way 'not to be led into temptation', answering the prayer we so often say.

✶ *Almighty and loving God,*
help me to protect myself against pollution of heart and
mind.

Friday June 27   *Matthew 6.24-34* ✶

Being God's providence

She fell asleep over the steering wheel of her van. It hit three trees and caught fire. People from stopped cars did not manage to stop the fire. A truck pulling a big water tank stopped. Its driver doused the burning car with gallons of water and extinguished the fire. The victim, though shocked, was saved. Some around the wrecked car spoke of synchronicity, others of serendipity. The driver of the water truck called it 'God's providence'. Before driving off he said a prayer.

Jesus asks us to trust God's providence, and not to worry about anything. God is our perfect assurance and helper in need. That is why Jesus – sent by God – helped the people around him. He did that as our human brother and friend. God works among us through human beings. Women and men, equipped with God's Spirit, do not let the hungry go hungry, the naked undressed, the homeless unsheltered and those in need without support. When we set God's Kingdom first in our hearts, no one has to worry about tomorrow!

✶ *Almighty God, let me be your hands to others*
and let others be your hands to me.

Saturday June 28   2 Corinthians 8.1-15
Generosity

In his letter Paul has his personal agenda. The Jerusalem community allowed him to develop his mission among the Gentiles with the provision that he 'remember the poor' (Galatians 2.10). This agenda was rooted in the divine / human solidarity of Jesus, who '... became poor for your sake' (8.9).

Paul does not ask the Corinthians to sell all they possess. He asks them to see their riches as benefices from God that allow them to have everything they need, and to do good works (9.8). Paul asks them to share with others in the way God and Jesus shared their riches with them. It is a privilege to be able to share in God's service to God's holy people!

Paul adds that this support is not only a question of balance and fairness, but also an issue of foresight and prudence! It is a question of a kind of insurance! The time might come, Paul suggests, that you and your community might be in need, and you will depend on others being willing – in their turn – to share their gifts from God with you.

✳ *Almighty provider of all,*
   let us share in your providence helping those in need.

TO THINK ABOUT

● Read the titles of a daily newspaper and check the references to infringements of the ten commandments.
● Why do the media seem to be so attracted by sin and sinners?

✳ *Come to the world!*
   Yes, God the Creator, come!
   Come, God, for it is your help we need in the world.
   Come and see how our people are destroying the world,
   without seeking what is in your heart,
   without seeking what is in your mind.
   Come and see how retaliation prevails among us.

   Rise, brothers and sisters and live together,
   for it will be well.
   Yes, if we seek peace,
   God will grant us peace.
   Peace, brothers and sisters, it is unity,
   peace and purity of heart,
   that will raise us up.   Ikole Harcourt Whyte, Nigeria
                    Adapted from Oceans of Prayer (NCEC)

LORD, HEAR OUR PRAYER

Notes based on the Revised Standard Version by
Lesley G Anderson

Lesley Anderson, a Panamanian, is Chairman of the Belize / Honduras District of the Methodist Church in the Caribbean and Americas. Previous to this he was Chairman of the Panama / Costa Rica District, and between 1987 and 1995 served with the Methodist Church Overseas Division (UK) as Secretary for the Americas, the Caribbean and Europe.

Prayer is our communicating channel with God. It is a spiritual response and the integrated dynamic of a Christian's life. There are many postures: standing, sitting, bowing, kneeling, prostration ... Prayers can take the form of

adoration, in recognition of God's uniqueness beyond our full comprehension;

confession of our guilt and sins;

intercession, a prayer for others;

petition, knowing we are dependent upon God for all things;

thanksgiving, for God is deserving of all our praise and thanks.

6th Sunday after Pentecost, June 29   *Matthew 7.7-12 **
Ask, seek and knock

This passage has no apparent context, but in Luke 11.9-13, it follows the parable of the friend at midnight and the Lord's Prayer. When you pray, 'ask', that you may receive, believing always that God will answer. 'Seek' that you may find God's gracious gifts through and in the power of the Holy Spirit. 'Knock' on the unconditional doors of God's grace and mercy and they will be opened to you. I have learnt all through life that God offers no limitations!

A dear friend of mine in Trinidad went through trial after trial with her son, who brought her to tears and prayer on bended knees. In every situation she learnt to pray like Jesus: 'nevertheless, not as I will, but as thou wilt' (Matthew 26.39).

In Panama, I recall an incident in which a father, a man of wisdom, although beaten up by his son, continued to love and pray for him. There are times in our experience when we need more than wisdom and love that we may not offer 'stones' instead of 'loaves' (4.1-4). Interestingly, Luke substitutes 'egg' and 'scorpion' for 'fish' and 'serpent'. Fish like bread was common and seasonally plentiful. Let us be reminded of verse 12, the Golden Rule, the general conclusion to Jesus' sermon: 'So whatever you wish that men would do to you, do so to them ...'

✳ *O Lord, my God, teach me in humility*
  how to 'ask, seek and knock' when praying.

Monday June 30   *1 Timothy 2.1-8* *
Pray for others
Timothy is challenged here to teach his congregations the use of public prayer and intercession. They should

● offer prayers of supplication, thanksgiving and intercession;
● give thanks for God's blessings on others;
● give thanks for events and things relating to others.

In the church I attend in Belize, some of us meet every Wednesday morning at 6.00am. to pray. We believe we have a responsibility to support others in prayer. Christlike love and goodwill do not discriminate. We pray for all – evil governments as well as good ones – that they may rule justly and in peace. God's will is that all persons should be saved. He is God of all, and Christ is both the Mediator and Redeemer of all (verses 5-7).

Paul reaffirms his apostleship (see 1 Corinthians 9.1 and 2 Corinthians 12.12), and teaches faith to the Gentiles (verse 7). He challenges all of us to pray, 'lifting holy hands' – a natural gesture in earnest prayer, especially used by early Christians – and not to enter into dispute with one another.

✳ *Lord, forgive us,*
  cleanse us,
  and teach us how to pray with sincerity for others.

Tuesday July 1   *2 Chronicles 6.12-21* *
God hears and forgives
Solomon (see 1 Kings 8.38-39) shares with us in this prayer the God of infinite goodness and righteousness. He is knowledgeable of all beings and things. He knows each of us intimately – he knows our joys and sorrows. This prayer is a showpiece of God's faithfulness to us and willingness to forgive. He is the same

148

yesterday, today and forever. The prayer is set to meet the needs of Israel, yet it includes a petition for the stranger.

Like Solomon, each of us can pray to God in faith and trust, giving him thanks for his love and forgiveness.

My mother-in-law, Beatrice, had no material wealth, but she was spiritually rich in heart and mind. Her prayerful and loving spirit reached out beyond her immediate family to others. As God will never reject us, so she never rejected anyone who came to her door in need.

Like Solomon, we can pray to God to meet our needs, and be willing as well to respond to a petition from the visitor, the stranger, the unknown, and the 'lost' in the crowd.

✳ *Lord, you are the only one to whom we may go:*
  help us to keep our faith and confidence in you. Amen

Wednesday July 2   *Matthew 6.5-15*
Learn *how* to pray
When I visited the continent of Europe, I was surprised to see congregations seated to sing and standing for prayer. Standing, however, was the normal attitude for the early Church.

In this passage, Jesus condemns a) the kind of prayer that is offered only to draw attention to ourselves (verse 5), and b) 'empty phrases' – idle, meaningless thoughtless words (verse 7 and 8). He encouraged praying 'in secret' and offered a model for prayer (verses 9-13).

The Lord's Prayer is Jewish in both language and thought. God is addressed as Father. There is both intimacy and reverence in calling God 'Our Father'. He is to be treated as holy, for his nature is holy. The Aramaic *Abba* (Romans 8.15 and Galatians 4.6) was an even more intimate form of address which was adopted by the early Church. Verse 10 speaks of the future establishment of God's sovereignty on earth. Verse 11 reminds us that we can pray for material blessings – bread for today and tomorrow.

Particularly Jewish is verse 12 where sins are referred to (in Matthew only) as 'debts'. (Might this reflect the Jewish year of Jubilee when debtors were meant to be released from their debts?) Forgiveness is dominant, because we have sinned, we intend to sin and we go on sinning. In verse 13 we pray that God will not allow us to enter into trial and temptation. When we do yield to temptation, God is able and willing to deliver us. Verses

14 and 15 are a liturgical addition, in which the Greek *gar* 'for' is the linking word.

✳ **Lord, teach me how to pray in the power of the Holy Spirit.**

Thursday July 3   Matthew 9. 35-38
Pray for the work of the Kingdom

In this reading we have a description of the work that Jesus was doing: teaching, preaching and healing (verse 35). His popularity had grown immensely and crowds followed him everywhere. The situation eventually became very troubling. The people 'were harassed and helpless, like sheep without a shepherd', like today's refugees whom I have seen in war torn countries of Africa, and in the former Yugoslavia, on my television screen – men, women and children. I saw despair on their faces and heard their cries of relief. Then I saw the wounded and the dead.

Verse 36 describes the sorrowful and heartbreaking state of affairs into which the people of Jesus' day had fallen. They were unprepared for the Last Day. They were receiving no spiritual guidance.

In verse 37 (see Luke 10.2), Palestine was like a field at harvest time in the Caribbean. The field was ripe and ready for reaping. The people were ready for the Messiah and to receive the good news that the Kingdom was at hand. Unfortunately, the preachers – the liberators – were not enough. There was a need for prayer. In Luke 10, the saying is at the beginning of the mission charge to the Seventy, after Jesus had called them to be his disciples. In Matthew it is a separate saying. Note the sudden change of metaphor from 'sheep' to 'corn'. The present mission of the Twelve was an answer to prayer.

✳ **Lord Jesus Christ,**
   we are thankful that you are the answer to all our prayers.

Friday July 4   Philippians 1.1-11
Pray for the Church

Christian believers are saints, holy persons, consecrated to God. Despite their differences, the apostle Paul has this confidence and certainty about the entire membership in the Church.

The Methodist Church in the Caribbean and the Americas

(MCCA) is in the process of restructuring and has introduced legislation to establish bishops and deacons (overseers and attendants) into its system (see 1 Thessalonians 5.12).

In the early Church, *Episkopos* (bishop) was the name given to those charged with administrative or financial responsibility. *Diakonos* (deacon) was the title of those who served, hence 'servant', 'attendant' (see Matthew 20.26). When all is said and done, the whole Church needs to go beyond restructuring to acts of praise and prayer to God for his many blessings.

The Pauline Thanksgiving (verses 3-6) is indicative of the joy he experiences, stemming from his unbroken and steadfast relationship with the people of Philippi. His prayers assure them of success in their undertakings. He is full of joy, he has their trust and is grateful to them all. They are linked together in prayer and in the cause of the gospel. He appreciates their love, sympathy and the presence of Epaphroditus. There is a depth of genuine love which we all need to experience. The strength of verse 11 rests on the word 'filled' (made complete) with the 'fruits of righteousness'.

✴ *Lord, we turn to you in acts of thanksgiving and prayer.*

Saturday July 5   *Genesis 21.1-21; Romans 8.26-27*

God's Spirit intercedes for us

In this graphic story of Sarah and Isaac, Hagar and Ishmael, is the painful human situation of jealousy and protection, hurt and cruelty. Isaac would become Abraham's heir in whom the promises of God would be fulfilled (verse 12). Paul made excellent use of this story to illustrate the persecution of Christians (see Galatians 4.29).

The 'skin' referred to in verse 15 was of sheep or goat. The openings were sown up and made watertight with pitch, a thick, dark, sticky substance obtained from the residue of coal tar or petroleum which was used for waterproofing, roofing and paving (in Trinidad, I lived near the famous Pitch Lake in La Brea).

During her time of suffering and weakness, Hagar sought to kill her son. God scolded her and, in his grace, comforted and met all her needs and that of her son. No direct words of prayer from Hagar are recorded. Maybe her sense of rejection was so intense that she could not articulate what she felt. But prayer is not only speaking to God; it involves hearing what God is saying to us, and Hagar did just that.

In the New Testament, Paul reminds us that when we suffer so much in persecution or rejection, if we have hope, we will know that the Spirit within is praying on our behalf and giving us support.

✳ *Lord, help us to pray in the power of the Holy Spirit and keep hope in you. Amen*

TO THINK ABOUT

● Read again Matthew 7.7-12. How do you ask, seek and knock in prayer? Is it important that you receive, find and have things opened for you?
● How prominent is thanksgiving in your prayer life?
● How do you sustain your hope in God while enduring suffering?

Almighty and most loving God,
We acknowledge your overflowing love
    and infinite glory.
Purify our hearts.
Teach us how to love and forgive.
Pour down on us the spirit of peace and reconciliation ...
Teach us your people how to survive, amid
    death and starvation,
    misery and destitution,
    torture and disappearances.
Lord, sometimes our faith trembles.
Lord, sometimes it is as if you have left us.
Lord, help us to trust you more
and to put our lives into your hands!
O God of unceasing love,
To you be honour, glory and praise. Amen Lesley Anderson

FOR ACTION

Form a prayer group or cell, and pray for Christians around the world who are enduring suffering for the sake of their faith. Decide how frequently or regularly you will meet.

Discuss new ways of interpreting the Lord's Prayer and write your own paraphrase of it.

ONE GOD – JUSTICE FOR ALL
The Book of Deuteronomy

Notes based on the Authorized Version by
Albert H Friedlander

*Rabbi Albert Friedlander is Dean of the Leo Baeck College (London UK), which trains Reform and Liberal rabbis, and he serves as minister of the Westminster Synagogue. His recent writings include a book with Walter Homolka – **The Gate of Perfection: the Idea of Peace in Jewish Thought** – and his own study of Christian and Jewish thinkers writing after the Holocaust – **Riders towards the Dawn**. He is Honorary President of the World Conference of Religions for Peace, and recently was invited to be the 'Martin Buber Professor' at the University of Frankfurt.*

The Book of Deuteronomy is the final section of the Pentateuch, and is, as the title suggests, a 'repetition' of the teachings of Moses. It is a farewell address, in which Moses reviews all of his teachings which have shaped the people in the wilderness and have made it a united community where 'the hewers of wood and the drawers of waters' share the Covenant of living under Divine Law. They bring the great insights of their desert experience to all the world.

It is a law and a vision given at a lawless time, and in a violent world. Other nations will oppose them, will try to destroy their understanding of the One God who must be served with justice. And so we encounter God in these texts as the God of war who protects the people and helps them to settle into the Promised Land. But when we examine all of the texts, including the Ten Commandments and the *Sh'ma* - that great affirmation of Jewish faith which bids us to 'love God with all our heart, with all our soul, and with all our might' – we begin to recognize the great vision of the God of Love and of Justice. We learn that the two must be combined by anyone who studies the biblical texts and wants them to be a guide for the daily problems of living in *our* violent world. Once we understand this, the various texts of the Book of Deuteronomy come to life and make us realize that this book, and indeed the Bible, is a true guide for those who have faith and for those who are seeking faith in a dark world.

We are our past, and also our future

Deuteronomy is the farewell address of Moses to his people. In these last moments of his life, he points to the great task which has been assigned to Israel. They are to pass over the Jordan, to the Promised Land, and must confront a mighty people, a well defended country, and cities with tall walls towering into the skies. Are they capable of it?

A lesser leader might try to convince the people that they are invincible, that they can do everything demanded of them. Moses knows that this is not the right way to handle this 'stubborn people'. Instead, he reminds them of their failures. In their journey through the wilderness, they consistently rebelled against God. They worshipped the golden calf, disobeyed Moses constantly, and finally saw Moses shatter the tablets of the Law and return to the top of the mountain to receive them once again for his people. Moses restored their future to them, but reminded them that they had to confront their past and acknowledge their responsibilities.

Some years ago, a German prime minister spoke of the 'grace of being born *after* the evil time' and *not* being guilty for the past. He was right about the guilt – but not about the rejection of history. We cannot claim credit for the good of the past without acknowledging responsibility for its evil. Only if we acknowledge our weaknesses, and live with them, can we move forward and be strong, as Israel learned on that day.

✴ *God, give me the wisdom to know myself,*
to acknowledge my past errors,
to hope for a future in which I will fulfil myself more.
May I never forget my weaknesses,
so that my knowledge of them
may become my strength. Amen

The Sanctuary and the daily Way

When Moses returned from the mountain top the second time, he placed the tablets of the Law into the ark which he had fashioned. And he told the people what this meant: 'And now, Israel, what doth the LORD require of thee, but to fear the LORD thy God, with all thy heart and with all thy soul, to walk in all his ways, and to love him, and to serve the LORD thy God' (verse 12). The basic teachings of the Commandments can be safeguarded in the Sanctuary; but they have to enter life itself, and one must 'walk in all the ways' and be committed to them with heart and soul. The experiences of their ancestors whom God had loved are shared by them: they not only received the law, but escaped from slavery and entered freedom. This, too, instructs them in the ways they have to walk. Verse 19 shows them that one must learn from experience as well as from the preserved texts: 'Love ye therefore the stranger: for ye were strangers in the land of Egypt.' When our own suffering leads us to love the stranger, we also come to love God. In that moment, the house of prayer and the street in which we live become one.

✳ *God, give me the strength*
   to love the stranger as well as my family.
   And may I come to realize that
   the fatherless and the widow are part of my family.
   Then I will come to love Thee and Thy Law.
   Let my heart become soft and gentle,
   and let my hands become strong in Thy service.
   Thus would I serve Thee. Amen

Tuesday July 8   *Deuteronomy 5.1-11*

A covenant with God

Moses reminds the people that he stood between God and the people so that they would not be overcome by the dread of the Holy, where the Revelation was wreathed in fire. There are boundaries between the Sacred and the profane, and one must learn to respect them. Even a commandment which is often discounted in our time serves such a purpose: 'Thou shalt not take the name of the LORD thy God in vain' is a basic insight which we ignore to our peril. Curses and blasphemies were seen as evil in older times; once one misuses sacred words in daily life, they lose the intensity and beauty they possessed in prayer. And swearing falsely in court shames the religion, the person, and the Divine Name. If we want to preserve the Sacred, we must not let it be invaded by the profane.

✳ *God, let my lips not betray my faith.*
   Let me see the beauty of sacred words,
   and let me bring that beauty into daily life,
   lest the ugliness of a world in discord

pushes back Thy realm from all of us. Amen

Wednesday July 9   *Deuteronomy 5.12-21*

Ten commandments for living

When Moses repeats the Ten Commandments in this farewell
address, he makes some minor but significant changes. This is
not in conflict with the text in Exodus; we view it more as an
enlargement upon the first revelation. In the first text, we sanctify
the Sabbath because God rested on the seventh day: time itself
becomes hallowed, a dimension of the Divine. Here, the
commandment to rest becomes a reminder that *every one* needs
to rest, that we must have compassion for those who work for us
and are under our control. Israel is reminded of its time of slavery
– we learn from our experience how oppression and suffering
destroys the human spirit. In Exodus, the text states 'remember'
the Sabbath. Here, we are enjoined to 'keep' it, to turn this
commandment into a rule for living. And there is a Sabbath prayer
in the Jewish tradition which says: 'to "remember" and to "Keep"
the Sabbath is the same word!'

✳ *Lord, help me to keep what I remember of Thy law.*
  May I learn to hallow time and space,
  so that the Divine rest at the beginning
  becomes the concern
  for all who labour in the world I inhabit today.
  In that way, may my day of rest
  truly bless my home and my neighbours. Amen

Thursday July 10   *Deuteronomy 6.4-21*

The One and unique God

This profound affirmation of the One God is the central prayer of
the Jewish tradition, the *Sh'ma,* recited by Jews from early
childhood and whispered at the moment of death. Christians
reaffirm it when they remind themselves of the teachings of
Jesus. Asked what is most important in religion, Jesus quotes the
Sh'ma (Mark 12.29-30). And then he turns to the other Jewish
text, Leviticus 19.18 'And thou shalt love thy neighbour as thyself'
(Mark 12.31).

Reading the Bible, we come to see the two religions walking
along the same way of love. And, entering the home of a Jewish
friend, we often see a small, beautiful capsule on the door post,

156

following the teaching 'and thou shalt write them upon the posts of thy house.' In that capsule, called *mezuzah*, these words are hand-written upon parchments, reminding all who enter of the teachings of the Bible.

✳ *May we truly talk of God's word when 'we sit in our house,*
and when we walk on our way,
when we lie down, and when we rise up.'
And may the knowledge of the One God
make us one humanity,
filled with love for one another and for God.

Friday July 11   *Deuteronomy 7.7-11*

God's love and human response

How does God choose a person or a people for a special task? Clearly, it does not have to be a person of special skills, great power, or someone in a position of influence. *Every* human being is fashioned in God's image and can grow into the task which may be assigned. This also holds true for a people. Israel was not chosen for its task as a priest-people because it was more numerous (it was a tiny group!) or because it was better than every other nation. It was chosen, quite simply, because God loved it, says our text. In human relationships, marriage is often based on economics, status, or family reasons. Yet we also come to discover that love triumphs over all other considerations, and that it becomes the special covenant of marriage. Both partners come to know the special duty they owe each other; and that is what is described in this text. Following the Divine laws becomes an act of love which acknowledges the love of God towards all who are created in the Divine image.

Accepting God's love means that we accept our duties, and thus show our own love.

✳ *O God, help us to accept and cherish your love,*
to make it the foundation of our life.
Then, truly, will we be sanctified. Amen

Saturday July 12   *Deuteronomy 8.12-19*

On giving thanks

We are to bless the LORD for the good which we receive (verse 10), 'lest, when thou hast eaten and art full, and has built goodly houses ... thine heart be lifted up, and thou forget the LORD thy God ... who fed thee in the wilderness' (verses 12, 14, 16).

Gratitude is one of the great virtues which sustains us in life. There is something very familiar to us in the description of those who become proud with riches and who say in their hearts, as the text describes, that '*my* power and the might of *mine* hand hath gotten me this wealth' (verse 12). I have often heard the quip, 'He is a self-made man and he adores his maker.' When we solely ascribe success to our own efforts, we downgrade others who are not as fortunate as we are, and we assume that what we owe will always be ours by right. But we are *not* in control of the world. Riches can be lost. If we equated them with ourselves, we are lost as well. But if we gave thanks for what has come to us, we will not be destroyed. And if we share what we have, we can never lose everything. More than that: a word of thanks at our table makes us appreciate that we are surrounded by blessings throughout life. Let us praise God at every meal, lest we become less than human. We might just say:

* *We praise you God,*
  Who sustaineth all of us with Thy bounty. Amen

TO THINK ABOUT

● From this week's readings, make a list of those areas of our faith which Jews and Christians hold precious, and reflect upon them.

● Read again Deuteronomy 8.12-19. What challenge does it make to our attitude towards our possessions and our general sense of achievement?

8th Sunday after Pentecost, July 13   *Deuteronomy 11.10-17*
The earth is the LORD'S

A curious text confronts us here, and Bible scholars have helped us greatly in their analysis. They show us that the Promised Land is different from other lands. In Egypt, the crops were nourished by wells dug by slaves, and by the Nile which was worshipped as a god. In Canaan, the land drank the water of the rain of heaven, and the harvest was sustained by Divine Providence. And God promised the people that 'if ye shall hearken diligently unto my commandments which I command you this day, to love the LORD your God and to serve him with all your heart and with all your

soul, That I will give you the rain of your land in his due season ...'
(verse 13). Everything depended upon the Covenant, the
agreement between the people and God. If they did not live
righteously, 'the LORD's wrath' would 'shut up the heaven that
there be no rain ...' (verse 17). No forces of nature had to be
propitiated, but ethical actions were a necessary part of farming
the land. Even today, ecology depends on ethics; the earth is the
Lord's and we are God's stewards.

* *In a land of riches, let me remember, O God,*
  that all comes from Thee.
  At a time of poverty, let me search for the moral way
  in which I share with others.
  And, always, let me search my ways
  so that the land be not poisoned by my actions. Amen

Monday July 14   *Deuteronomy 14.22-29*
The tithe and the Levite
These days, the tithe has become much more of a voluntary
contribution to our religious institutions. Yet there are still areas of
religious life where the individuals and the religious organization
give or require a tithe. Several European countries still maintain
the 'Church Tax', where a percentage of all earnings are
deducted as part of the income tax, and are then returned to the
different religious institutions. Yet it is better to follow the insights
of this text, and for all individuals to assume their own
responsibilities towards their religious faith. Churches and
synagogues depend upon the donations of their members – they
are not business firms. And the religious functionaries – 'the
Levite that is within thy gates; thou shalt not forsake him; for he
hath no part nor inheritance with thee' (verse 27) – they too are
not 'in business' but serve religion and must receive their due.
Some have accepted the vow of poverty, but we must not force it
upon them. In a world of materialist values, we may not degrade
them in order to diminish their authority upon us.

* *Lord, help me to accept responsibility in all areas.*
  Let me support those who give me support in dark times.
  May my gifts not be exacted from me,
  but let them be free will offerings,
  in the spirit of my faith. Amen

Slavery and freedom

Slavery can take on many forms. In our time, economic slavery is so much part of our society that we do not need the reminder of verse 11 ' the poor shall never cease out of the land' – but we must *not* make this an excuse for doing nothing about it. In the Bible, we see a society striving to be just to its weaker members. The 'seventh year of release' cancels debts; but it also recognizes the problem of credit drying up in the sixth year when no one is willing to give a loan. In later times, in the Talmud, the rabbis interpreted the text by noting that this applied only to direct loans. Loans through a 'bank' (they named it a *prosbul)* were collectable. But the Bible also insisted upon justice on the part of the affluent, who must consider risky loans to the needy as an act of charity. The poor were not to become slaves. And slaves should not remain slaves. Branding them by boring a hole in their ear in public if they refused manumission was a way of forcing them to accept freedom. 'Why the ear?' asked the rabbis. And they answered: 'Because with that ear they heard freedom announced to them. If they rejected freedom, that ear should be marked for all of their lives.'

✳ *O Lord, teach me to accept freedom with its responsibilities*
    and its joys. May I share it with others,
    and may my dreams and hopes grow in a world
    where freedom must become a reality for everyone.
    Amen

Justice and judges

The deep gates of the cities and towns of ancient Israel were the courts of law where citizens could listen to the courts' decisions. There, they could see that judges would 'judge the people with just judgment'. But this passage in the Pentateuch is really intended as instruction to the judges themselves. The words are still valid today: 'Thou shalt not wrest judgment' (verse 19) – don't twist and distort the law! 'Thou shalt not respect persons, neither take a gift' – do not favour the rich since they have power; and do not favour the poor because they are needy: justice must be impartial. And, in a corrupt society, we still know that bribes are possible: judges may not accept gifts!

The text also warns us against kings. Even a good king – Solomon – multiplied 'horses ... wives ... and silver and gold' for himself (17.16, 17). Basically, the injunction warns against dictatorial, absolute rulers; but there was also concern that the people would turn away from the laws of God and live by the laws governing all neighbouring countries. If there is a king, let him study the Law, and live by it. And this is a proper injunction for all rulers, in ancient times and today.

✳ *We pray for our governments and our courts.*
May they always act justly,
and strive for the good of the people.
And may just actions and just laws
be part of our home and our land. Amen

Thursday July 17   *Deuteronomy 19.4-7, 14-19*

Cities of refuge

It is difficult to overcome the past and its rigid customs. Israel lived in a world where the laws of blood revenge were still enforced – 'a life for a life' – even if an accidental death occurred. But if one could not yet change that society, one could at least prevent the worst excesses. By creating 'cities of refuge' as sanctuaries where one could flee if one had taken a life accidentally, this biblical innovation broke the chain of blood feuds. Otherwise, the relative who had revenged the death would also be the subject of the next blood feud and had to be killed in turn. To this day, the concept of sanctuary is present within religious institutions; and we come to understand that laws have to develop and grow. The past continues to be respected in our text: 'thou shalt not remove thy neighbour's landmark' (verse 14) recognizes that a society should not be overthrown violently, and that property rights are respected. The improvement and growth which must take place exists within the structure of the law; and, as the American poet Robert Frost wrote: 'Good fences make good neighbours.'

✳ *God, help me to grow.*
May my passions never ignore my sense of justice,
and may I learn the meaning of life within a community
where understanding of the neighbour
enables me to see the difference
between evil actions and accidental tragedy.
Sanctuaries are needed in our time;
help me to respect them, and all boundaries. Amen

Responsibility for others

Life is filled with temptations. Children still chant 'finders keepers, losers weepers', and we relax our ethical standards in the market place: 'let the buyer beware'. Yet from the beginning, the Bible enjoins us not to take advantage of others. Lost property must be returned; and every effort has to be made to find the rightful owner. Similarly, compassion for animals extends beyond our possessions: 'thou shalt not see thy brother's ass or his ox fall down ... and hide thyself ... thou shalt surely help him lift them up again.'

One of the most interesting laws is: 'When thou buildest a house, thou shalt make a battlement (parapet) for thy roof' (verse 8). In the Babylonian Code of Hammurabi, it was decreed that if a neighbour's child played upon your roof and fell to its death, your own child should be cast off the roof. In the Bible, one builds a parapet in order to avoid blood guilt. And, in the case of an accident, the law calls for compensation, not for death. Behind the laws, there stood awareness for the rights of others, even of animals. 'Thou shalt not take the dam with the young from her nest' (verse 6) was a law of compassion for birds where one also saw a pattern of family life. Today, much of that compassion seems to be lacking.

✳ *O Lord, help me to understand*
that others need our protection,
both people and the animals around us.
The more we reach out to them,
the closer we will come unto Thee. Amen

Accepting the Covenant

There are moments in history which shape a nation: the Magna Carta at Runnymede, the Constitutional Assembly in Philadelphia, the end of Apartheid in South Africa ... At Sinai, the children of Israel entered an agreement with God which also became their constitution. In many ways, it was the forerunner of the pre-amble of the American Constitution which echoes much of what we find in today's text: 'Ye stand this day all of you before the LORD your God ... your little ones, your wives, and thy stranger that is in thy camp ... that thou shouldst enter into the covenant with the LORD thy God, and into his oath ... that he may establish thee today for a people unto himself, and that he may be unto thee a God ...' (verses 10-13). And the text continues to point out that this applies also to those who are not present, and to those not yet born. Just so, we are born citizens of a country, bound to observe its laws – ignorance of the law is no excuse – and must live by the Covenant made for us. This applies to our faith as well. God's people are linked to the Divine by the revealed law; and this text is our own constitution, our agreement, our 'testament' with God.

✳ *O God, let us live by the agreement*
   which endures through the generations
   between Thee and Thy children.
   Then the Holy Scriptures will live for us,
   and we will live through Thy divine word. Amen

TO THINK ABOUT

● Read again Deuteronomy 15.1-3 together with Luke 6.30-34. What challenges do these two passages make to problems of credit and debt today?
● What challenges does Deuteronomy 22.6-8 make to our stewardship of the earth?

FOR ACTION

Make your own clear copy of the *Sh'ma* (Deuteronomy 6.4-9) – in calligraphy if you can – and place it in a prominent place in your home where it will be a constant reminder to you.

IN EVERY PLACE
1. A new creation

Notes based on the New Revised Standard Version by
Leta Hawe

Leta Hawe has served within the Presbyterian Church of Aotearoa-New Zealand as Deaconess and Minister. She now lives in active retirement in Wanganui, and is particularly involved in the work of the local Hospice.

The village store appeared timeless: stable and unchanging. Regular customers might grumble about the limited range of products, but appreciated the friendly unhurried service.

Then the unbelievable happened! A large notice appeared: 'Under new management'. Changes were swift and radical. The old had gone; the new had taken over. Nothing remained the same.

Neither can life remain the same when we are 'converted' to Christ, nor as we are renewed over and over again by the power of the Spirit. 'New' implies change which may be resisted by those who prefer the status quo, but welcomed by others who recognize the need for improvement.

'New' is a gospel concept, indicating the complete transformation that occurs when we enter into fellowship with the living Christ, and allow the Holy Spirit to work through us to change the world.

9th Sunday after Pentecost, July 20   Hosea 6.1-6 *
Hope of genuine renewal

In every crisis, Israel turned to God, confident that if they repented God would forgive. They were sure that God was on their side, but Hosea recognized the superficiality of their sacrifices and prayers. He distrusted this facile penitence. It was as short-lived as the morning dew that vanished in the Palestinian heat.

The people of Israel needed to be made alive again, and this could only happen through an act of genuine repentance, a return to the ways of God. If only they could show as a nation that their intentions were serious and that their loyalty to God stemmed from genuine devotion, their sacrifices and burnt offerings would again be effective.

Ritual as a substitute for compassion is meaningless, but ritual as a sign of a worshipping heart is acceptable to God.

✳ *If there is a credibility gap between what I do in worship and my daily witness, help me to be aware of it.*

Monday July 21   Matthew 9.9-13 *

A new inclusiveness

Time may have dimmed the radical nature of Jesus' ministry: his refusal to be bound by tradition or influenced by the deep-rooted prejudices of political and religious leaders.

In calling Matthew, Jesus was not condoning his way of earning a living. Tax collectors were notoriously dishonest and universally hated. They were collaborators with their country's oppressors. Many became wealthy at the expense of their compatriots who they mercilessly exploited, and who were powerless to withstand their corrupt ways.

In identifying Matthew as a follower, Jesus demonstrated that Matthew and others like him were not excluded from God's love. Jesus did not imply a lack of interest in the faithful, but emphasized that he actively seeks the sinner (see Luke 15). Jesus is Saviour of all, including those who are ignored by the dis-ease of society!

✳ *Jesus Christ, whose love reached out to all,*
   transform my attitude that I may reflect your
      inclusiveness.

Tuesday July 22   2 Corinthians 5.14 to 6.2

A new lifestyle

It is common practice today for firms and organizations to formulate a 'mission statement' to express the reason for their existence and to set out objectives.

Here Paul sets out a mission statement, defining what it means to be a Christian. This new life is a complete transformation. The centre of life is no longer self but Christ.

Christians cease to be motivated by a desire for self-fulfilment, personal success or advantage. And why? 'The love of Christ urges us on' (verse 14). Our actions stem from a radical remake of our old selves. We are not merely altered or improved. We are a new creation.

I was with a group studying Psalm 51.10 when a Maori lad excitedly exclaimed, 'I see what it means! "Lord, put a new engine inside me; not just a rebore either!"' With a new engine installed, a new quality of performance is guaranteed.

This new creation is a gift from God. With the gift there comes responsibility: to be agents of reconciliation. Having experienced the power of God's transforming love, we are to express that love in every aspect of our living and to point others to the source of that love.

✳ *Create in me a clean heart, O God,*
  and put a new and right spirit within me. Psalm 51.10

Wednesday July 23   *Matthew 7.15-29*
Is the change obvious?
Jesus drew attention to the credibility gap between the words and practices of those who falsely claimed religious authority, and Matthew's use of this saying probably reflects a similar situation in the Early Church. Their practices failed to reflect the ways of Christ.

This question applies not only to church leaders but to all who follow Christ. We must admit that there are occasions and situations when we are poor advertisements for our faith.

People are seldom argued into the Kingdom, but they may be persuaded by a Christ-like lifestyle. Jesus made it clear that we shall be judged by our fruits. Creeds into deeds would make for a more convincing way of life. Many of Jesus' parables emphasize doing the will of God (e.g. Matthew 25.31-46).

'If you were on trial for being a Christian, would there be enough evidence to convict you?' These words on a poster constantly challenge me.

✳ *May we not be hearers only,*
  but doers of God's will.

A costly change

Zacchaeus, ridiculed for lack of height and hated as a tax collector, carried a double burden, even if the power he wielded in his work compensated for a lack of stature.

In his determination to see Jesus, he showed signs of a potential yet to be realized. No one could deter him. He was resourceful, and he was a risk-taker, prepared to face yet more scorn through his attempt to attract Jesus' attention.

The encounter that followed resulted in a new Zacchaeus, ready to make amends for the wrongs he had committed.

In this graphic story of his demonstration of gratitude, he took the radical step of breaking with the past and undertaking restitution far beyond what the Law required. Judged by the world's standards, Zacchaeus had become poorer, but he gained something of greater value: a peace and joy the world cannot give. He experienced a new freedom: no longer bound by desire for wealth or power.

Does our commitment to Christ alter our attitude to and use of possessions? Are we prepared to accept the challenge 'to live more simply so that others may simply live'? Is our attitude toward material wealth a barrier to total commitment?

✷ *Lord Jesus Christ, do I own my possessions,*
   or am I possessed by them?

Resurrection power creates new life

Prior to his death, Jesus promised the disciples 'The one who believes in me ... in fact, will do even greater works than these, because I am going to the Father' (John 14.12). The apostles were discovering the fulfilment of that promise. As they went about, proclaiming the presence and power of the risen Christ, their reputation grew. People, recognizing that these ordinary men were gifted with extraordinary powers, brought the needy and distressed to them for help and healing. They expected results and were not disappointed.

Miracles do happen today. People come alive in the power of the risen Christ, overcoming the fears, anxieties and inadequacies that diminish them as individuals.

Some of us limp along in a twilight zone of faith. We never

experience life in all its richness until we trust the resurrection power and enter into a close relationship with the risen ever-present Christ.

✴ *Risen Christ, source of our hope,*
  we rejoice with awe and wonder at your ability to
    surprise us
  with your healing, renewing power.

Saturday July 26   *Acts 19.11-20*
Demon-possessed or God possessed?
People have always been attracted and influenced by 'signs and wonders'. Paul took his lead from Jesus who consistently refused to accede to the pressures and expectations of those who looked for 'a sign', and avoided anything that could be interpreted as magic.

In the first century, exorcism was widely practised, and some practitioners were ready to use any means to achieve their ends. But the sons of Sceva learnt that the name of Jesus was not a 'magical charm'. It became clear to people that God's way had nothing to do with magic and that a greater power was at work.

As a dramatic symbol of their break with the past, many exorcists publicly burned their charms and books of spells which had been so profitable. They did not hesitate to consider how they would survive as they gave up things they depended on for their livelihood. Are *we* ready to demonstrate total commitment to Christ by abandoning things which give us a sense of security? What of church structures and practices to which we adhere so rigidly? Do we sometimes allow them to become barriers to our growth?

✴ *Now to him who by the power at work within us is able to*
  accomplish abundantly far more than all we can ask or
  imagine, be glory in the church and in Christ Jesus to all
  generations, forever and ever. Amen.   *Ephesians 3.20*

TO THINK ABOUT and FOR ACTION
● What changes have taken place in your life as a result of your commitment to Jesus Christ?
● What changes in your life, or the life of your church, have you resisted? Why?

Is there a relationship, attitude or situation needing to be made new? Decide on the steps that should be taken **now**.

168

IN EVERY PLACE
2. Opportunities for mission

Notes based on the Revised Standard Version by
Akuila Yabaki

Akuila Yabaki is an ordained minister of the Methodist Church in Fiji. He first served in Britain as a circuit minister under the World Church in Britain Partnership in the 1980's and later in 1990 became World Church Secretary for Asia and the Pacific for the British Methodist Church.

Mission is more than the movement of 'mission partners' from North to South. It is the business of every church in every part of the globe. Every church, however small, is able to give as well as receive. As Christians move across boundaries of nations and cultures to share their good news of what God has done, and continues to do, they follow those who went before. This week, we see lives changed as in the case of Jonah and the apostle Paul. We see that mission is as much about being received by people in their homes as battling through prayer with powers that dominate the world. It is about the Spirit challenging and opening new doors of opportunities.

10th Sunday after Pentecost, July 27   *Jonah 3.1-5 **
Reluctant messenger

God often chooses the most unlikely person to take on an impossible task, like Jonah, a rebellious individual who had different ideas about how to deal with the people of Nineveh. Just as Jacob wrestled with the angel, Jonah had his own battle with God. Prayer is not a request made to an immovable God but an inner struggle in which we the servants seek to be honest with God. Do you see prayer as a struggle or simply asking for things?

Jonah had to be won over for mission to begin. The word of the Lord came to Jonah 'the second time'. The book of Jonah describes a person's internal struggle to come to terms with God's purpose for his life. Many people experience the same dilemma. One may have to shed old prejudices or rise above ethnic or religious differences to become the person God can use. The message once delivered had its desired impact; warning and judgment brought the whole city to its knees. From the greatest to the least, people's lives were changed, all humbled before God. How many reluctant messengers could God use if only they were willing to respond?

✴ *Make me a captive, Lord,*
   And then I shall be free;
   Force me to render up my sword,
   And I shall conqueror be.   George Matheson (1842-1906)

Monday July 28   *Daniel 7.9-14*

Engaging the powers

Visions in the Bible have a way of inspiring hope because God is about to intervene to empower and restore broken communities. So this vision of the Ancient of Days on the throne over ruined principalities and powers provides encouragement. In our own strength we cannot possibly triumph over massive structures and systems which dominate our world today. There are principalities and powers, the great socio-spiritual forces who get in the way of God's rule being realized. Not only do systems obstruct God's rule but they summon loyalty to themselves. In dealing with these powers we are to reckon with powers which may not be defeated for a very long time. Yet these are limited and time-bound.

And God is ever present. The Ancient of Days was there in the beginning. In our hymns and praise we declare that empires rise and fall but God who was in the beginning, is now and shall be for ever. When the book of Daniel was written (c.167 BC) the Jewish people had been under occupation for over four hundred years – several life spans but not for ever! We are to be persistent in prayer for the coming of God's Kingdom. It could be a 'long haul' and powers will thwart God for 'a season and a time' (verse 12), but our prayers will ultimately prevail.

In Jesus' messianic consciousness, 'son of man' meant that he was to die on the cross. Jesus the crucified was vested with power, authority and kingship. The Church is the gathered peoples of different nations and languages who unite to proclaim his dominion over all life and that his rule is everlasting. The church has no mission but Christ's; it serves under the Son of Man, to gather all peoples into his service.

✴ *Lord teach us afresh the meaning of power*
   and how it should be used,

170

and may we have confidence in your power to guide.
   Amen.

Tuesday July 29   *Matthew 10.5-10 **

In our own backyard

The mission mandate to all nations (Matthew 28.18-20) is not to distract attention from work nearer home, 'the lost sheep of the house of Israel' (verse 6): increasing materialism in the West and hunger for the gospel in our own backyard. Mission at home is often less inviting than in far-off places and to be a prophet among one's own people can be the most lonely and excruciating experience. What difference does it make for messengers to be sent and charged in the name of Jesus? We are under orders to move according to God's call. The signs of the Kingdom are evident as new communities are raised to new life; communities healed as well as engaged in healing. Is this your picture of the Church?

Messengers are to trust in the power of the message. To be weighted with so much provision for the journey would be a mark of anxiety and unbelief. The poor in spirit are better able to see that the values of the Kingdom are values of the world in reverse. As I write (at the end of 1995), the new national budget has been announced in the British Parliament: five thousand extra police in three years and 10,000 extra close-circuit TV cameras to ensure security and comfort. So much for a budget for anxiety and success! The gospel encourages us to live generously and simply so that others may live.

✳ *The task thy wisdom hath assigned*
   O let me cheerfully fulfil,
   In all thy works thy presence find,
   And prove thy good and perfect will.
                                          Charles Wesley (1707-88)

Wednesday July 30   *Matthew 10.11-15 **

Finding time for people

The simple instruction that the apostles should stay with those who receive them, is a strong reminder that hospitality, however basic, has an essential place in sharing the gospel. They were sent to be with people and share with them in the familiarity of their homes. True worth is a discovery made through identifying with people and gratefully receiving what they have to offer. A cup of cold water or 'cuppa tea' can be a meeting point for sharing which leads us to make that important discovery. In an age of mobility and speed travel, finding time for each other – sharing hopes and pains – have become healing moments where the peace of God is shared. Such rare moments are more important than ever before.

The test for any church ministry is whether it is able to assist people to meet each other and share God's peace. Do changes in structures and communication systems being proposed in the Church actually lead people to listen to one another better, and to bear one another's burdens in the love of Christ?

Rejection of the blessing is possible. Endowed with the freedom which God the Creator has provided, we all have the ability to choose. The choice to refuse the messengers, and with it the peace that only God can bring, means that we have brought judgment upon ourselves. We can, if we choose, take the decision to cast ourselves outside the scope of God's saving activity. There is a 'Rubicon' to be crossed; it is a life and death decision.

✳ *Lord, motivate us by your Spirit*
to make time, to listen, to feel the pains of others
and to open our hands, not only to give, but also to
receive.

Thursday July 31   *Acts 9.1-19*

Turning point

When he fell under that blinding light on the Damascus Road, Saul who later became Paul was already living a religious life. As a Pharisee with a burning zeal for the law, and in defence of it, he took the offensive against those who were followers of what he thought was a heresy called 'the Way'. He fought to have it stamped out. Then came the transforming religious experience; the turning point. The same person, gifted with a remarkable intellect, was now to pursue the Christian cause with zeal and devotion; an advocate, no longer an enemy.

In the question, 'Why do you persecute me?', the crucified Christ identified himself with persecuted followers. If we declare that we belong to Christ, it means being part of a persecuted movement first called 'the Way'. Might we also see ourselves suffer for the faith which we hold?

172

Through the loving hands of Ananias, Saul's life was restored. In 'the house of Judas', in a street called Straight, help and hospitality were provided. God uses other servants within the Church with their own gifts – less spectacular but just as important. God's mission is often a crossroad where fellow travellers meet and touch one another's lives. Recall such persons who may have helped in your spiritual journey. God's ministry of grace reaches us though others.

✳ *God of grace, thank you for your servants who were there*
  when I needed a neighbour,
  and who helped me along the way. Amen.

Friday August 1   Acts 9.20-31

Living with risk

Paul's old friends became his enemies while new friends were still unsure about him. Paul took his hearers to the heart of the matter as he proclaimed Jesus saying, 'He is the Son of God' (verse 20). His hearers were breathless, aghast and confounded; here was a changed person with a message of such power. For some, it might have been a passing shock but there were others who were simply closed to change. Do we fail to respond to the new because we have given up believing that things could be different?

The gospel calls for change: it is good news to those who are open and trustful of the God who is at work in the world. But it is bad news for those set and fixed in their ways, who would rather things continue as they have always been.

Paul once again turned to fellow believers to help establish his new identity. Barnabas – a name which means 'encourager' – helped to build bridges of relationship and removed fear and suspicion. Where are such leaders to be found? Those who promote dialogue and understanding that there might be peace in Church and society?

✳ *Lord because our knowledge of you is partial,*
  and we have to live with risks and uncertainties,
  make our faith strong enough to obey your command.
    Amen

Breaking new ground

Years into his ministry, Paul gave his own personal account of the remarkable transformation which made him an apostle. Paul was not seeking attention, or a place of honour. He had to defend his bridge-building ministry to the Gentiles; a departure by which the gospel turned enemies into friends. By whose authority could a newcomer dare make such a distinctively new shift, widening the area of mission? Paul replied that he was answerable to a higher authority; to the one who set him apart from birth and called him by grace. Paul stood firm and alone on an authority which was higher than that of 'flesh and blood'.

Fifteen days with Cephas could have provided a meeting of minds. Peter must have shared a first-hand knowledge about the life of Jesus: a discussion on the state of the Church in Jerusalem and future plans. Differences were to emerge between the two great apostles about what should be the Church's attitude to gentiles. Such differences, without causing division in the Church, led to a positive division of work; Paul and Barnabas were designated for new work among gentiles and others for work among Jews. Can we think of issues which divide the Church today which, if handled with humility and patience, could open rather than close doors for new opportunities?

✳ *O Sending Spirit, forgive us for insisting*
that things which are changeable are not to be changed,
and embolden us to turn our differences
into new opportunities for service.

TO THINK ABOUT AND ACT

● Do you think the church grows despite persecution or because of it?

● Try and learn something of the life of the Church in places where there is persecution today. Pray for that Church.

● Daniel 7.9-14 is about a vision of powers being overthrown. What are the massive institutions and systems of domination which get in the way of God's rule today?

● Familiarize yourself with the work of Amnesty International and similar organizations which advocate human rights? Be an advocate through prayer and action.

IN EVERY PLACE
3. Opposition

Notes based on the Revised English Bible by
Salvador T. Martinez

Salvador T Martinez teaches theology and ethics at the McGilvary Faculty of Theology, Payap University in Chiang Mai, Thailand. He was executive secretary for theological concerns of the Christian Conference of Asia. He is an ordained minister of the United Church of Christ in the Philippines sent to the Church of Christ in Thailand as an international associate under the joint auspices of the United Church Board for World Ministries and the Division of Overseas Ministries of the Disciples of Christ (Christian Church).

'Persecution', says the apostle Paul, 'will indeed come to everyone who wants to live a godly life as a follower of Christ Jesus' (2 Timothy 3.12). Even family members and friends can be obstacles to Christian discipleship. This is especially true in Asian societies where other faiths are in the majority. People are so bound to tradition, community and the family. One of the most painful of all experiences is to be ostracized and rejected by one's immediate community. Faced with real threats to our faith today, what do we do?

11th Sunday after Pentecost, August 3   Matthew 10.16-20 *
The Spirit's witness through us

When God sent Moses to bring the words of deliverance to the Israelites, he complained of his inability to speak. The Lord assured him: 'Go now; I shall help you to speak and show you what to say' (Exodus 4.10-12).

In today's reading, God promises something better. When the follower of Christ is delivered before rulers and councils, there is no reason to be anxious about what to say for 'it will not be you speaking, but the Spirit of your Father speaking in you' (verse 20). The apostle Paul makes an interesting point: those who are led by God's Spirit are God's children and the Spirit enables them to cry, 'Abba! Father!' because it is the Spirit who dwells within that bears witness (cf. Romans 8.12-16, Galatians 4.6). Paul further adds that as children of God we are God's heirs, 'fellow-heirs with Christ', provided we suffer with him and so we share his glory. In his darkest hour, Christ also called upon 'Abba, Father,' to remove the cup of suffering, but left it to God to do his will. Are we able to pray as our Lord prayed?

✳ *'Abba, Father, all things are possible to you; take this cup from me. Yet not my will but yours.'* Mark 14.36

Monday August 4 Matthew 10.21-25 *
Enduring till the end
Thailand has had its share of Christian martyrdom. In September 1869, two newly baptized Christians, Noi Sunya and Nan Chai, were martyred at the behest of Prince Chao Kawilorot, then ruler of Chiang Mai. When asked why he ordered their execution, the Prince answered: 'They have embraced the Christian religion.' He added that he 'would continue to kill everyone who did the same. Leaving the religion of the country was a rebellion against him and he would so treat it.'

Presbyterian missionaries, stationed in Chiang Mai, were advised to leave at once for their safety, but Dr. Daniel McGilvary refused: 'I could not see that it is the will of Providence that the mission be abandoned.' Because of the perseverance and dedication of the early missionaries, there remains a growing witness in Thailand today. 'Everyone will hate you for your allegiance to me, but whoever endures to the end will be saved' (verse 22). Do we have the courage to stand up for our faith today? Think of the challenges that face you in your country and local community.

✳ *Thank you, O God, for the faithfulness*
of those who have gone before us.
May we have the courage to follow their example.

Tuesday August 5 Matthew 10.26-33
No reason to fear
This passage gives three unassailable reasons why a true disciple should never be afraid of opposition. First, 'There is nothing covered that will not be uncovered, nothing hidden that will not be made known' (verse 26). The word of God is powerful. It should be told as though we are not afraid of anyone, because

we know that truth will be vindicated.

Secondly, there is no reason to 'fear those who kill the body, but cannot kill the soul.' Rather, fear God. 'The fear of God' liberates a person from fear itself. 'Let us fear therefore,' St. Augustine exhorts, 'that we may not fear.' The Psalmist says, 'The fear of the Lord is the beginning of wisdom' (111.10a). Reflect on these words found over an English hearth:

'Fear knocked at the door.
Faith answered, 'There's no one there ...'

Thirdly, Jesus said that as God cares for a sparrow that falls to the ground, nothing can surely happen to a disciple who serves and trusts him without God's knowing and caring.

✳ *Fear has been real to me, Lord.*
Help me to trust only in you – my true security.

Taking up the cross

The Gospel puts it very succinctly: a person's worst enemies could be under his own roof. The last and perhaps greatest single obstacle to Christian discipleship is the family. Jesus taught us to love and honour our families (Matthew 15.3), but love for family should not stand in the way of Christian discipleship.

Discipleship involves 'taking up the cross' (cf. Mark 8.34-35; Luke 14.26-27). The disciples knew what this meant. The cross was Rome's instrument of punishment for anyone who dared to challenge the status quo. Jesus was nailed to the cross precisely for doing that. He went where people were wronged and set things right. What is the meaning of the cross for us today?

Taking up the cross is to go out where violence and extortion are committed against innocent people and doing something on their behalf to bring about justice. It is to be where the world is most in need and become involved with God in setting right some of the terrible agonies of a world that has gone wrong.

✳ *O Lord, teach me how to be your disciple*
in my own place and time
and give me what it takes to be one.

Baptism through suffering

As part of his desire to conciliate the Pharisees and Sadducees, King Herod Agrippa I instituted a systematic persecution of Christian leaders, hoping to discourage their followers. First, James was put to death by the sword. Peter would surely have suffered the same fate were it not for the intervention of an angel. But the earliest Christians countered Herod's persecution with prayer. They prayed 'fervently', and their prayers were 'answered'.

It is not easy to understand the mystery of God's will. This is faith. We pray demanding nothing of our will, only God's. To do otherwise is to make a mockery of God.

The death of James echoed Jesus' reply to James and John: 'The cup that I drink you shall drink; and the baptism I am baptized with shall be your baptism' (Mark 10.39). The words refer to the imminent suffering of Jesus on the cross.

✴ *O Lord of the cross, make me worthy to be baptized*
  with the baptism of fellowship in your sufferings
  in my life as well as in death.

Suffering for righteousness

I Peter was probably written at a time when to profess faith in Christ might result in the death penalty. In spite of great opposition, Christians are challenged to live differently. They are privileged people (2.4-10), and so they are to be worthy of their calling (2.11-12). They are to be ready to suffer for righteousness' sake (3.13-17). Their suffering, like that of Christ's, is undeserved, yet merits God's approval (2.20-21). Suffering is essential for the progress of the Christian's life on earth, as well as for its final fulfilment. As Christ himself entered glory through suffering (cf. Luke 24.26), so Christians are also called upon to share in his sufferings (Matthew 5.11-12). The Christian is to rejoice in his suffering, for in doing so s/he glorifies God. Can we go on trusting God in the trials we go through, and continue to do good? Reflect on your own experiences and those of others known to you.

✴ *O God who suffers, help us to endure suffering*
  and to rejoice and be faithful till the end.

Martyrs of faith

John relates his vision of the martyrs of faith – of all nations and languages – clothed in white robes standing around the throne praising God. They were nearest to the throne of God, ahead of angels and others, pre-eminent before God to whom they ascribed blessing, glory, wisdom, thanksgiving, honour, power and strength.

They were triumphant over persecution. They had overcome opposition, not by escaping from it, but by enduring steadfastly and faithfully through it. Their faithfulness was rewarded with the right to enter into the very presence of God.

Our great Saviour is pictured here as the divine shepherd who guides the faithful to 'springs of the water of life' and who 'will wipe away every tear from their eyes'. Even in the end, God shows his loving concern, ministering both to the physical and spiritual needs of the faithful. God our Saviour is the saviour of the whole person.

✳ *O divine shepherd, you satisfy the hunger and thirst*
of my body and soul.
Help me to praise you even in the midst of difficulties.

TO THINK ABOUT

Think of times when you felt you were personally threatened because of your faith. Reflect on ways that God delivered you from these onslaughts.

Think of Christians in other parts of the world who are facing opposition because of their faith. Reflect on ways in which you might be God's agent in bringing deliverance to them.

FOR ACTION

Identify a person who may be facing real persecution because of his faith. Pray for that person. Better still, write a letter of encouragement to him or her today.

AN EXTENDED FAMILY

Notes based on the New International Version by
Ebere Nze

Eberechukwu Nze, a Nigerian theologian and former Principal of Methodist Theological Institute in Umuahia, has travelled widely and represented the Methodist Church Nigeria in many international conferences and seminars. He is now Bishop of the Nochi Diocese, Abia State, Nigeria.

The extended family structure is commonly found in the southern countries of the world. Its character is more religious than social when compared with the nuclear family which emerged along with the process of industrialization in the West. The African family, for example, is a network of relationships established by marriage, birth and adoption. It is one of the main 'caretakers' of life, health and culture.

Like the extended family, the Church is an inclusive community with an inclusive message to proclaim to the world. Its fellowship welcomes all who accept its faith and claim its common heritage. At the birth of this Christian community (Acts 2.42-47), the fellowship which brought believers together provided opportunities for a common meal, caring for one another and sharing spiritual experience and resources. What a wonderful world it would be, if all peoples discovered that the extended family system provided a pattern of relationship for the world and its various cultures to emulate.

12th Sunday after Pentecost, August 10
Matthew 12.46-50 *; 8.18-22

Radical demands

The family is an organized social structure which makes radical demands. Its welfare and solidarity depend on obedience to its rules and obligations.

In this text, Jesus was not rejecting his natural family. Rather he was expressing the inclusive nature of the family of God's people which includes all who are in tune with him spiritually. In this way, he showed the higher priority of his spiritual relationship to those who believed in and followed him. His statement in 8.22 indicates that the spiritually dead can be left to bury the physically dead. To follow Jesus, we need to be spiritually awake to give our full attention and commitment to living as members of God's family.

This family includes everyone, whatever and whoever you are. Do you belong to it? If you do, it asks you to surrender your total self to the Lord of life.

✳ *Holy God, whether we live or die, we belong to you.*
Cause us to make a full surrender of our lives to you
that nothing may prevent us from continuing
as members of your family. Through Jesus Christ we
pray.

Monday August 11   *Matthew 13.53-58*

God's power has no limits

It is said that 'familiarity breeds contempt'. But in the case of Jesus' ministry in Nazareth, his home town, the people also had a limited understanding of the power of God. They could not see God acting outside their tradition, or that God might use anyone he wills to proclaim the gospel at any time and anywhere.

Herod had received a report of the activities of Jesus (Matthew 14.1). So the ordinary folk must already have known of the miracles and the great and prophetic teachings of Jesus. It was unreasonable therefore, after their initial amazement, that they should disbelieve and dishonour Jesus just because of their familiarity with his origins. His appointed presence at Nazareth was a missed opportunity of salvation for them.

God is God and God's wisdom is unsearchable. The Holy Spirit works through familiar and strange people in achieving God's purpose for all. The Holy Spirit projects the message not the messenger and the message is greater than the messenger.

At the River Jordan, a familiar river, God asks us to listen and hear Jesus as a Son in the context of his universal family (Matthew 3.17). Jesus' family was not limited to the family of his birth who lived in Nazareth.

✳ *Great God of wonder, help us to see beyond your*
messengers,
that we may be humbled to hear your message of
salvation
through your Son Jesus Christ our Lord. Amen

181

The strength of love

One role of the family is to provide company where there is loneliness and love where there is none. From John 7.5, we learn that the brothers of Jesus did not believe in him. Maybe that was why Jesus, in today's reading, could not rely on them to care for his mother after his death but committed her to the company and love of his extended family. It is interesting to note how these women were variously connected with Jesus, shared a tremendous love and supported him with their presence even to the point of risking their lives as they stood and watched the crucifixion. And it must have been a strong bond of love that moved Jesus on the cross to think of the sorrows of others.

In his agony, and when the salvation of the world hung in the balance, his thoughts turned from his own bitter experience of rejection to his mother's loneliness. This demonstration of the strength of love challenges the quality of our love and service to others in the community. *Be an instrument through whom God will provide love for someone today.*

✶ *O God, make me an instrument of love today*
that others may know your love through my life. Amen

The flavour of nobility

To this day, this chapter is read on Friday evenings by committed Jewish families as part of the traditional ceremony that welcomes in the Sabbath. It expresses great respect for the role of the woman in the family, within which a good wife has a tremendous influence. And her influence is experienced by the whole community. Excellence cannot be hidden.

The Christian is a child of God, of noble birth. Yet many Christians who serve in public life shy away from letting this God-given nobility infect those around them. Where are the Christians who recognize that they are people of noble birth? The quality of their commitment and service to the community will influence and attract others to love Jesus. Let your life today be an example to those who wish to know our Lord.

✶ *May the power of the Holy Spirit, which gave us a noble birth*
through our faith in the transforming work of the cross,
help us to live nobly to the end.

Family ethics

Through giving and receiving from one another the family grows in mutual love, and develops a sense of solidarity. Every family thrives on reciprocity. The concept of the family suggests obligations of mutual obedience. Everyone is interlinked so that irresponsible actions by any of its members create conflict and destroy peace and harmony. In using the example of the family to admonish Christians at Colossae to practise true fellowship, Paul begins where people are, but he lays down principles which are still relevant.

A strength of the Christian faith is that it provides a structure of morality for daily routine: the peace of the home, that of communities and nations, stable marriages and good neighbourliness. All these depend on simple respect for basic principles like those listed in today's reading. Reverence and love for one another can achieve greater results than force, human wisdom and logic.

✷ *Loving Father, we confess*
that the things we can do, we do not try.
May your Holy Spirit give us a new heart of obedience,
that we may follow the simple rules of life
and so live in harmony with others.

The great institution

Marriage is one of the greatest institutions God created. There are various patterns of marriage across cultures, but the basic principle of commitment for life is the same. In some cultures, marriage is contracted along the kinship line, just as in biblical Judaism. In some, the bride's family seem to hold most authority; in others it is the bridegroom's family. But wherever we look, we see marriage instituted by God to provide a pattern of unity and stability in the world.

In the choice of Rebecca, Abraham's servant easily located her through the family's belief that God had ordained that she would be Isaac's wife. The simple prayer said to God beside the spring was answered, and Rebecca appeared before him.

God in his infinite wisdom puts us in compatible units. In the process of socialization, the personality pattern we acquire in the home brings about the way that each of us behaves to other members of the family and work together to resist harmful factors from without.

✳ **Dear Lord, in all our endeavours,**
you go before us to prepare the way.
Help us to trust your leadership in all things.

Saturday August 16   *Ephesians 4.14-21*
Unity in diversity

In today's reading, unity comes from the interdependent support of every part of the body. It is a perfect example: the very body that feels the pain and discomfort of an accident or disorder also experiences social problems and conflict which arise from ignored obligations in home and community. Jesus Christ is the head of the Church, which can only be a well co-ordinated body when every member allows him to take control, just as every healthy human body is obedient to the brain.

In a pluralistic world, every Christian needs to remain steadfast and intimately connected with Christ. His presence can keep us from being swept away by winds of change and false philosophies. To maintain our link with Christ our head is to remain in solidarity with God.

Christ is the head – or centre – of the Christian family and this image of the body also reflects the unity intended for Christian marriage. Our life today does not have to consist of alienation, but can be one of interdependence and unity of purpose.

✳ **Jesus, with Thy church abide;**
Be her Saviour, Lord, and Guide,
While on earth her faith is tried;
We beseech Thee, hear us.   *T B Pollack (1836-96)*

TO THINK ABOUT and FOR ACTION

● If you have time, read Ephesians 5.1 to 6.9. What basic principles are still important to marriage and family life today?
● Can a husband love his wife as Christ loves the Church, and vice versa?
● How can we help children to discover their true place in today's family and community?

IBRA is an extended family, with work in over 80 countries. As a member of this family, have you responded to the International Appeal? See page 66.

ISAIAH
1. Words to a prosperous society

Notes based on the Revised English Bible by
Pauline Webb

Though officially retired, Pauline Webb is still frequently heard, presenting the Daily Service on Radio 4 or giving a Pause for Thought on Radio 2. She was previously in charge of religious broadcasting on the BBC World Service. Prior to that, she worked for the Methodist Church Overseas Division and served for a time as Vice-Moderator of the World Council of Churches. She is still active as a Methodist local preacher and writer.

The Bible has been called a 'book which has a bias to the poor'. But it also has a clear message for the rich. In the Hebrew Scriptures, riches were often regarded as a sign of God's blessing, but with that blessing came also a call to responsible stewardship. The prophet who has given his name to the book of Isaiah was himself apparently a prosperous person, with easy access to the royal court. He was married, with a family of two children, and lived in Jerusalem in the eighth century BC. At first the country was enjoying the relatively stable and peaceful reign of King Uzziah. But the prophet Isaiah was a man of vision who could see beyond the immediate comfort of the wealthy to the needs of a wider community. His own deep spirituality led him to an awareness of God's call to justice and compassion. He warned the rich against complacency and complicity in oppression. When disaster fell upon the nation the prophet saw in that defeat a judgment upon the people, but he never gave up faith in God's mercy. His words call us today to seek spiritual resources for the pursuit of justice and peace in our own times.

Recommended reading:

David Stacey *Isaiah 1-39 Epworth Commentaries* (Epworth 1993)
Kenneth Leech *The Eye of the Storm* (Darton, Longman and Todd 1992)

Worthless worship?

At first it sounds as though the prophet is condemning all religious rituals, even suggesting that prayers are futile. But these words must be read in the context of Isaiah's own practice as a devout Jew. For him reverence for the Sabbath and the keeping of holy festivals would be part of God's law. So it is all the more shocking to realize that he is warning the people that not even their traditional worship is acceptable to God if they persist in injustice, or are indifferent to the plight of the poor.

They are like the people whom Studdert Kennedy (known as 'Woodbine Willie') once described as those who 'have one mind for the sanctuary and another for the street; one conscience for the church and another for the cotton factory'. But Isaiah speaks positively too. God is reasonable and will forgive those who want to make amends. True worship means not only giving worth to God, but also recognizing the worth of all his people. Spirituality and social justice are two sides of one coin.

Prayer: (said with hands uplifted, palms uppermost)
✷ **Lord, I come with open hands.**
 Wash them from the corruption of wealth;
 open them to generous impulse;
 strengthen them in the struggle for justice;
 and use them in the service of others for your sake.

Worthless values

A prosperous nation enjoys trading with other lands and enters into all kinds of alliances. Isaiah is warning the people of Judah that they are in danger, not only of enjoying others' wealth, but of absorbing their values too. The word translated here as 'idols' is derived from a word meaning 'worthless'. Compare the material obsessions of our modern society with those described in verses 7-9. In an article about young people in *New Society* in February 1980, Jeremy Seabrook wrote, 'a whole generation has been delivered to private enterprise for their most exalted spiritual experiences – their spiritual needs are being met now, not by religion but by the artefacts of the same world, the film and junk fiction industries.' The prophet warns the people that underlying social injustice, moral laxity, and insincere worship the nation's fundamental sin is arrogance before God, and, like all pride, this is heading for a fall.

> * The dearest idol I have known,
>   Whate'er that idol be,
>   Help me to tear it from Thy throne
>   And worship only Thee.   *William Cowper (1731-1800)*

Tuesday August 19   Isaiah 3.1-15

Worthless leaders

Anarchy is a terrible prospect for any society. The prophet here suggests that unless the appointed leaders of the people take their responsibilities seriously they will be supplanted by rebellious, callow youths who will despise the traditions and experience of their elders. Those who hold positions of authority in the realm of politics, or in the armed forces, in the legal profession, or in the arts and sciences are called by God to be concerned for the welfare of all the people. If they fail to act justly, then society disintegrates. The prophet imagines the Lord summoning influential leaders to court and accusing them of bringing about the destruction of the nation through their own arrogance and unjust treatment of the poor.

> * *Pray today by name for those who hold positions of responsibility in the various parts of your community: your Member of Parliament and local councillors; teachers in the universities and schools in your area; editors and journalists in the national and local media; judges, magistrates and lawyers; police officers and prison warders; social workers and probation officers. Pray that they may do their work with integrity and with concern for the well being of the whole of society.*

Wednesday August 20   Isaiah 3.16 to 4.1

Worthless women

Far from being the tirade of a misogynist, these are the words of a prophet who takes seriously the role of women, and believes that their behaviour can both affect and reflect the moral tone of the nation. He returns to the same theme later in Isaiah 32.9-12 when he accuses women of failing to be aware of what was happening in society as a whole. Too many of the wealthy women of Isaiah's day seemed to him to be obsessed with their appearance, decking themselves with expensive ornaments and cosmetics. The jewellery and cosmetic trades are still flourishing. Ought this to be of greater concern to us as we assess the

187

priorities of our own spending? Note that the prophet warns that when disaster befalls the nation it will be the women who will be the most vulnerable victims. This is also true today.

✳ *Lord Jesus, who received graciously*
the extravagant gift of a woman,
forgive us when we are too extravagant
in attending to our own wants
and too niggardly in caring for the needs of others.
Help us to be concerned particularly
for women who are victims of war and violence
and to do what we can to bring back beauty into their
*   lives. For your sake.*

Thursday August 21   *Isaiah 5.1-7*
Worthless vine
Popular songs often contain profound truths. In this passage the prophet takes what was probably a secular vintage song and uses it to express God's love for the nation of Judah. However fond of his vineyard a farmer might be, and however much labour he may have expended on it, if it produces poor fruit then it has to be destroyed. In verse 7 the prophet gives his own comment on the meaning of the song. Here he plays on two Hebrew words in a punning manner. God has looked for *mishpat* (justice) and had found *mishpach* (violence). He had expected *zedaqah* (right relationships) and had found *zeaqah* (tears of bitterness). The similarity of sound emphasizes the link between justice and violence, between bad relationships and bitterness. Where there is no justice, there can be no peace; where there is wrong conduct, there are inevitably tears.

✳ *Lord, help us to plant the seeds of love,*
rooted in justice that shall produce a harvest of peace.

Friday August 22   *Isaiah 5.8-17, 26-30*
Worthless behaviour
The prophet here lists a number of 'woes', of reasons for God to judge the people of Judah sternly. All the examples he quotes of their decadence will be familiar to any who observe our contemporary scene. Some are greedy for land and build fine houses whilst others are homeless; some drink excessively and

live only for pleasure; some become addicted to their vices, like an animal tethered to its stall; others reverse moral values and cease to distinguish between right and wrong; and some are so arrogant that they think they can get away with injustice. Yet, the prophet declares, the Lord of all the nations will call them to account. He is rallying his forces and finally his purposes will be fulfilled, even through the growing strength of those who were apparently Judah's enemies. Are we able, like the prophet, to see even in the threatening events of our time, the hand of God's judgment?

✳ *Think first over the events of the day's news. Which items speak of the decadence of our society, and which hold hope of deliverance? With your concentrated prayer try to lend your strength to all the forces of good you are aware of at work in our world today.*

Saturday August 23   *Isaiah 6.1-13*

Worthless despair

In today's reading the prophet's mood changes from one of despair over the contemporary scene to awesome wonder in the presence of God. Though firmly rooted in the life and times of his own society ('in the year that King Uzziah died') he is caught up into a sense of the eternal holiness ('otherness') of God. But this is no escape for him. His deep spiritual experience becomes also his call to personal commitment and social action. He is charged with a vocation to speak both words of judgment and words of hope to the people of his own day. Neither the sense of his own unworthiness, nor his scepticism about his people's readiness to hear him, are accepted as an excuse. Those whom God calls, he also cleanses and then equips for the task.

✳ *Lord, on the eve of your holy day,*
    make me fit to give you worship that is worthy.
    Conscious of the sins of my own people,
    I am aware too of my own sin.
    Give me clean hands and a pure heart.
    Let me hear your word speaking not only to me
    but also to the society in which I live.
    Send me, Lord, even me, into your world
    as a servant of your word of judgment and of hope.

TO THINK ABOUT

- How would you define 'spirituality'? In what sense does it provide an escape from secular reality and in what sense does it provide an entry into it?
- Note the kind of sins in society that Isaiah attacks. Which sins are taken seriously and most often preached about in modern society?
- Examining my own budget, what are the priorities of my expenditure? What does this say about my own scale of values?

Reflection:

Blessed are the poor ...
not the penniless
but those whose heart is free.

Blessed are those who mourn ...
not those who whimper
but those who raise their voices.

Blessed are those who hunger and thirst for justice ...
not those who whine
but those who struggle.

Blessed are the pure in heart ...
not those who act like angels
but those whose life is transparent.

Blessed are the peacemakers ...
not those who shun conflict
but those who face it squarely.

Blessed are those who are persecuted for justice ...
not because they suffer
but because they love.

P Jacob, Chile
Quoted in The Power and the Glory –
URC Prayer Handbook 1987

FOR ACTION

Invite someone who holds a position of responsibility in your local community to an informal discussion about what are the values that determine their particular policies.

ISAIAH
2. Words in crises

Notes based on the Good News Bible by
Alan Greig

As a minister of the Church of Scotland, Alan Greig's first ministry was in the Ayrshire village of Hurlford, after which he served for seven years as a mission partner with the United Church of Zambia. Since 1992 he has been the minister of Kintore Parish Church near Aberdeen.

When Isaiah of Jerusalem became a prophet (c.736/35 BC), the glorious days when David and Solomon reigned in Jerusalem were long gone, and both Israel and Judah were at the mercy of more powerful nations. For almost fifty years, Isaiah brought God's word to the people of Judah as they lurched from one crisis to the next. This week, as we study some of these words, we shall identify some principles to help us in the crises we face.

14th Sunday after Pentecost, August 24   *Isaiah 7.1-16*
Words to those who rule

In the period 735-733 BC, King Ahaz and the people of Judah faced a crisis. Ahaz refused to join Syria and Israel in an anti-Assyrian coalition, and so Syria and Israel attacked Judah and Jerusalem. In panic, Ahaz appealed for help to Tiglath Pileser, the Assyrian king (see 2 Kings 16.5-9).

Although 8th century Judah was not a democracy, it was a kingdom built on the belief that Yahweh, its God, had chosen David and his descendants to be its rulers. They were, therefore, answerable to God. Using words and signs, Isaiah counselled against the king's policy, and encouraged him to put his trust in Yahweh – 'If your faith is not enduring, you will not endure' (verse 9b).

Prophets like Isaiah have shown us that it is right for people of faith to challenge policies they believe to be wrong. In a democracy people can influence government policy by making their views known through letters and petitions, and at election time through the ballot box. In non-democratic countries, however, it is more difficult and often dangerous to criticize those in power.

✳ *Pray for a strong Christian influence in your land, and remember Christians who live in countries where it is difficult to challenge government policies.*

Monday August 25   *Isaiah 8.1-18*

Don't follow the crowd

The context of today's passage is the same as yesterday's. The prophet's words reinforce the message that the threat to Judah from Syria and Israel is not a serious one. Isaiah's wife gives birth to a son, and the boy is given the symbolic name 'Quick-Loot-Fast-Plunder'. God promises that before the boy can speak his first words, Syria and Israel will have been defeated by the Assyrians.

Verses 11-13 provide important teaching in times of crisis for people of faith. When times are difficult, there is a great temptation to hide in the safety of numbers. It would have been easy for Isaiah to accept national policy in the interests of a quiet life. However, as verse 13 makes clear, the believer's first responsibility is to God – 'I am the one you must fear'.

Today, we come under many pressures to conform to the ways of the world. To resist can often lead to ridicule and a feeling of isolation, especially when practising Christians are in a minority. Like the prophet, let us remember that God has the first call on our loyalty.

✳ *Father, help me to follow your way, even when I seem to be swimming against the tide.*

Tuesday August 26   *Isaiah 9.1-7*

The Prince of Peace has come

A change of national leadership often brings with it a period of renewed hope and confidence. The coronation of a new monarch, the election of a new government, even the replacement of one dictatorship by another, can give a nation a sense of expectation that something new and exciting is about to happen. The experience of history, however, is that all human leaders are fallible and fail to satisfy people's aspirations.

Read again Isaiah 9.1-7. These inspiring verses are among the best known by Christians in the Old Testament. In their original context, they were referring to the birth or accession of a new king of Judah – a successor of the great king David. This king would base his rule on right, justice and peace under the authority of God.

When Jesus was born seven centuries later, this special 'Messiah' was still awaited. Christians have seen how today's reading points to Jesus, 'the first to be raised from death and who is also the ruler of the kings of the world' (Revelation 1.5b).

✳ *Lord Jesus, thank you for bringing the good news*
of the Kingdom of God – the Kingdom that really matters.

Wednesday August 27   *Isaiah 10.5-23*

The folly of human pride

God made it very clear to Isaiah that he had used Assyria as 'a tool' to achieve his purposes (verse 15). But success had gone to the Emperor's head, and he failed to recognize the authority and power of Judah's God. Such pride and arrogance would inevitably lead to disaster.

In the crises of our day, God continues to work through people to achieve his purposes. All Christians are called by him to the task of mission in the world. The tasks of preaching, teaching, healing, caring and befriending urgently need to be undertaken in the name of Jesus. Lest we boast of any success, let us remember that we are tools in God's hands, and that all the glory should go to him.

✳ *Our loving Father, and Father of ALL*
We thank you for having brought us together
in this land to learn to love you
and one another ...

Give us courage, we pray, to stand up
for your truth.
Make us apostles of your love, justice,
hope, reconciliation and peace.
               Stanley Mogoba, Southern Africa. From Oceans of Prayer
                                           (NCEC)

Beware of false religion

The last three readings for this week refer to events in the reign of
Ahaz' son, Hezekiah (727-698 BC). Judah had rebelled against
the Assyrian Emperor, Sennacherib, and looked to Egypt for help.
The revolt was unsuccessful and resisted by Isaiah.

After a prophecy of Jerusalem's doom and restoration (verses
1-8), there follows an attack on religious insincerity and a lack of
spirituality. Faith has been replaced by a formal religion that owes
more to human rules and traditions than to the worship of the
living God.

Sometimes crises drive people to religion rather than the living
faith. But the practice of religion cannot be a substitute for a
saving knowledge of the living God. In the crises of life today,
God offers us friendship in Jesus Christ. Jesus says, 'Come unto
me, all of you who are tired from carrying heavy loads, and I will
give you rest' (Matthew 11.28).

✳ *Ask God to help you deepen your relationship with him.*

Listen to and obey God's word

The attempt to overcome the crisis, by seeking an alliance with
Egypt, is mocked by the prophet and, to emphasize the root of
Judah's problems, Isaiah is instructed to write a permanent
record of the people's disobedience (verses 1-14). The message
is clear: in a crisis the first priority of people of faith is to follow
God's word.

The fact that you are reading these notes suggests you are
keen to learn what God is saying to you. Through the work of the
United Bible Societies, the whole Bible is available today in over
300 languages, and portions of it in over 2000 languages. More
and more people have access to God's word in their own tongue,
and at a price they can afford.

Studying God's word can be a painful process because it
identifies our sin and calls us to repentance, The wonderful news,
however, is that God is merciful and invites us to return to him
(verses 15-18).

✳ *Thank God for the Scriptures to guide us. Pray for the
translation and distribution work of the Bible Society in
your country, and the work of the United Bible Societies.*

The importance and power of prayer

When it seemed that the Assyrian army was going to capture Jerusalem, King Hezekiah went to the Temple and prayed for deliverance (see verses 1 and 15). God's answer to the king's petition, which is the basis of our reading today, condemns the arrogance of Sennacherib and reassures Hezekiah that Jerusalem would be saved. And it was!

During Isaiah's prophetic ministry, the people of Judah experienced many crises, and he maintained that the root cause lay in a *failure to trust God.* Isaiah believed that God was holy and powerful, but that he took a keen and loving interest in the affairs of his people.

To be able to trust someone, we need to be able to enter into a relationship. That is why the reading of the Bible needs to be accompanied by prayer. In prayer, we can confidently share our lives, including our crises, with God and he can speak to our situations. Never forget that because God became a human being in Jesus, there is understanding and compassion at the very heart of God.

✳ *Jehovah! Great I AM, who was and is and is to be,*
   hear in love the cry of your people for life.
   Your people need bread –
   but grant that amid hard realities and hunger
   we may understand that we do not live by bread alone.
   Give to our leaders true wisdom;
   save us all from economic, moral and social decay.
   May your Church, with the gift of the Spirit,
   rightly discern the things that make for peace,
   for survival, and more –
   for life in all its fullness:
   and may we be bold to speak your word.
   Franklin Roberts, Caribbean. From Oceans of Prayer (NCEC)

TO THINK ABOUT and FOR ACTION

Think of a crisis you faced up to recently. How much did your faith in God help? What Bible passages did you find particularly helpful? Has the crisis deepened or weakened your faith?

Identify an area of government policy that from a Christian standpoint you believe is wrong. Find the most appropriate way – in your country – to make a protest and influence public opinion.

ISAIAH
3. Words to exiles

Notes based on the Good News Bible by
Magali do Nascimento Cunha

*Magali do Nascimento Cunha is a Brazilian Methodist laywoman
who works as a journalist with KOINONIA Ecumenical Presence
and Service in Rio de Janeiro.*

Isaiah 40-55 is one of the most beautiful and inspiring passages
of the Bible. It was written in a period between 538 and 515 BC
after the Babylonians had invaded Judah, destroyed the temple
and the city of Jerusalem and took the directing class of Judah
into captivity. Just the miserable people escaped. The situation of
the scattered people was so sad that the prophets assumed the
task of giving comfort and hope.

The words of Isaiah are still alive today. The large mass of
people who live in the southern countries, and groups of people
who live in rich countries, have faced humiliation and exclusion.
They are exiled in their own land, feeling hopeless and
desperate. Good news is needed to show that change is
possible. That is God's promise!

15th Sunday after Pentecost, August 31   *Isaiah 40.1-11*
A new order is possible
Exile. Difficulties. Suffering. Oppression. In the midst of all that,
words of comfort and courage come from the prophet of God.
Good news! The Lord comforts and encourages his people who
have suffered enough.

Exile was a punishment. It was the result of years of
oppression and injustice practised in Judah. The people
themselves had provoked that. But God cares! 'Grass withers
and flowers fade ... People are no more enduring than grass. But
the word of our God endures forever.' And the word of God is a
word of forgiveness and comfort.

Today, it is not necessary to go far away to see the sufferings
of our world. The way its leaders choose to rule their peoples

reminds us of abuses committed in Judah that generated oppression and injustice. For the poor countries of the south these sufferings are stronger, but they are present everywhere. But a voice cries out: 'Prepare in the wilderness a road for the Lord! Clear the way in the desert for our God!.' A new order is possible. All of us are called to believe, support and struggle for it.

✳ *Our God,*
thank you for being a God of forgiveness and comfort.
Help us to share the good news of salvation and hope,
and to struggle against the sufferings of our world.

Monday September 1   *Isaiah 40.12-31*

God renews our strength

Fifty years in exile. Hope of going back home was almost finished. The people of Judah were tired of suffering and transferred to God their tiredness. They felt abandoned and forgotten.

How many times do we feel like the people of Judah? How often are our lives full of difficulties of many kinds? In Brazil it is common to hear poor people – those who are excluded from all possibilities of dignity and life – cry out: 'God has forgotten us!' In rich countries too, with all their progress and development, God seems remote from everything that makes sense, and groups of people who are excluded from all welfare and dignity think they have been forgotten by God.

To inject courage and hope into the people, the prophet presents God, trying to answer a question: 'Who is the Lord?' How can we describe what he is like? Actually it is an appeal to the memory of the people. He invites us to remember that God is the Creator of all things. His power is so great that it reduces to shadow and nothing all the powers of the earth, all human knowledge.

Are the people tired? In a very inspiring way, the prophet calls their attention to the Lord who never grows tired or weary. Those who trust the Lord for help will find their strength renewed. What a relief for all of us!

✳ *Praise be to you, our Lord, for your power and strength.*
Forgive us when we complain against your will for us.

Do not be afraid!

It is a very nice feeling to be back home, even after travelling on holidays. At home we feel safe, comfortable. We have those we know best around us; we have a space that is ours. It is good to travel and know that we will be back.

After 50 years in exile the people of Judah were in despair. The images used by the prophet illustrates it well: deep waters, fire, hard trials. Of course they were afraid! Especially for the future. There was no longer hope to go back home. They were disheartened.

The prophet remembers that Yahweh, the Lord, is the Liberator. People can count on him. There is no reason to be afraid because God is ready to rescue them from all troubles and let them go back home, to feel safe and comfortable.

In our lives, many times we pass through deep waters or through fire. There are moments when hard trials seem to hurt us. We could list those things that provoke despair and fear in our lives and in our people's lives. The words of God through the prophet are still alive: Do not be afraid! You are mine! I am with you! It is a promise that will never fail. We can never forget that.

✳ *Almighty God, we trust your promise of salvation.*
Renew in our hearts the conviction that you are with us
despite all troubles.

Mission is open to all contributions

Cyrus, the Persian king, is introduced by the prophet as the one whom God had called to save Judah and restore the people to their land. The way the Lord insists on saying to Cyrus 'Although you do not know me' is very significant. God had called Cyrus to that mission although he did not know the Lord of creation and history.

This attitude of God shows that the act of taking part in God's mission is not confined within the limits of religion and church. A stranger to God's people is called to help to save this same people. That means: all contributions are welcomed when the target is the salvation of the people, to rescue their dignity. It does not matter if those who are involved have not known the Lord before. What matters is the struggle for life, against all injustice. The victory will show the power of the Lord from one end of the world to the other, and so people will know that there is no other god.

The building of God's Kingdom is not a privilege or a monopoly of Christians. The prophet teaches us that we will see with the eyes of faith that liberation is already happening in many places.

✳ **Thank you Lord, for giving us the chance**
to take part in the process for the salvation of our people.
Send your victory and strength to us.

Thursday September 4   *Isaiah 49.1-7*
The value of the people of God

The prophet relates how the people of God become aware of their mission as a people chosen to be the Lord's servant. It is a recognition that, despite all sufferings and difficulties, the people have value, a value given by the Lord.

How wonderful is the Word of God! How powerful! It is not difficult to imagine the effect of the prophet's words on those who were feeling weak and disheartened in exile. It is the same for people who live in countries like those in Latin America: dispossessed, despised, hated by the nations, struggling to survive. This is the power of the Word of God: we can read it today and it continues alive, ready to serve, strengthening those who feel weak and disheartened, those who experience similar suffering and humiliation, exiled in their own land.

By the simple fact of resisting and surviving, the poor, the excluded in our societies, fulfil their mission by denouncing injustice. Their right is not to be imprisoned by the legalist world, but rests in God's promises of salvation.

We are God's servants, and so we are valued. Praise be to God!

✳ **Lord, you are the source of our strength.**
Help us to be the light of our world and serve you,
to bring back the scattered people who try to survive.

God is faithful

Oppression has never been accepted by God in any way. It is a blasphemy against his name. God has always been a presence of liberation and it is never too much to remember it. The prophet calls everyone to remember how God turned the people free from Egyptian slavery and invites them to experience a new Exodus with no hurry or need to escape. That is the good news for everyone and an invitation to celebrate.

God is faithful to his name and his promises. The true messengers of the gospel are those who announce the victory of the people, not those who preach 'religious doctrines' ... Evangelization has to do with liberation because God is there beside the suffering people.

What are the announcements we have made to our people? Do we really believe that at the end there will be victory over all suffering and humiliation for our brothers and sisters? Are we sharing hope with them? Are we preaching a gospel of salvation and liberation or are we imprisoning people in 'religious doctrines'?

God is faithful and, as the prophet says, in time to come we will acknowledge that he is the Lord and that he has spoken to us.

✳ ***Dear Lord, help us to share your good news of salvation and, every moment,***
    to acknowledge your sovereignty and power.

Suffering servant: an image of the people

In Brazil, Carlos Mesters – biblical scholar and prophet of our time – has taught us to read this text of the prophet with the eyes of a people who have suffered like the servant of God. He used to say that the prophet did not dream, but he saw. And what he saw and described was the servant, certainly identified with the people, the poor people of all ages and places.

Today, who is carrying the sins of society? Who is paying the price of all suffering and rejection? The promise of glorification can be also given to the people. It is this promise that sustains the resistance and helps them to survive. The poor people represent a cry for justice.

It is not necessary to emphasize that this passage was lived literally by Jesus Christ. And when we read it, either because of the value of the text, or because of the traditional use of it in our liturgies, the image of the suffering Jesus automatically comes to our minds. But Carlos Mesters, our prophet, reminds us: this text was written more than four centuries before Christ and the person who wrote it did not have before his / her eyes the image of Jesus, but the image of the people. The prophet was seeing, not dreaming ...

✳ *Praise be to you, our Lord,*
when you give dignity and life to our world.
We praise you for your mercy and love
which rescue us from death.

TO THINK ABOUT

● Sometimes we face situations that lead us to despair and weakness, like the people of Judah. Inspired by the words of the prophet, how can we be strengthened to overcome our difficulties?

● The prophet refers all the time to good news to the exiled people. For the people of Judah, good news meant to go back home and have their land back. Think of the situation of your people. What sufferings do they face? What is the good news to be shared? What does God's victory represent to your society?

FOR ACTION

Do you know a person, or a group of people, who suffer any kind of humiliation or exclusion? If not, try to identify one. Humiliation and exclusion are present everywhere – including next door – because they are a fruit of human sin. Share the good news of hope with them, not only by words but also by concrete acts of solidarity (sharing food, clothes, denouncing the injustices they suffer, searching for alternatives to change their situation). People need to know and feel that they are valued by God and consequently by the Family of God.

201

ISAIAH
4. Words to a disappointed society

Notes based on the Good News Bible by
Anesia Nascimento de Jésus

Anesia Nascimento is a journalist and Anglican priest from Brazil, working in the UK as a mission partner with the Grassroots programme based at the Luton Industrial College.

The prophets were a bridge between God and the people. They had the ability to recognize God's project and the people's situation. God called them to rebuild his alliance with the people which they had broken by acts of injustice and infidelity. Isaiah (a third prophet in this book) proclaims hope to encourage a people who had returned from exile, feeling deserted, unsure and lacking any clear vision which would unite them with other previously dispersed Jews (also returned to their homeland). It was a complex situation. The people ignored God's commandments. Oppression, exploitation and slavery were rife. The prophet called them to turn again to the living God. These readings also encourage us to ask: *How do these words from Isaiah relate to our society and our experience of 'exile'? Where do we see God's light? Where are God's prophets today?*

> For all the saints
>> who went before us
>> who have spoken to our hearts
>> and touched us with your fire,
>> **we praise you, O God.**
>
> For all the saints
>> who live beside us
>> whose weaknesses and strengths
>> are woven with our own,
>> **we praise you, O God.**
>
> For all the saints
>> who live beyond us
>> who challenge us
>> to change the world with them,
>> **we praise you, O God.**   *Janet Morley, Christian Aid 1989*

Hope

To write poetry is for many people a waste of time; for others it is an escape; and for a few it is the ability to translate reality into symbolic language. Isaiah was one of them. In this reading, the exiled and returned nation is visualized as an arid land pregnant with life, giving birth to a new creation. The people of Judah, who had been dead, who had no land, no freedom, who were afraid (an experience which those who had remained in Judah did not have), will become a new community. God is already among them, and through their encounter with God they will be born as one new people.

To a decadent society these words spoke powerfully: 'Be strong and do not be afraid.' The prophetic voice does not come from the intellect but from an experience of pain and exploitation to resurrect God's people from helplessness and self-pity.

✳ *Lord God, make us prophets,*
pregnant with your word in this world.

Liberation

Isaiah was called to proclaim liberation to the poor – those who had been excluded and prevented from receiving their just rewards. Society must change. There must be an end to exploitation. The people must seek justice, a new relationship between rich and poor. God calls them to rebuild the city through a common agricultural policy (verse 4-9). After slavery it is important for liberated people to walk to the freedom in which foreigners will no longer exploit them; they themselves will participate in making decisions for their own future. If there is oppression, that has to be faced so that justice and right may prevail (verse 8).

Speaking in the synagogue at Nazareth, Jesus read this text (Luke 4.18-19) and it became the synthesis of his mission. It is our mission as well. We need to ask: *Which people are excluded by society today? Where are they? Where do you find 'exiles'?*

✳ *Almighty God,*
we pray for those who are excluded in our society,
and that we may become agents of transformation.

Challenge

The prophet speaks to Jerusalem, telling her that her guilt has been paid for: the Almighty has forgiven her people. They should not be overwhelmed by the invincible Babylon (where they lived as exiles), because now God has a gift for them: one blessed country where people may enjoy themselves, where plunder cannot be replaced by another form of exploitation and oppression. Their country has to be a place where the gratuitousness of God can be expressed, where everyone is invited to participate as equals. If a country wants to enjoy material abundance it does not have to oppress its people. Abundance comes when food is shared, as in a party.

The most significant party for Christians is Holy Communion, where everyone has the same bread and drinks the same wine. This is not a vague act; it is prophetic. We are saying that all meals are unjust when we are eating fruits that come from the exploitation of others. *What have you done to change the system that excludes many brothers and sisters where you live?*

✷ *Give us O God, your bread,*
  the bread of justice and peace.

Listen

Memory is revolutionary. It is the way people keep going. The Jews in exile knew that. Before any books of the Bible were ever written, there was the stage of oral tradition. People spent hours and hours, listening to one another. They sat around their fires, in camps, just to listen to their own history, their own journey. Getting to know the past, they were able to reflect on their present and to glimpse the future. The power of memory and the ability to listen have produced crazy poets and revolutionaries.

We seem to have lost that capacity. We want to talk about what our contemporaries are saying – often words of no lasting value. We need to relearn the art of listening. Suffering people are crying. Listen to God's call. Too often we choose death. We are politically ignorant, socially distant 'good Christians'. But where there is memory, there is strength for struggle.

✷ *Give us, O God,*
  the ability to listen to your call in your little ones.

Reflect

There was more than one country in which people suffered hardship and slavery (verse 2). Judah had this in common with her neighbours. The exile was a time for reflection and renewal. It was a time of encounter: between God and the people, and the people with each other, between slavery and freedom, the living God and idolatry. There was time: time for ups and downs, time to ask forgiveness of God. There were times of conflict, but also moments to grow in hope and faith.

I do not think that many of us like the idea of reflection and evaluation. We are so afraid of facing our own mistakes and wrong doing. And so we keep busy. If we want to advance and grow, we need to spend some time reflecting, thinking how we can do better, learning from our mistakes. Hope is born in this process. It is born out of the pain, the fears and the conflict. Hope is not something vague; it has to do with life, with people. Where there is hope, there is strength to continue. But how can we keep going if we do not realize what has been achieved?

✳ Help us, O God, to reflect on our lives
and the life of our community,
that we may learn from the mistakes of the past.
Give us the courage to change what is wrong.

Turn to the living God

God is responding to his people's provocation, but God is also saying that he will create a new earth and a new heaven. God can see a blessing even when his creation has deserted him. God, who is a living God, does not accept the sadness of the people. This passage was written a long time ago. The prophet tried to put into words what God must feel, seeing his people so far away from him.

What about today? Is it possible for us to write a poem like this of God's anger with his people? *What makes God angry today?* Poverty, oppression, exploitation, consumerism, individualism ... so many things. What have we done with the life God gave us? Where are the gospel values in our lives? We have worshipped other gods – money, the world market, the media ... This passage is an invitation to recognize the new idols we have created and which separate us from one another and from God.

* *Help us to be faithful to your commands.*

Begin building – NOW!

When the exiled people returned to the land of Judah, God's promises did not materialize straightaway, and so the community became decadent again. The prophet had to call their attention to God. God had not forgotten them. The dream would come true, and they had a part to play. All feelings of superiority must be abolished; their arrogance must be substituted with humility. The new earth will come by God's action.

We are called to be co-builders, today where we are. The call for change, for the creation of a new order is not for the future; it has to be established here and now. And we will be as glad as a child at her mother's breast.

Why have faith in a new heaven and a new earth encouraged the struggle and hope among exiled peoples today?

* *Our Father in heaven,*
may your name be held holy,
your kingdom come,
your will be done,
on earth as in heaven.
Give us today our daily bread.
And forgive us our debts,
as we have forgiven those
*   who are in debt to us.*
And do not put us to the test,
but save us from the Evil One.   *Matthew 6.9-13 (NJB)*

TO THINK ABOUT

Reflect again on the many questions asked in this week's notes.

ACTION

If you have not already begun, begin to reflect, evaluate, dream of the future and act. Encourage others to do so too.

THE KINGDOM OF GOD

Notes by
Burchell Taylor

Burchell Taylor, a Jamaican minister, has been pastor of Bethel Baptist Church in Kingston for twenty five years. He has studied at Calabar Theological College, Jamaica and the Universities of London, Oxford and Leeds (UK), and now teaches at the University of the West Indies. He is married and has three sons.

In the synoptic Gospels, the Kingdom of God is the central theme of the proclamation and teaching of Jesus. His miracles are also signs of the 'inbreaking' presence of the Kingdom (Luke 11.20; cf. Matthew 12.28). Jesus did not try to define the Kingdom. It involves the sovereign and redemptive purpose of God, too profound in significance, and too multi-dimensional in meaning, to be captured in a single definition.

It is not surprising that in the parables, Jesus' most distinctive way of teaching, the Kingdom occupies centre stage. This method gave him greater freedom to bring out its various aspects and characteristics. In the parables, the Kingdom is presented as God's promised new order of righteousness, justice, peace and joy. It represents both divine gift and demand, God's gracious redeeming action warranting prompt human response, and action in acceptance. It is a reality already present, having been inaugurated in and by the ministry of Jesus. It is, however, yet to be manifested in its fullness in the return of Jesus.

A vision of the Kingdom commits us to live according to its values and standards, and so provide evidence of its presence. It also anticipates the perfect manifestation of such values and standards in its full and final establishment. The gospel is the goodness of the Kingdom which holds out reconciliation, liberation, and hope for the captives, alienated and oppressed.

For further reading

A M Hunter *Interpreting the Parables* (Philadelphia: The Westminster Press 1960)

Douglas R A Hare *Matthew Interpretation: A Bible Commentary for Teaching and Preaching* (Louisville: John Knox Press, 1993)

Matthew 19.13-15*; Psalm 8.1-2

Yes to the powerless

The focus is on children and the contrasting attitudes of the disciples and Jesus towards them. The disciples displayed the traditional attitude while Jesus demonstrated a new approach that was subversive of tradition and its wider implications. The children are typical of the powerless. They had no rights, no status or value save that which would have been arbitrarily granted to them to suit someone else's interest. They would have been barred from Jesus without any significant resistance. There would be no arguable grounds on which a case could be made for their admission. They were powerless in every way.

Jesus set aside the action of the disciples who sought to bar parents from bringing children to him. By graciously welcoming and blessing them, he radically challenged the existing attitude to children and, by extension, the powerless generally. He assigned and affirmed their identity and value. He showed care and concern for those who were not socially, culturally and religiously affirmed – the voiceless, the defenceless, and the powerless.

This is good news. Jesus characteristically used the occasion to make it clear that it is to those who are powerless that the Kingdom of God is open. Those who are prepared to acknowledge their powerlessness and who are willing to accept the Kingdom as a gracious gift from God, will have entry. We all need to know this, and abide by it, to receive the blessing of the Kingdom that we need above all else.

✻ *Lord, grant me grace to see myself in a true light*
that by faith I may accept your welcome to life
in and through Christ.

Monday September 15   *Matthew 19.16-30 **

Sorry, no entry

It is most interesting that this story follows immediately upon that of the children and Jesus' declaration of those qualified to enter the Kingdom (verse 14). This rich young man possessed everything the children lacked. He had status, wealth, privilege, authority, and his religious and moral credentials were equally impressive.

His need for eternal life inspired him to ask Jesus how it may be obtained. Eternal life is the life in and of the Kingdom of God.

His sense of need brings to our notice that this was not something he thought was attainable by what he possessed. Apart from this, there was nothing he could not afford.

He suddenly discovered that all the credentials he brought with him – social, economic, moral and religious – could not qualify him for the life he sought. He had to be willing to give up all that gave him his sense of control over life, his sense of security, and his perceived ability to provide for himself whatever he wanted. This he wasn't prepared to do. He barred himself from the life of the Kingdom by his refusal to accept powerlessness. He was not willing to accept entry on the terms of God in Christ.

We deprive ourselves of entry into the fullness of life if we are not willing to enter it on God's terms. It is a matter of great grief, but it is only by God's way of grace.

✳ *Help me, O Lord, not to be so possessed by anything that I may not be free to entrust myself to your graciousness.*

Tuesday September 16   *Matthew 13.24-30*

Evil in the midst

The promise of the Kingdom, the evidence of its 'inbreaking' presence and witnesses to it, do not mean the immediate elimination of evil from our midst. Wheat and tares growing together are an undeniable reality. People of faith must be wise enough to recognize this and realistic enough to admit it. They must be humble and patient enough to realize that the task of dealing effectively with evil is best left in the hands of God. God will deal with it in the fullness of the time of the final establishment of his Kingdom by Christ.

We must also exercise restraint in our response to the presence of people who are influenced by the power and force of evil, and whose lives reflect the influence of evil more than anything else. This restraint must not be confused with tolerance or careless compromise. It retains its moral sensitivity, but attempts no judgment that presumes anyone irredeemable. It is ever mindful that final judgment belongs to God. It is easy to overreach ourselves in thinking and acting otherwise, and do more harm than good to others as well as to ourselves. Heeding the warning of our Lord is vital.

✳ *O Lord, give me the practical wisdom, humility and patience*

to react as you wish to the failures of others in our midst.
Help me to remember my own weaknesses
and my dependence upon the grace
and mercy of your forgiveness in Christ.

Wednesday September 17   *Matthew 11.25-30*

Opting for the oppressed

Jesus, who shares a unique relationship with God and full knowledge of God's will and purpose, issues a reassuring invitation and promise to the oppressed (verses 26-30). This is in keeping with God's own way of revealing to the least – to infants – what he has not revealed to the learned elite (verse 25).

This is the wisdom of God's liberating purpose in Jesus. It gives hope to men and women who are made helpless by burdens they have had to bear. This is demonstrated in Jesus' special concern for the handicapped, diseased, poor, captives, the excluded, those for whom impossible standards of conduct are set and upon whom unreasonable demands are made. These are truly the oppressed.

Oppression, whether attributable to our lack of wisdom as we try to make sense of life, or to our vulnerability to the forces and powers of injustice and unrighteousness, is never far from us in one form or another. Jesus offers hope and liberation to the oppressed. He offers a relationship with himself, renewal of life and shared responsibility in his service. He does not offer release from accountability, but gives a new opportunity for discipleship as the fulfilment of life's purpose. This means that we have Jesus as Liberator, Teacher, and Exemplar.

✳ *Lord, thank you for the yoke of your service*
 which is joy, freedom, responsibility
 and the discipline of discipleship.

Thursday September 18   *Matthew 13.44-46*

It's worth it all

The Kingdom is already a present reality to be encountered. It is, however, not so obvious as to be taken for granted. We may become aware of its presence by surprise encounter in the daily routine, like the farmer, or as a result of a deliberate quest, like the pearl merchant. Once encountered, the Kingdom is discovered to be of such immeasurable worth that it deserves and demands to be possessed without fail. This is the thrust of the message of these two parables. To possess it is to sense an unparalleled privilege, and to recognize its availability is a matter of immense joy. No opportunity should be lost in seeking to possess it, and whatever it takes to do so is worthwhile. Nothing is too great or too valuable to risk.

In the face of the gift and demands of the Kingdom, no competing claim on us should be allowed to stand in the way. Nothing should be considered too precious to give to receive the Kingdom. To seek the Kingdom is life's priority. To possess it is joy unspeakable.

✴ *Lord, deepen my insight*
  that I may discern the Kingdom and its worth.
  Give me the wisdom and courage to be prepared to give
  whatever may be necessary for the Kingdom's sake.

Friday September 19   *Matthew 13.33*

More than meets the eye

Leaven is rarely spoken of positively in the Scriptures. This is one of the rare occasions. Whenever it is spoken of, however, whether negatively or positively, its capacity to work imperceptibly but with potent influence is the feature most emphasized.

Here the Kingdom of God is likened to leaven. It is inaugurated by Jesus. It is already making its impact for good, but in a manner not immediately obvious. Hiddenness and apparent insignificance must not be regarded as inactivity and ineffectiveness. The Kingdom is already at work, and in due time the full effect of its creative and transforming presence and influence will become obvious.

This Kingdom is to be judged by its own values and its own vision of things, and not by the world's. Preoccupation with the spectacular, high level publicity and instant results, are generally regarded in the world as marks of effectiveness and greatness. If this is applied to the Kingdom's active presence in the world, then it can lead either to discouragement or derision. To the eye of faith, however, there is already enough to signify that the Kingdom's influence is radical, practical and total in its impact. This is like the leaven's impact on the dough which eventually becomes obvious. The contrast between what seems to be now and what will be then is stark. It is a matter that calls for steadfastness, patience and hope in commitment now.

* *Lord, help me to judge by your standards and to be*
    guided
  by the values of the Kingdom
  that I may not be deceived or discouraged by the world.

Saturday September 20   *Ephesians 5.1-5* *
Show the difference

Those who by faith have become members of God's family are
expected to display a quality of life that is in keeping with the
nature and character of God, whose family it is. The paradigm of
how this is to be done (and the inspiration for it) is Jesus Christ,
the faithful and beloved Son of God, in and through whom the
family is brought into being. It is through him that the privilege to
be called children of God is realized.

The key virtue of this life, and controlling factor in its self-
expression, is Christ-like self-giving love. Where this is in
evidence, respect for others (which is also intimately related to
self-respect), will be an integral part of our daily practice. Self-
gratifying exploitation and abuse of others in deed and word have
no place in such a life. A lifestyle which contradicts this is an
indication of not belonging to God's new order to which the family
of God belongs and testifies. Indeed it attracts the judgment of
exclusion from this new order. This is undoubtedly a fearful
prospect. We should not be deceived. Our life with God in Christ
has a distinctive quality and pattern. It is a challenging alternative
to what prevails in the present, and a fitting sign of our future with
God.

* *Help us Lord, to make your light shine in and through us*
  in our daily life, and that you may receive the glory due to
     you.

TO THINK ABOUT and FOR ACTION
● What does powerlessness mean in your context?
● Where do you see the 'inbreaking' presence of the Kingdom?
● How and when should Christians speak out against evil social
  and political structures?
● What did Jesus mean when he said the Kingdom of God is
  'within you'?
● Think of ways to ensure that children's insights are heard and
  respected in your church and community.

WORK

Notes based on the Good News Bible by
Peter Millar

Peter Millar, minister of the Church of Scotland and member of the Iona Community, is now warden of Iona Abbey. He and his wife Dorothy served for many years with the Church of South India, and together have written on a wide variety of subjects.

The Wild Goose, a Celtic symbol of the Holy Spirit, is the logo of the Iona Community. © *The Iona Community*.

'... Geese in formation fly seventy-five per cent faster than single geese. Iona, down through the centuries, speaks to us above all about the experience of the Holy Spirit in community.'

One dictionary defines 'work' as 'effort directed to an end' but our immediate association is with 'employment'. However we define it, the subject of work arouses passions and controversy at a time when many (all over the world) are unemployed, under-employed, or facing redundancy. It is a political issue but it is also a spiritual one.

What is the relationship between Christian faith and work? How do we as Christians respond to the issues of justice which surround work? How do we challenge unjust work practices? How does a Christian express his or her faith in the workplace? And how do we respond to the struggles of those who can find no work? Hard questions, and our biblical passages this week raise many more.

Lord Jesus,
as we look at these readings
from your Word,
help us continually to connect
our personal faith
with the complex questions
surrounding work,
unemployment
and redundancy.

An upside-down gesture

No, it's not an easy parable. Where would we be if we used it as a model for current labour-management relationships? What the boss did runs counter to our sense of fairness. Little wonder the guys who toiled all day long under a blazing Palestinian sun were grumbling! They had a genuine complaint.

The landlord was adamant. He refused to take on board their complaints and insisted he was free to be equally generous with all. Even as we seek to understand further dimensions of meaning within this parable, we must not lose sight of its problematic nature. A fair wage for a fair day's work is something which millions, especially in the countries of the South, are not experiencing.

But here the boss appears to operate by the standard of grace, not of merit. He gives with a sense of abandonment: a kind of upside-down gesture. And in acting this way, he gives us an insight into the Kingdom. For that Kingdom is all about upside-down activity in which free-flowing compassion matters so much more than narrow legalism. Remember the old Rabbinic saying: 'Some enter the Kingdom in an hour; others hardly enter it in a lifetime.'

✴ *Lord, allow our lives to be transformed*
by your limitless love
which is new every morning
and comes to us without legal constraints.

Monday September 22   *2 Thessalonians 3.6-15 **

Finding work

They were waiting in excited idleness for the Lord's return, truants from work, as they lived expectantly for the Second Coming. Paul wasted no sympathy on them: they should be back at work, earning an honest day's wage. It was a strong admonition, 'Whoever refuses to work is not allowed to eat.' It reminds us of the Jewish saying: 'He who does not teach his son a trade, teaches him to steal.'

The stress here is on *refusal* to work. But what of our young people, in their thousands, who daily scan the notice boards for a possible job? And then, having seen a job, are rejected in an interview because they lack experience?

Many of the younger folk who come to work as volunteers with the Iona Community are unemployed, not because they have refused jobs but because no opening has appeared. They have such a lot to offer to our society. Their stories would make one weep. As the rejection slips multiply, so the level of confidence erodes. It's a vicious and tragic circle, constantly repeated.

Most would agree with Paul's understanding that we have an obligation to work. Yet how do we deal with the contradiction that the survival of our present western economic order is actually dependent on millions being either unemployed or under-employed? For me, that is both a political and a spiritual issue.

✳ *Lord, help us to stop and listen*
to those who are trying to find work
amid escalating unemployment.

Tuesday September 23   *Exodus 31.12-18*

A day off

A day of rest – a sacred day. And for the children of Israel this day was, in itself, a sign of the covenant, a permanent marker between the living God and his people.

Does such a day make any sense in our frenetically paced societies, in which most of us find it hard to stand still for even a single moment? Who needs a sacred day when so many other goodies are on offer? We do! We who are the heirs of an incredible technological revolution of mobile phones, plastic cards and E Mail, with our potions and pills, seven-days-a-week shopping, rushed and constantly over-anxious.

Slowly – as if from a long sleep – we are awakening to the basic fact that without some 'sacred spaces' in our rushed lives, we become totally overwhelmed. Spaces in which, as Brother Roger of the Taizé Community says, 'We can hand everything over to God in humble prayer' – places of renewal and of inner restoration.

Our 'day of rest' may not be Sunday, but a sacred day remains a precious gift from God. In our fast-paced world we can still make that amazing discovery – that Christ does come close if we take a moment to listen to his gentle voice.

✳ *Lord, help me to discover a time of quietness*
in order to hear your words
amid all my endless busyness.

A time for work

The words in this chapter seem to spring out of the page. They are almost too familiar. And in the midst of all his questions, the writer asks: 'What do we gain from all our work?' (verse 9). A valid query. It is a question most of us ask at one time or another. What are we achieving through all our efforts?

Perhaps God will never give us a clear answer. Much of life is a mystery, but I do believe that our work – however we define it – is important in the wider purposes of God.

Cardinal Newman's wonderfully eloquent reflection on this subject has always moved me deeply. Although written a long time ago, his words have a freshness and immediacy:

> ' God has created me to do Him some definite service. He has committed some work to me which he has not committed to another. I have my mission. I may never know it in this world, but I shall be told it in the next. I am a link in the chain, a bond of connection between persons. He has not created me for naught. I shall do good. I shall do His work. I shall be a preacher of truth in my own place, while not intending it, if I but keep His commandments. I can never be thrown away. The Lord knows what He is about.'

✳ **Lord, thank you for a time to work**
and for giving me some definite service in this life.

Thursday September 25   *Luke 16.1-12*

Accountability

William Barclay, in his famous *Daily Study Bible* noted that this particular parable involved about as choice a set of rascals as one could meet anywhere. And as one reflects on this story, it becomes clear that steward, master and debtors were all folk seeing a quick profit one way or another. In that sense they were contemporary people.

The parable reminds us that not infrequently those involved in financial dealings are much more clued up than those who work for the church! It also points out that the way we go about small tasks is the best proof of how we tackle larger ones. And it underlines the fact that serving God is never a part-time job.

As a member of the Iona Community, I have to account to my

fellow members about how I use my money. No easy thing! Yet in this accountability lies a powerful and meaningful spiritual discipline. I am accountable for my money, not just to God, but also to those who walk the Christian path with me.

And yet so often we are unwilling to 'account' for our money to anyone else. It is a private affair. But is it? I think that it is good – at least from time to time – to be honest to others about our use of money. As we seek to be disciples of Christ, can we in fact do anything less than this?

✳ *Lord, may I be willing to account for the use of my money to my fellow-believers.*

Friday September 26   Luke 15.11-24

Escape from work?

We all want to do it at some point. Run away! Be free! Forget the daily routine. Who wants to work when we can take the cash and have a rave? Why walk anywhere if we can be in a fast car?

Each week in the UK, millions of pounds are spent on the National Lottery. There are not many winners, but if a million pounds did come our way, would we go into work the next morning? Doing something different with our lives is always attractive, and we can understand the prodigal son, even if he did go a bit over the top. One of the reasons why so many want to escape from their work is because it is so intolerably boring. It gives no fresh energy. We count the days to retiral. For the fact is that vast numbers of folk are in dead-end jobs with no possibility of change.

So maybe the question becomes – can we discover ways to touch in on new energy even when our jobs seem pointless? Can we discover a new creativity within ourselves when everything around is dragging us down? That's a hard one and it does not avail itself of an easy answer, yet the father's words to the son who stayed at home are both affirming and comforting (verses 31-32).

✳ *Lord, even if I am stuck in a dead-end job,*
   help me, each day, to be aware of your presence
   of life and hope.

217

Work as service

The idea of our work (for those fortunate enough to have paid employment) as being a service is not common. Yes, we may think of ordained women and men as serving others, but what about those who distil whisky or check income tax returns, or are involved in multi-million dollar deals?

In our minds, do we understand these kinds of jobs as 'serving' in the way mentioned here in Matthew's Gospel? And this piercingly direct reply of Christ to the anxious mother is hardly in tune with the drive to reach the top which permeates many cultures. Who wants to be a 'servant of the rest' when, with a bit of elbow-twisting, a promotion becomes possible?

In a competitive, acquisitive society, it's not easy to act as a servant in this biblical sense. Yet we are spiritually impoverished if we are unable to discern an element of service in all of our jobs. And we should be prepared constantly to challenge attitudes which see status only in well-paid, prestigious jobs. Even Christians sometimes despise the lowly paid as 'not having made it'. At the Reformation, Martin Luther spoke of this connection between work and service when he wrote: 'The freedom of Christians is realised in our becoming Christs to each other.' Christs to one another in our place of work? It's an enormous challenge, but perhaps one we can't avoid as we seek to see Christ in every situation.

✻ *Lord, we ask for strength*
that we may live courageously and compassionately
as friends of Jesus.

TO THINK ABOUT

● From your own experience, how do you understand the many issues surrounding work, unemployment, under-employment and redundancy?
● Are you in any way actively involved with those trying to challenge the desperately low wage levels throughout the countries of the South?

FOR ACTION

Can you encourage your local church to become more involved with local young, unemployed people? Have you spoken with your local Member of Parliament on these issues?

HOW MUCH FAITH?

Notes based on the New International Version by
Eileen Jacob

Eileen Jacob, a member of the Church of South India, is retired and living in Hyderabad. Previously she taught in a city grammar school and was superintendent of a village hostel for girls.

Jesus was often grieved by the smallness of faith he found in his disciples and in others whom he met. And he rejoiced whenever he found great faith. If faith 'even as small as a mustard seed' (Matthew 17.20) is sufficient to enable us to move mountains, why do we find it so hard to believe? Why are we so prone to fear and doubt, so unable to grasp our potential as children of the living God?

Faith is a free gift of God to his children. But to receive it may cost us dear. Let us see why.

---

*19th Sunday after Pentecost, September 28 Matthew 21.18-22 ***
Fruitful faith

I suppose at some time or other, all of us have experienced the bitter disappointment that ensues when some plan or person on whom we pinned our hopes, and for whom we did all we could, fails to respond in the way we expected. If you have time, reflect on today's reading together with John 15.1-8 and Isaiah 5.1-7. God is seen looking in vain for the fruit of his efforts to promote the life and growth of his people, deeply disappointed when failure to bear fruit indicates a dying plant.

To bear fruit, both as a Christian community and as individuals, God's gift of faith has to be nurtured in a life of prayer – that means a continual awareness of God's presence and a constant effort to do his will. 'Remain in me and I will remain in you' (John 15.4).

✳ *May wisdom herself take root in you,
grow strong and tall within you;
May she touch what is old and dead
and make you beautiful and fragrant
like cedars and olive-trees;*

May she spread out her branches and shelter you;
And as the tree of life sustains and heals you,
so may your fruits and leaves be a source of life for the
world. Alison Geary, UK. From Oceans of Prayer (NCEC)

Monday September 29   Joshua 6.1-20 *

The obedience test

Faith is inseparably linked with obedience. Obedience is the outward proof of inner faith. And perhaps the greatest test of obedience is not so much in doing something difficult, that requires courage and stamina, but in doing something that seems foolish. Remember how hard Naaman found it to obey the simple order to go and wash himself seven times in the river Jordan? An army of soldiers marching round and round the city they wanted to conquer, and expecting the walls to fall down when the trumpets blew and they all shouted! Joshua was humble and obedient enough to trust God's orders, mad as they must have seemed to him and to the soldiers. And they saw the reward of their faith. 'My thoughts are not your thoughts, neither are your ways my ways,' declares the Lord (Isaiah 55.8).

How can a morsel of bread and a sip of wine minister Christ to our souls? 'Do this in remembrance of me,' says Jesus. This is God's crazy way of continuing to give himself to us. Two or three ordinary people presenting to God in prayer a problem that has eluded the best efforts of world leaders – how can this help? 'I tell you that if two of you on earth agree about anything you ask for, it will be done for you by my Father in heaven. For where two or three come together in my name, there am I with them.' (Matthew 18.19-20).

✴ *The foolishness of God is wiser than man's wisdom,*
   And the weakness of God is stronger than man's
        strength.   1 Corinthians 1.25

Tuesday September 30   Hebrews 11.17-22,29-31 *

The family of faith

'God has no grand-children.' There is a lot of truth in this saying, and we must heed John the Baptist's warning to those who trusted in an inherited faith (Matthew 3.9).

But there is a community of faith. It is a tremendous privilege to belong to a family, a Church, a nation whose heroes and heroines of faith have blazed the trail for us.

In 1995, I had the joy of sharing in the bi-centenary celebrations of the London Missionary Society / Council for World Mission. The programmes were designed to help us to thank God for all those who in the past had responded to God's call and served him in many ways, to hear God's call to us now, in our day, and make a worthy response. Behind us was the great 'cloud of witnesses', beside us a vast crowd from many nations who represented the fruit of their faithfulness, and before us the challenge to pass on the torch of faith undimmed to the next generation.

✷ *Lord, you do not ask us to travel the way of faith alone. We thank you for the great family of faith to which we belong.*

Wednesday October 1   Nehemiah 4.7-21

The work of faith

Nehemiah was a very different person from Joshua. He exercised wise caution. He planned meticulously. He rallied and encouraged the people and proved that he cared for their safety and well-being. He was with them at their place of work and in time of danger. But Nehemiah's great natural gifts of leadership were under girded by a faith in God not less than Joshua's. Faith is not to be equated with foolhardiness. God may ask us to do apparently crazy things at times but normally he expects us to exercise the talents and good sense he has given us.

Human Rights Trust produced a report on the appalling conditions in the Tihar jail in Delhi. Greatly distressed I spent a day lifting the situation to God in prayer. Within a year I saw pictures on my television screen of the gutsy woman police officer, Kiran Bedi, interacting with the prisoners, and learned of the transformation she had brought about by her dedicated work there. Was this God's work? Or Kiran's? Can we separate the two? God *can* act without us but generally he chooses to work through us.

✷ *Lord, increase my faith in you, so that you can accomplish your work through me.*

221

Faith which sees

The reality of Hezekiah's physical and mental suffering is obvious. At the time he could see no meaning in it. When God wonderfully restored him and extended his life he was able to look back and say, 'Surely it was for my benefit that I suffered such anguish' (verse 17).

The words in Hebrews 12.11 have been well-illustrated in the programme on our Indian *Doordashan* TV entitled 'Going On'. Weekly episodes depict true stories of people who have suffered some debilitating disease or other great tragedy in their lives which rendered them helpless and dependent. The initial reaction usually is one of anger, bewilderment, frustration or depression. But the programme shows how, helped by loving family or friends, these people have learnt to 'go on', and to demonstrate wonderful triumphs of the spirit which would never had been possible if life had flowed on smoothly. Inspired by such examples of faith and courage (and they are all around us!) can we learn to *see*, even in our darkest hour that, 'This is good for me?'

✳ *Jesus, looking at his approaching crucifixion, said, 'The hour has come for the Son of Man to be glorified.' He could see the reality even beforehand – by faith.*

Unexpected faith

What all the profound teaching, the hoary traditions, and meticulous observances of the Jewish religion could not accomplish, was wrought in this centurion by the rigorous discipline of army life. It taught him to recognize the power of authority and the unquestioning obedience and trust required of those under authority. Acknowledging the authority of Jesus he unquestioningly submitted to him.

Jesus frequently showed that faith is not confined to one nation, nor to those who make a public profession of faith. If only our eyes are open we can see amazing proofs of faith in the most surprising people – like the distraught mother (Matthew 15.21-28), the grateful prostitute (Luke 7.50) and the noisy beggar (Luke 18.42).

God's gift of faith, like his gift of rain, is showered upon all without partiality. And those who are homeless, with no roof over their heads, nor walls to protect them, are the ones who get wettest! Are there ceilings on our expectations, or walls of prejudice preventing us from receiving the full outpouring of God's gift of faith?

✳ *Forgive us your faithless people*
for ignoring the signs of your kingdom
growing in such unexpected places
and surprising ways.

URC Prayer Handbook 1992

Saturday October 4   *Matthew 14.22-33*
Sustaining faith
Was it presumptuous of Peter to think he could do as Jesus did? But Jesus did call him to come. Was Peter's faith more in his own ability to overcome his fears and walk the waves, rather than in Jesus' saving power? It took no small courage to step out of the security and protection of the boat onto the storm-tossed sea. Yet his faith could not sustain him. Doesn't it happen to us all? With much enthusiasm, and what we regard as great faith and courage, we step out in response to Jesus' call, leaving behind us all that represents our security. And in no time at all we are floundering, sinking and crying out, 'Lord, save me!'

It seems that we need to pass through such experiences of failure, of defeat, of helpless dependency, before strong faith in God alone can be deeply rooted in us.

✳ *Though the fig tree does not bud*
and there are no grapes on the vines,
though the olive crop fails
and the fields produce no food,
though there are no sheep in the pen
and no cattle in the stalls,
yet will I rejoice in the Lord,
I will be joyful in God my saviour.   *Habakkuk 3.17-18*

TO THINK ABOUT and FOR ACTION
Using this week's readings and your own experience consider:

● How is faith measured? What is it that makes us conclude that a person has faith in God?

● How can faith be nurtured? What makes it grow?

Identify from among people known to you someone whose faith seems great and someone who is young in faith. Plan ways in which you can learn from the former and encourage the latter.

LIVING IN GOD'S WORLD
1. Religion or politics?

Notes based on the New International Version by
John Hastings

We are tenants on a planet owned by God. Living in God's home entails a responsibility to maintain it as a place of comfort, creativity, fairness, beauty and peace.

Politics is about the organization of society – protecting the weak and removing social evil. Religion too seeks to bring people into harmony with God and one another. The vision of a new heaven (theology) and a new earth (politics) is in both Old and New Testaments (cf. Isaiah 65.17 and Revelation 21.1). Politics is more than party squabbling and rivalry, and religion is more than securing people's allegiance to spiritual creeds. The Bible presents them as one whole. Archbishop Desmond Tutu said, 'I am puzzled which Bible people are reading when they suggest religion and politics don't mix.'

20th Sunday after Pentecost, October 5   *Matthew 10.1-4*
Creative tension

Jesus included in his team Simon the Zealot. Three or four others may have been of the same nationalist persuasion – 'daggers drawn' with the tax-collector Matthew, one of a despised group who oiled the machinery of an unwanted administration. Philip would have been treated in 'pure' Jewish society like an immigrant. Jesus took followers for training from both ends of the political spectrum. Even if the Gospel record rarely gives a hint of it, there must have been heated arguments. Jesus knew that mutual enrichment would come through tolerance and compromise. They stayed together, right up to the time of Judas' betrayal – and that wasn't the result of a quarrel. To develop as human beings we need creative tension. Jesus welcomed people with spirit who were prepared to be entangled with controversial and risky involvement in politics. In my experience, such people make fine Christians, even if the Church disowns them.

Naturally we choose like-minded friends: it makes for a cosy life. But both politics and religion challenge us to learn to live with widely differing neighbours, however much we dislike their views.

A prominent civic leader once accused me after a service of being a Communist, because my sermon had been about oppression. He hadn't realized that the word 'oppress' occurs 115 times in the Bible (even in the Authorized version)!

✳ *Lord, save me from preferring a quiet life*
so that I may be with you in the rough and tumble
of human controversy.

Monday October 6   *Matthew 17.24-27*

A spiritual case for disobedience

Many people today live under duress. Taxes rankle if you can't accept the legitimacy of those who govern you. What can you do? Assert your rights and refuse to pay for what you consider immoral? Protest about particular issues? Jesus seems to be saying, Yes, you can claim exemption from paying, but you also have a duty not to offend those who have power to multiply oppression.

We don't have access to easy money from the jaws of a passing fish. Perhaps Jesus was referring humorously to Peter's income as a fisherman – every paid worker has a 'fish' with a coin in its mouth.

There are major and minor issues, even if deciding between them isn't always easy. We have to salute those who are prepared to go to jail to make a moral protest. Sometimes we may feel called to join them. If no public protests were made about the production of weapons of destruction, might that not be a greater evil? It can never be said that civil disobedience is always wrong. There is an enigma in Jesus' words. In respect of the Temple-tax, both Jesus and Peter could claim to be 'sons'. But even though the Roman 'unbelievers' benefited from the tax collected, Jesus was accepting their patronizing authority. Was he suggesting we have a world-citizenship – and therefore duties which are world-related as well as parochial ones?

✳ *Help us, O Lord, to declare your way*
both through our obedience to just authority
and by our disobedience to evil decrees.

Do you put boundaries round God's domain?

Jesus seems, on the face of it, to put religion and politics into separate compartments. Sadly this is the way too many people make use of this text. Jesus' drift is clear enough – Caesar has a claim over you, and you can't evade it. But as soon as you think more deeply, you realize that for Jesus there's nothing which Caesar claims which doesn't already belong to God: he couldn't have meant that Caesar has an area all to himself.

Romans 13 also can be read as either staunch pro-State or a strong anti-State passage! A Caesar can only hold power by God's permission. But for those who know their Scriptures, God doesn't ask for a token sacrifice, or a 'tax'. As in Psalm 50.10-11,

'every animal of the forests is mine,
and the cattle on a thousand hills,
every bird and creature ...'

He wants us to live affirming that trees, cattle, politics – all things, not just religion – belong to God. So Jesus left it open for his hearers to decide that nothing could be Caesar's – for a bigger reason than that his right to rule over Israel might be in question. Both Bonhoeffer and Niemoller denied that Hitler could claim any dues. All citizens have the responsibility of applying the supreme rule Paul gives: 'Love is the fulfilment of the law'.

✳ *Lord, we offer to you*
    every part of your world that passes through our hands.
    May our practice of citizenship
    help towards the redemption of all our laws by love.

Wednesday October 8   *1 Kings 21.1-24*

Oppressors must be confronted

For over eight months in 1971, I witnessed the viscious oppression of a people by their own government. Egged on by hurt politicians who had refused to accept the verdict of a democratic poll, President General Yahya Khan set about forcing the eastern wing of Pakistan into submission by bombs, guns and bayonets. Millions were killed in cold blood. Hundreds of thousands of women were raped. Ten million fled into India as refugees. Even giving relief was a terrible trauma. Though I failed to get World Church support – politics got in the way – I eventually took a peace mission to confront the President about his army's atrocities. He refused to call a halt. We reported our failure to the Indian Prime Minister, Mrs Indira Gandhi, and a fortnight later the force of a superior army aiding the freedom fighters created a liberated Bangladesh.

We were saddened that eight months of terror reigned without stirring any high-level protest against the inhumanity unleashed on the innocent in the name of preserving Pakistan's integrity. Even as we talked with the President in Rawalpindi, a massive fleet was sailing into the Bay of Bengal to aid the oppression.

If only Elijah's action could be replicated again and again wherever people are oppressed. The role of the people of God cannot be merely to accept and adjust to all political *faits accomplis*, but to speak the word of the Lord directly to the oppressor.

✳ *Lord, I am ashamed to ask you to forgive my silence*
at the unjust oppression of the innocent.
I can only beseech you to change it.

Thursday October 9   Luke 1.46-55
Radical Motherhood
The Magnificat is not just a hymn of a humble, grateful mother filled with extraordinary grace. It is tantamount to a blueprint setting out the revolutionary force. When Fred Kaan's version of the Magnificat 'Sing we a song of high revolt ...' came out in 1968, many in Britain were scandalized. What a nerve, they said, turning so sacred and precious a canticle into a political manifesto! They had been singing the words of this song, weekly or daily, for many years without realizing they were political dynamite or that Mary brought political awareness to her motherhood! Prayerfully reflect on this Namibian version:

✳ *As on the day of the Exodus, he is stretching out*
his mighty arm to scatter the oppressors
with all their evil plans.
He has brought down mighty kings
from their thrones
and he has lifted up the despised;
and so he will do today.
He has filled the exploited with good things
And sent the exploiters away with empty hands;
and so he will do today.
His promise to our mothers and fathers remains new and
*   fresh*
to this day.

Therefore the hope for liberation
which is burning in me
will not be extinguished.
He will remember me, here now and beyond the grave.'
                    Zephania Kameeta, Namibia. From Why O Lord?
            (World Council of Churches) Psalms and sermons from
                                Namibia © 1986 Geneva, Switzerland

Friday October 10   *Acts 25.1-12*

When secular justice is best

In appealing to Caesar, Paul showed that he believed his own
people would be too prejudiced to give him a fair trial.
Nationalism, racism and sectarianism are the enemies of a just
society. Unlike Paul, people of religious faith today tend to
distrust secular powers. Yet so often they themselves are
prejudiced by the anti-secular bias of their upbringing. Beware of
religious brainwashing! Being religious doesn't make it any more
excusable than political brainwashing. Not only is it less
excusable (because listening to God should help our lives to
correspond more to his justice), but also it is more dangerous
because it claims, falsely, the stamp of 'spiritual authority'. The
church 'pot', sadly, often has no room to call the State 'kettle'
black.

Apartheid was promoted in South Africa by the Dutch
Reformed Church, exalting white Afrikaners as God's chosen
people. In Northern Ireland, while individual Christians have
worked sacrificially for reconciliation and peace, the Churches
institutionally have tended to fuel rather than solve the political
conflict. These are examples of what goes on everywhere. All
Churches need to examine themselves as to the extent to which
they inculcate prejudice.

✳ *Do we seek first the Kingdom of God and his justice?*
                                                    Matthew 6.33

Saturday October 11   *Revelation 13.1-10*

Faith fuels freedom

John's insights are born of a grim political situation. Christians at
the end of the first century would have understood his allusions.
Whereas in many countries, nineteen centuries later, Bible study
may be over-spiritualized (read again the introduction to notes for

March 16-29), John's first readers had to live out their faith against harsh realities, including threats of torture and execution. Roman Emperors claimed to be divine (verses 1 and 4). Cruel dictatorships won popular support by demonstrating miraculous healing and claiming eternal life (verse 3) – an anti-Christ always looks very much like Christ. Power itself still mesmerizes enough people to ruin a nation under the slogan 'might is right' (verse 4).

At times of terrible persecution the cry goes up: Why is it allowed to go on? For John, the political tyrant (the beast) draws strength from Evil itself (the Dragon – verse 2), which has its own potent life-force. But there is an alternative life-force which is more powerful, though it is seen in physical weakness.

My wife and I lived in Bangladesh for over six years under the corrupt dictator Ershad. People eventually took to the streets to confront his guns with their bare hands. A young man named Nur Hossein became a martyr, with freedom slogans painted on his chest and back, when he was shot in a Dhaka street on 10 November 1987. Ten years previously in Santiago, on the way to confronting the Minister of the Interior of Chile with the names of hundreds of 'disappeared' people, I had been encouraged to see the tell-tale little 'R's etched on walls to proclaim *resistanzia* to the brutal Pinochet regime. The life-force of political freedom is closely related to that of faith. Those who endure have access to inexhaustible reserves, for they belong to the Lamb.

✷ *Lord, align me with all who are persecuted*
  for righteousness' sake,
  Please use my prayers to help build up their spiritual
      resources.

TO THINK ABOUT

What decisions have been taken recently by your government, nationally or locally, which suggest that the guiding reasons and objectives have more to do with party interest than with the public good? Are all your Church's decisions free of sectarian bias and self-interest?

FOR ACTION

After careful preparation, and perhaps forming a small deputation, take up any of these issues with your MP or an appropriate church officer.

LIVING IN GOD'S WORLD
2. For the sake of tomorrow

Notes based on the New Jerusalem Bible by
Terrence Fernando

Terrence Fernando, a young Sri Lankan, is a priest of the Roman Catholic Church in Sri Lanka. In 1994/5, he responded to an invitation to serve as a Partner in Mission with the Grassroots Programme (UK), and CAFOD.

Week of prayer for World Peace

In this week's readings, we begin with God's vision of peace which is expressed in the story of the garden of Eden. This garden's initial beauty and peace is an image of how the world might have been if we had not marred it, but it is also a vision of hope for the future. Hope never dies, even in the most intractable situations. And we can all work for peace. We can begin through prayer and meditation, radiating peace to all round us. *Each day, pray the Universal Prayer for Peace:*

> *Lead me from death to life,*
> *from falsehood to truth*
> *Lead me from despair to hope,*
> *from fear to trust*
> *Lead me from hate to love,*
> *from war to peace*
> *Let peace fill our heart,*
> *our world, our universe ...*
> *Peace, peace, peace.*

And then work together in community, taking appropriate actions – political and social – to make the world a better place.

21st Sunday after Pentecost, October 12   Genesis 2.4b-17
Our oneness with nature

The natural world is a gift, given to us to be protected and nourished. It is important to correct our wrong attitudes. Coming from an Asian Buddhist country I have seen how village people respect their environment. There is no intention to dominate creation, but to live at peace with it. Nature is part of us. It is a misunderstanding to say that Christianity teaches that humanity and nature are separate, and that nature only exists to meet our needs. 'Yahweh God took the man and settled him in the garden of Eden to cultivate and take care of it' (Genesis 2.15).

Humanity today is not only engaging in a war between fellow human beings but also, without mercy, killing trees, rivers, mountains, animals, soil and the whole of nature. Greed is the motive. And we kill ourselves in the process. Today God calls us to repent and correct our relationship with creation: to make peace with it and dominate it as God dominates it.

What does it mean to dominate? God's domination is one of loving kindness to all creation.

✻ *Enjoy the earth gently*
Enjoy the earth gently
For if the earth is spoiled
It cannot be repaired
Enjoy the earth gently.   *Yoruba poem, West Africa*

Monday October 13   Genesis 2.18-25

One flesh, one body

It is interesting first to compare the Priestly account of the creation of human beings in Genesis 1.26-27 with the earlier Jahwist account in today's reading. In the Priestly account, the word 'man' represents both male and female and neither has superiority over the other. And the Jahwist account in 2.24 reduces the superiority of men by saying that male and female must become 'one flesh' in marriage.

A person who is not at peace with him or herself cannot give peace to others. Peace must start within, and then it can foster and burst forth in families. Family must be the first place where our children learn about peace. But today, in most cases, married partners imitate the pattern of market economy: a short-term contract. Instead of mutual respect, many partners exploit one another for pleasure. Children are merely the by-products of business. There are no efforts to listen to and understand each other, and to make decisions together. Our generation does not know how to forgive, pardon and to persevere in total faithfulness. *How do we rediscover the family values which are fast disappearing in today's society?*

✻ *Loving God, help us to teach our generation*

that marriage is not a business contract
but a holy bond between two people
who are responsible for each other's integrity
and development before God.

Tuesday October 14   Isaiah 51.1-6
Hope for the world

In Sri Lanka, since 1983, violence has brought deep sorrow to many rural and urban communities. The price of war is the decimation of a generation of young people. The issues are complex and seemingly intractable. Yet we do not lose hope.

This was Israel's experience in exile in Babylon in the sixth century BC. Almost a whole generation had been wiped out. But the prophet did not despair. 'Consider the rock,' he said, 'from which you were hewn' – Sarah and Abraham, the childless couple who became the parents of the nation. Just as God eventually blessed their marriage with a son in their old age, so he would again raise up from this depleted exiled community a new generation of young people. Joy and gladness would once more fill the nation's homes. God's justice and salvation in this local situation will be recognized by other nations, 'the coasts and islands' (verse 5) and give them hope. In recent years too, many peoples have taken courage from the signs of God's activity in the ending of apartheid in South Africa, and in the beginnings of a Peace process in the Holy Land itself.

✳ *Loving God, whose saving justice is inviolable*
and whose victory is forever,
deepen our sense of hope and give us the will
to work together for peace in your world.

Wednesday October 15   Psalm 96
Perfect glory

What is the difference between mystics and people who just follow the trend of today's society? One of the greatest differences is that mystics see reality with the naked eye. They are not satisfied by social formulas. They take the risk of turning away from convention to discover for themselves the secrets of life. Only such people can proclaim with confidence to the whole world the words of the Psalmist –

'... The Lord is king,
the world is set firm, it cannot be moved.
He will judge the nations with justice' (verse 10).

Today, we are conditioned by various formulas presented to us by evil powers. Our values and attitudes are formed by them, and our understanding of reality narrowed. The Psalmist invites us to sing a new song to the Lord, to exercise the freedom of children of God by putting aside these narrow formulas, to look at creation with pure eyes, without fear and without restrictions, so that it won't be long before we really see. Then we will sing with the Psalmist of the power of God and work with God in making this world a better place.

✳ *Be silent and spend a few minutes reflecting on God's image that is within yourself. Then, remaining aware of that image within, look at the things around you.*

World Food Day, Thursday October 16   *1 Samuel 2.1-10*

Responding to hunger

While I was studying for the priesthood (1989-1991), my country Sri Lanka was in turmoil. Many very poor young people, wanting to change the system to a better one, rebelled against the government. About 60,000 were killed or 'disappeared' during that time. Coming from a middle-class family, and being sheltered in a Roman Catholic Seminary, I was not affected. I was sympathetic to their struggle but did not want to get involved until someone in the struggle challenged me.

'Have you ever experienced hunger?' he said. 'Yes,' I replied. But he laughed and said, 'No you haven't. Because of work you may have postponed a meal and felt hungry, but it was kept for you! Here we have no food at all. You have never experienced that hunger!' He made me ask myself: What is my response to that hunger which makes millions of people go to sleep hungry every day? Does my faith in God and his salvation have anything to do with this? How can I live my faith if I do not respond to the voice of the poor? For God is on their side (verse 8).

Make a firm commitment today to get involved in working for a better world where all can find their daily bread with dignity.

✳ *Lord, help me to respond to the hunger of humanity*
by committing myself to some collective action.
I believe any system which is against your will
will one day be brought down.
Help me to hold on to that hope
and work hard to make it a reality.

God's values

Our generation neither knows how to forgive nor how to forget. To refrain from taking revenge is one of the hardest demands of Jesus. But he gives us a reason for his commands, and why we should go the 'second mile' – 'that you may be children of your Father in heaven' (verse 45). We will never experience this great fact by hitting back, but forgiveness brings the joy of exercising the image of God within us.

Today we are encouraged by the media, not to be as perfect as our heavenly Father, but to be as successful as most businessmen. But if we engage in this adventure, we become mere machines, operated by the Evil One whose model we will ultimately become – just the opposite of Jesus' values.

To follow Jesus' way is not to climb the ladder of success. It may even mean taking action to bring about the downfall of large multi-national companies that exploit developing countries. We need, therefore, to remind ourselves that we are created in God's image. It is God's values that we must learn and practise.

✳ *Loving God, you have shown us*
that only love has the power to redeem, and
that loving enemies is not passive submission to gross
     injustice
but is seen in the active transformation of what is wrong
     by a greater power.
Let your love fill me and work through me.

Perfect like God?

In a recent article about reducing stress, were the words: 'Thou shalt not be perfect, nor even try to be perfect.' Most psychotherapists would agree with this rather than the words of Jesus in verse 48. Are there examples in your own experience of people who may have suffered remorse as a consequence of aiming at perfection? We are all conscious sometimes of setting for ourselves unattainable targets.

So what did Jesus mean? Is perfection something we should strive for – forgiving enemies, blessing those who curse us, not taking revenge ... Are these unrealistic and unattainable? Will we never achieve the perfection for which we were created?

Jesus tells us that it is the wish of God that all his children shall be like him. This is only possible when we depend on God's grace with a fully open heart which yearns to be like him, and it is only possible when we really join in the struggle with our sisters and brothers who share the same adventure of living in God's world. Only in relation to each other, and in a community of love, can we really understand what it means to be like God. There is no room for personal perfection in the Christian faith, but only the perfection of *individuals in community.* So when we open our lives to those around us and try to rid ourselves of selfishness in co-operation with our sisters and brothers, we will understand and experience the words of Jesus. Verse 48 is not unachievable nonsense, but something we can achieve with the help of our brothers and sisters with God's blessing.

✳ *He whom I enclose with my name is weeping in this dungeon. I am ever busy building this wall all around; and as this wall goes up into the sky day by day I lose sight of my true being in its dark shadow.*

I take pride in this great wall, and I plaster it with dust and sand lest a least hole should be left in this name; and for all the care I take I lose sight of my true being.

From Gitanjali, Rabindranath Tagore
(Macmillan General Books 1957)

TO THINK ABOUT

● Am I aware of the world economic system which makes millions of people hungry every day?
● If we believe all humankind is made in God's image and likeness, how do we as Christians engage in this society which seems to put possessions and profit before people?

FOR ACTION

● Remember those who hate or dislike you, or put obstacles in your way. Send a stream of love into them and prayerfully wish them to be happy and loving.
● Each day, remind yourself that you want to experience the beauty of God through directing loving thoughts to every living being. In this way, you will radiate God's supreme Love.

INTERNATIONAL BIBLE READING ASSOCIATION

1020 Bristol Road, Selly Oak, Birmingham, Great Britain B29 6LB

ORDER FORM – For 1998 Books

Please send me the following books: *Office Ref: 98101*

Name: _____

Address: _____

_____

_____

_____ Post Code: _____

To qualify for 1998 books at the prices shown, this order form must be used (photocopies not accepted). Your order will be dispatched when **all** books are available.

Code	Title of Book	Quantity	Unit Price	Total
ZYW0895	Words For Today 1998		£3.99	
ZYL0896	Light For Our Path 1998		£3.99	
ZYF0897	Finding Our Way Together 1998		£4.99	
ZYP0898	Preachers' Handbook 1998		£4.99	
ZYE0213	Everyday Prayers		£4.95	
ZYM0325	More Everyday Prayers		£4.95	
ZYL0575	Looking At The Cross		£4.50	
ZYL0684	Looking At Advent		£4.50	
ZYL0762	Looking At Pentecost		£4.50	
ZYL0781	Looking At Easter & Ascension		£4.50	
ZYL0871	Living Prayers For Today		£11.99	

I enclose cheque/PO (Payable to IBRA)

Please charge my ACCESS/MASTERCARD/VISA
Card No:

Expiry Date: _____

Signature: _____

Total cost of books	
Post – UK free Overseas – add £2.00 per book	
Donation to International Fund	
TOTAL DUE	

Payments in Pounds Sterling, please

The INTERNATIONAL BIBLE READING ASSOCIATION is a Registered Charity

LIVING IN GOD'S WORLD
3. One world

Notes based on the Revised Standard Version by
Lourdino Yuzon

Lourdino Yuzon, a Filipino, is the organizing minister of the newly formed Cosmopolitan United Church in Dallas, Texas. When this church (composed mostly of immigrant and American-born Filipinos) is established, in two or three years' time, he is committed to returning home to take up the challenge to share the task of relating the Christian faith to Philippine realities. Previously, he was Dean of the Divinity School at Silliman University in Dumaguete City in the Philippines. He has also served as Joint Secretary for the Council for World Mission and Evangelism of the Christian Conference of Asia.

'Unity in diversity'. This is what God intends the world to be. We are not meant for dull uniformity, but for rich diversity. We belong to different races, cultures and religions. Yet we have many things in common. Basic to all else is the fact that God is our Creator. We are God's people. Because we are meant for God, we are also meant for one another. Our readings affirm that worshipping our Creator God inescapably means that we should learn to live with people who are different from ourselves.

---

*22nd Sunday after Pentecost, October 19   Matthew 26.6-13 **

A Messiah anointed

Usually a ruler is anointed at the beginning of his or her term of office. The anointing of Jesus, however, was unusual. It took place towards the end of his life and ministry and was carried out by a woman, perhaps of ill repute. He was anointed in preparation for his burial after an untimely death, not at the beginning of a long reign. But he was not a political Messiah according to popular expectations. He came as *the* Messiah who ruled by self-giving love, not by dominating power. His love for sinners and outcasts was a sign of his reign. Anointed for burial, he was crowned as King. His crown was a crown of thorns; his throne – the cross.

As the Messiah, Jesus deserved a gift fit for a monarch. Paradoxically, it was a 'non-person' who showered him with extravagant love.

✳ *Gracious God,*
thank you for giving yourself to us in Jesus, the Christ.
In and through him,
we who are non-people have become your people.
Help us to love you above all else,
and our neighbours as well.

Monday October 20   *Isaiah 45.14-25* ✳

The hidden God

'Truly thou art a God who hidest thyself' (verse 15). This does not mean that our longing for God's presence is futile. Rather, it means that we tend to look for God in the wrong places. For the Hebrews, signs of God's presence were all over the place: their deliverance from captivity, the orderly world of things and God's liberating truth and righteousness.

As in the days of Isaiah, we see signs of tension, alienation and conflict between nations. In the midst of all these we wonder where we could find God. God is not in the earthquake, wind and fire. God speaks to us in a still small voice that impels us to strive towards truth, justice, righteousness, peace and inclusive communities.

✳ *Loving and caring God, open our eyes,*
unstop our ears,
and quicken our hearts,
so that we may discern your presence in our midst.

Tuesday October 21   *Amos 5.1-15*

Seek God and live

The prophet Amos challenged his people to choose life instead of death. The people were religious, but what happened to them at the sanctuary was divorced from their day-to-day life. Religious rituals did not bear the fruits of righteousness and justice in the way they related to the poor and the oppressed. Therefore, they were doomed. Yet to Amos, the people were not without hope. What they needed was to enter anew into a right relationship with God and with their fellow human beings. That involved ethical obedience: to hate evil and do good through positive acts of justice.

We worship God, not only with what we think, feel and say, but also by what we do. Receiving the gifts of the Spirit is inseparable from bearing the fruits of the Spirit (Galatians 5.22-23). By our example, people will know whether we love and worship God with our whole being.

✳ *Holy and righteous God,*
we ask you to cleanse our hearts of all evil desires
and create in us a desire to do justice,
to love kindness,
and to walk humbly in your sight.

Wednesday October 22   *Psalm 15*

A call to moral purity

In some places of worship, devotees enter the sanctuary barefooted. That is a sign of respect for a sacred place. Psalm 15 demands moral purity of those who worship God. This is both an inward attitude and outward action. One's character should be reflected in specific social situations. The morally blameless person does not slander others or spread malicious gossip. Such people value others for who they are, not for what they have, and refrain from making profit by not charging excessive interests on loans. They are true to their word and will not resort to 'white lies'. Their whole lives are transparent.

To be 'in Christ' is to be a radically new person, inwardly and outwardly. To worship the most holy God inevitably means leading a morally upright life.

✳ *Loving God, mould us in the image of Christ our Lord.*
Cleanse us of all unrighteousness.
May we come before your presence and reach out to
others
with clean hands and pure hearts.

Thursday October 23   *Genesis 11.1-9*

God above all gods

The story of the tower of Babel is re-enacted every time human beings play at being gods. This can happen when human efforts, even towards supposedly worthy goals, become ends in themselves and men and women forget they are creatures, not the Creator. To ensure public order and discipline and unite supposedly fractious Filipinos, President Marcos imposed a dictatorship. People were forced to think, act and speak the way he wanted. Initially, his 'new Society' looked like the arrival of the kind of community of which Filipinos dreamed. Underneath that facade, however, chaos was waiting to break forth.

Like the builders of the tower of Babel, Marcos' intentions may have been good. But he overstepped his creaturely boundaries and played 'God'.

✳ *God, give us grace to accept with serenity the things that cannot be changed,*
courage to change the things that should be changed,
and wisdom to distinguish the one from the other.
Reinhold Niebuhr (1892-1971)

United Nations Day, Friday October 24   1 Corinthians 12.12-27

All for one – one for all

The human body is a living organism. Its well-being depends upon the proper functioning of its parts which are inseparable from one another. The same is true with the Church. When one member is regarded as all-important, and others as inconsequential, it cannot thrive. Within the whole human family there are many races, ethnic and linguistic groups, religions and cultures. They are inter-related. They are meant for one another. Despite their differences, they share a common humanity. Together, they ensure the well-being of the whole human race. Apart from one another they fall prey to communalism and ethnic cleansing.

The United Nations is a sign and symbol of what nations can, and should do, if they learn to respect and accept one another.

✳ *Lord God, you are the One whom we seek together,*
the Life which is part of us all;
the Truth and the mark of mystery,
the Love and Joy that makes us whole.   Adapted from
'God is the One Whom we seek together' by Colin Gibson,
in Alleluia Aotearoa, 1992 (New Zealand Hymnbook Trust)

In praise of the living God

A line in a popular melody exhorts us to 'count our blessings instead of sheep'. The ancient Hebrews had every reason to be grateful to God. It was God who called them into being as a chosen people. God was faithful to the Covenant as shown in God's saving deeds in their history. Unlike the lifeless gods of their neighbours, God created the heavens. God reigned over them and over the whole world in justice, righteousness and peace. Their God was not some distant, aloof and unconcerned deity. God cared. God was in, with and around them. God personally saw to it that people lived just, righteous and peaceful lives.

In the power of the Holy Spirit, the same God is present in the world today. God continues to bring about wholeness to human lives and to the world. As our reading puts it, God is the living reality we encounter in our places of worship. To the living and Creator God be the glory and praise!

✳ ***Creator God, your creatures raise***
to you and our Redeemer praise;
we sing your Holy Spirit's power;
among us even till this hour.   *David Beebe*
From Touch Holiness: Resources for Worship, ed. Ruth C Duck
and Maren C Tirabassi (The Pilgrim Press, Cleveland Ohio
1990)

TO THINK ABOUT

Where do you see God bringing wholeness to nations and communities today?

What is your vision for the world for the year 2000?

Which Bible passages express that vision for you?

FOR ACTION

Find out more about the work of the United Nations. Your local Library should be able to help you.

LIVING IN GOD'S WORLD
4. Living with anticipation

Notes based on the New Revised Standard Version by
Melvyn Matthews

Melvyn Matthews, the Vicar of Chew Magna with Dundry, two villages south of Bristol (UK) was a University Chaplain and Lecturer for many years and has worked as the Director of an Ecumenical Centre for reconciliation and peace. He has written a number of books on the spiritual life.

Patrick Leigh Fermor in *A Time of Gifts* describes how he set out as a young man to walk across Europe to Constantinople:

'To change scenery; abandon London and England and set out across Europe like a tramp – or as I characteristically phrased it to myself, like a pilgrim or a palmer, an errant scholar ... All of a sudden this was not merely the obvious but the only thing to do ...'

This kind of spirit, always looking for a further shore, is sadly out of fashion as we approach the end of the millennium, but it is the basis of a life of faith. People are expectant beings, and need to live constantly in hope to be truly human and deeply religious.

As we read this week's passages, mainly about Noah, let us allow them to call us out into new life, expecting to find God in new ways. The story of Noah is not so much about God's judgment on an evil world as about the hopefulness of one man in the face of hopelessness, and of God's hope in us symbolized by the rainbow. Noah is not so much the one pious man who was saved, but the one who, like a sea captain, set sail upon the sea of faith, always looking for new shores and new truth to burst forth from God's hand. The narrative calls us to launch ourselves forward with more trust in the journey of faith, always looking out across the waters of the flood to find signs of life and eventually the rainbow of his promise.

The torch dance of welcome

When I worked as a priest in Africa, the bride was always late for her marriage ceremony – up to an hour and a half on one occasion! I had to be ready to perform the ceremony with as much joy as if she had been on time! In other cultures, and in the biblical culture of Jesus, it is the bridegroom who has to come to the bride for the wedding and, apparently, can be just as late!

The lamps in this parable were probably torches used to illuminate wedding processions at night. They consisted of sticks wrapped in rags and soaked in oil, and the girls would dance with them until the flames went out. As Jesus tells the story, some of the torches have dried out and more oil has to be poured over them. Jesus uses it to call us to respond with openness and joy to the arrival of God in our lives, always believing that he is near.

This parable occurs in a section of Matthew's Gospel which is concerned with our readiness for the coming of the Messiah. It reflects the situation of the early Church, where there was difficulty and disagreement because of the apparent delay of the end of the world and the return of Jesus. If we can reach behind this to the original parable we find a tale about not losing our sense of readiness. Do we take the reality of God so seriously that we can come to terms with its sudden appearance in our lives at any time? If God comes, will we cope when his reality bursts upon us? Will we have oil enough to perform the torch dance of welcome? Or will we have dried out long ago?

✳ *God, when you come, however unexpectedly,*
  may we have watched so well as to be ready
  to dance with welcome.

Monday October 27   *Genesis 6.9-22*

The righteous man

Noah is, along with Adam, a Patriarch of every human being of whatever race or nation. Just for a moment, before the biblical narrative launches into the story of one people, it pauses and looks around at the general human condition and asks what it is that God wills for all humanity. The narrator sees that whereas 'the earth was corrupt' there is one just man who has resisted evil: 'Noah was a righteous man, blameless in his generation; Noah walked with God' (verse 9). He is asked to carry the future of the human race with him into the ark, and because of him the human race is given a blessing and a future. 'The world is saved on account of the righteous man' (Benno Jacob).

This theme recurs through the biblical narrative – that even one person matters. One person building an ark as an act of defiance against the prevailing climate, an act of independence and devotion to God – this has immense cosmic significance and forms the basis for the activity of God in continuing to bless all things. God needs our righteousness, however insignificant it may appear, in order to be able to bless creation.

✳ *God, we are surprised to hear that you need us.*
  Give us the courage to stay with what we know to be just,
  however great the injustice around us may seem. Amen

Tuesday October 28   *Genesis 7.1-24*

All saved together

The poetic phrases of verse 11 – 'on that day all the fountains of the great deep burst forth, and the windows of the heavens were opened' – show us that this flood is more than just too much rain – this is chaos bursting into order, the beyond breaking into the midst. The 'great deep' is seen as the intrusion of chaos upon the ordering that God has made and so the story portrays the reversal, apparently by God's own choice, of the creation of the world. The order and peace - *shalom* - originally established is now allowed to revert to disorder and chaos.

In that original order and peace, men, women, plants and animals exist together and are part of the same creation. The same coherence is preserved in the ark, for animals and human beings enter the ark of salvation together. We should not dwell on how possible it was for Noah to have brought every species of animal into the ark and kept them alive: the point of the story is to show that both clean and unclean animals were saved, and then that people and animals were saved from the disaster together. Human beings do not exist in isolation.

✳ *God, we are all part of the same bundle of creation.*
  When disaster overwhelms us,
  help us not to make distinctions where you make none,
  and to enter the ark of salvation together. Amen

God needs our hopefulness

Noah is shown to be impatient, always yearning for land, like the captain of a ship, always watching for a landfall. The birds he sends out are biblical equivalents of telescopes – indeed, not so biblical, for in the early days of sailing ships, mariners used to carry birds with them and let them loose at sea, so that they could watch the direction they flew and follow them to land.

Noah is a paradigm of humanity. If we want to remain human, then we shall do as Noah did and continue, even in the face of disaster, to send out birds to look for a chance to start again, to set up camp and start a business, have a family, build an altar, start a civilization ... God puts us in the position of always having to look forward. Only by looking and moving forward, even when we don't know how long this will take, we discover what we are really like and what we can do and be.

When the Pilgrim Fathers set out in the Mayflower from Britain to America, one of them said, 'God has always some new truth to break forth from his word.' The story of Noah is an extraordinary parable of hopefulness and how that hopefulness, however small, is not just blessed by God but actually bears the blessing of God, for without our hopefulness God cannot act.

✳ *God, when we send out birds, they are like straws in the wind,*
   little gestures of hope in an empty world.
   Give us faith that you are waiting for them too
   so that we can begin the great story of love together.

God's image in us restored

The first verses in this chapter remind us of the creation story. There too, human beings were made in God's image, were commanded to be fruitful and multiply, and were given dominion over the created order. It is almost as if the creation has to be repeated. This time, however, in between the original creation and its restoration (in this passage), there is the disaster of the flood. The final truth is not the flood, but the restoration of the image of God in all things. We need to endure the flood in order to be ready to accept and own the restoration of God's image in us. Perhaps we were so careless of it that we needed, almost, to lose it – or in biblical imagery, to have it taken from us – before we could appreciate it.

Where disaster comes we mend better, or in the words of Dame Julian of Norwich '... when we come up and receive that sweet reward which grace has made for us, there we shall thank and bless our Lord, endlessly rejoicing that we ever suffered woe'. It is almost as if the biblical narrative is saying that we needed the flood to find out who we really are, and that we can only hold these truths – about God's image dwelling in us and sharing in the work of creation – to be self-evident when we see them through the perspective of the flood and can see the rainbow at the end. Whatever comes, it will not finally destroy.

✳ *God, give us eyes to see what you are trying to give us in and through the disasters which come our way. Amen.*

Friday October 31　　　　　　　　　　　　　　*Matthew 24.36-44*

Believing the good news

A British television comedy programme called *'Allo, 'Allo* showed the behaviour, exaggerated beyond belief to make you laugh, of a small group of French people during the occupation of their country by the Nazis during the Second World War. René, the bartender, was always dithering, never knowing whether to collaborate with the invaders or to resist, to be loyal to his wife or to succumb to the charms of the barmaid. Every now and again a woman leader of the Resistance would appear to give a message about the imminence of the invasion by the Allies. Her catch phrase was, 'I will only tell you once.'

Human beings are like René, dithering about themselves and their dilemmas, occupied by evil tendencies and never knowing whether to give in to them or not. The Resistance leader is like Jesus, announcing the imminence of the Kingdom and the need to turn away from confusion. She tells us the battle is over if only we would believe it; but we turn back to our dilemmas and refuse to believe that anything can be resolved.

In these verses Jesus compares his people to Noah, who, unlike René, was watchful for the signs of the coming of the Kingdom and ready to respond, believing that the dawn of God could rise over us all. Is the Kingdom a possibility for us, as it was for Noah? Or will we, like René, turn back to wallow in our unsolved perplexities?

✳ *God, when you knock on our door, give us courage to believe that it could be you, and that the new dawn is possible for us and all humanity. Amen*

God builds the Kingdom with us – from the other side

This beautiful passage contrasts the stability of Jerusalem with the confusion of the present when our rigging hangs loose and the sail refuses to spread. In this vision of Jerusalem the old terrors are over, the oppression of unjust taxation (verse 18) is gone and the land stretches out before you in peace, and Zion is secure. Here there are broad rivers and streams protected by the king. Everything will be divided fairly and forgiveness reigns.

The Bible constantly holds out a vision of this kind, not just as a chimera, to take our minds off the difficulties we face. This reality is promised. What we cannot do is to lose sight of its possibility in the struggle for justice today in the societies we inhabit. If we begin to think it is not possible, then we have lost the capacity to build it. Life is not just struggling on to keep things going as best we can. It is having a vision of what can be and working to build that kingdom, confident that God is building it as well, from the other side as it were, until we meet.

It's a long way off but inside it
There are quite different things going on:
Festivals at which the poor man
Is king and the consumptive is
Healed ...
It's a long way off, but to get
There takes no time and admission
Is free, if you will purge yourself
Of desire, and present yourself with
Your need only and the simple offering
Of your faith, green as a leaf.   *R S Thomas*
From 'The Kingdom', taken from H'm which appears in
'Later Poems 1972-1982' by RS Thomas,
reprinted by permission of Papermac

✶ *God, you are waiting for us*
to send out the dove of anticipation from the ark of our
*   desire.*
Help us to release him into the future
so that he can return
with the gift of faith, green as a leaf, in his beak,
and we can rejoice to know that you are King forever.
*   Amen*

TO THINK ABOUT

What are you really looking for in life? What are your real hopes and desires? Have you had the courage to keep looking, or have you just given up? Do you believe there is anything 'out there' for you to look for?

If you belong to a Christian group of any kind, ask them what they are looking for. What sort of society are they trying to build? Do they think it is possible? Ask them why they have stopped sending birds out from their ark.

FOR ACTION

Spend some time working out what the person you love most is hoping for in the relationship you have between you. Talk to him or her about whether it is possible to achieve what s/he wants. Then ask the other person to ask the same questions of you.

HOLINESS

Notes based on the New Revised Standard Version by
Simon Barrow

Simon Barrow is an adult education and training officer in the Anglican Diocese of Southwark (London, UK). He works with inner city parishes and has a practical concern for the link between spirituality and social issues.

For many people in today's world, 'holiness' has about it the ring of suffocating piety, while 'lordship' is often uncomfortably associated with those who misuse religion for violent or oppressive ends. But as biblical metaphors these terms mean something quite different. Over the next two weeks, our readings show that God's holiness is the basis for the renewal of human hope, and that God's lordship not only judges all human systems of domination, but opens up a fresh understanding of power and its responsible use.

---

a. Holy is the Lord

8th Sunday before Christmas, November 2   *Exodus 3.1-15*
Holiness that liberates

Both the sovereignty (lordship) and unutterable purity (holiness) of God are testified by the three signs contained in this passage, the foundation text for the whole Judaeo-Christian religious pilgrimage.

First we have the flaming bush and the sight of the 'back of God', symbols of mystery and unapproachability in our midst.

Next, we have Yahweh hearing the cry of an oppressed, minority people – demonstrating the intimacy of God's intentions for humanity and the moral quality of divine holiness as a passion for justice in society.

Lastly, there is the promise of the covenant (implied in verse 13), the offer of unending faithfulness from the One in whom past, present and future are alone fulfilled (verse 14).

Far from being a pious irrelevance, the holiness and lordship of God have radical consequences for the ordering and purpose of all human life. It is the freeing of slaves rather than a purely religious epiphany which characterizes the locus of divine salvation.

✳ *Spirit of freedom and unity, direct our lives*
into the ways of justice and peace, for your name's sake.

Monday November 3   *2 Chronicles 5.2-14*

Two kinds of sovereignty

The origins of the Holy One of Israel lay in the story of a nomadic people enslaved in Egypt, freed by the agency of God, formed around a divine covenant (agreement) of mutual faithfulness, and now – in the period of monarchy and settlement – established through a Temple hosting the key religious symbols of those remarkable events.

A royal lineage was established in direct contravention of Yahweh's will, according to the first book of Samuel. Nevertheless, Chronicles is royal history and tells of the triumphs of Solomon in that vein. But many other upheavals recorded by the Chronicler also demonstrate the demanding nature of God in the face of a people who frequently neglected justice and the service of the poor. So what we have here is far more than hagiography. It is a constant reminder of the character of the liberator God (verse 10) – in strict contrast to the kind of 'lordship' represented by earthly kings and emperors.

✳ *Spirit of light and life,*
deliver us from the temptations of power
and the neglect of the needy.

Tuesday November 4   *Psalm 50*

Sacred integrity

What preserved Israel as a nation dedicated to a holy God, Yahweh, was their extensive sacrificial system. Here they recalled the divine presence on Mount Zion (verses 2, 5) and committed every action and event of their lives (verse 8) to the service of God.

This was fine in theory. In practice, ritual obedience proved open to three kinds of abuse. The first was that of limiting the universal dominion, or lordship, of God – rather than using specific religious moments to draw attention to God as the originator and liberator of all creation (verses 10-11, 15).

Then again, sacrificial loyalty could easily become empty rhetoric when it was not properly matched by holy – that is, just and true – behaviour. This concern (verses 16, 19) is strongly echoed by the eighth century prophets, Amos and Hosea.

Lastly, the definition of a people dedicated to a holy God through sacrifice was heavily dependent on tribal and familial loyalty. This sacred bonding was especially at risk when the meaning of the ritual was surrendered in everyday life (verses 18, 20). The antidote to these failings, suggests the Psalmist, is thanksgiving – an attitude of grateful devotion (in actions as well as words) to the character of God as the creative and freeing source of all life. This is the practical prescription which bridges the huge cultural and social gap between our own times and those of a strange and ancient people.

✳ *Spirit of holiness,*
fill all our words and actions with your justice.

Wednesday November 5   *Psalm 99*
Living out of the past
This Psalm can perhaps best be understood by starting at the end and working back to the beginning. For ancient Israelites, formed by the Exodus and preserved in hope through all kinds of national trial, Mount Zion (verse 9) was, above all, the place of holy remembrance. God's faithfulness in the tumult of life was to be found in the present, most certainly, but it was also located in the great figures of the past (verse 6), and in the historical and symbolic events (verses 7, 8) by which the mysterious ways of the Almighty could be attested.

The people of Yahweh were a people of memory. They lived towards an unknown future in the strength of a constantly rekindled past. It seemed to them (verse 4) that God's reign of justice had already come. What it required for active fulfilment was a transforming attitude of acknowledgment and acceptance (verses 1-3).

Today we have a very different sense of history. Memory is often obliterated by the pace of technological change, and hope is displaced by the despairing search for security in material comfort. What we need is not a backward-looking response to the challenges of the modern situation, but rootedness in a future promise arising from the past. And if this distinction appears peculiar to us, we need look no further than the historical hope in the holy God of Israel to see what it might mean.

*❋ Spirit of power and might,
  kindle in us a strong belief that your commonwealth of
  love is what drives our future.*

Thursday November 6   *John 6.60-71*

Who is the Christ?

The Gospel of John is littered with paradox. Having told his
followers that unless they eat his flesh they cannot be united with
him (John 6.53), the Johannine Christ now says (verse 63) that
the flesh is useless. Having elsewhere stated that no one can
come to the fatherliness of God except through him, he now
states the opposite (verse 65). Perhaps understandably, some of
the disciples gave up in despair.

There is, however, meaning in riddles. The stating of
opposites in absolute tension was a fairly common Jewish
rhetorical device to point towards that divine truth which lies
beyond contradiction. In this case, the Gospel writer's clear intent
is to show that the loving mystery of God is decisively revealed in
the humanity of Jesus, the Holy One of God (verse 69).

That the divine purpose should be disclosed in a person – and
ultimately in the fullness of all personhood (John 10.30) – was a
hope rooted deep in the Jewish faith. That it should take shape
through an obscure rebellious Galilean prophet, and that it might
embrace even the one most alienated from God (verse 70), was a
matter of shock and surprise. God's love comes to be seen as
both terrifically specific and fiercely indiscriminate.

*❋ Spirit of grace and truth,
  may your tender purposes consume our wilful flesh.*

Friday November 7   *Acts 14.8-20*

War among the gods?

In a strongly pluralistic age, the intense religious tribalism of much
of our biblical heritage can be at best uncomfortable and at worst
offensive. But in this story we witness the seeds of a more
accommodating approach to the sovereignty of the God of Jesus
Christ in a multi-faith world. In the context of their own religious
understanding, the people of Lystra received Paul and Barnabas
with warmth and enthusiasm. Their alarming attempts to deify their
visitors horrified the early Christians. But if, as in the Orthodox
tradition, God becomes human so that humanity might be assumed

into God, maybe their confusion glimpsed the truth nonetheless!

The message of the apostles was one of God's grace mediated through creation and in the joys of human relationship. Such generosity of spirit seemed alien to Paul's former co-religionists, and they turned their anger on him. Today also the overflowing grace of the Christlike God is too much for some who call themselves Christian. There are still those who wish to keep God all to themselves, and to deny the universal generosity (verse 17) which is at the heart of God's holiness.

✳ *Spirit of wisdom and knowledge, enable us to embrace all cultures and nations in your boundless love.*

Saturday November 8   *Revelation 4.1-11* *
An open heaven

The authorship of the Book of Revelation is uncertain, but we know that it derived from sources close to the Johannine community and that it was written to encourage and inspire Christian communities suffering under the weight of Roman oppression. In this setting, John's Apocalypse envisages a time of final conflict between the powers of darkness and the suffering love of God, revealed in the Holy Lamb (Revelation 5.6). Many commentators believe that the ascription of Babylon as the kingdom of evil is a reference to Rome's imperial system, veiled under threat of persecution.

This passage with its mysterious and impenetrable imagery, holds out for a time when God will be all in all. The image of a door in heaven vividly portrays the unveiling of God's holy ways – the dethroning of evil and the triumph of the purposes of love.

In an age of continuing violence and injustice against the vulnerable, Christians are called to be people of the Lamb, seeking to flesh out God's promises in all spheres of life.

✳ *Spirit of suffering love, sustain us in times of trial and keep us loyal to your promise.*

TO THINK ABOUT
● In what ways does God's holy lordship differ from the ways in which human beings typically 'lord it' over each other?
● What practical witness can we and our church community give to this difference?

---

b. A holy people

An insistent call
The book of Leviticus (meaning 'And God called') and the first ten chapters of Numbers are all about the institution of a covenant agreement between a holy God and a holy people. These writings address the important question as to what happens when the glory of God appears in the midst of everyday life. How can holiness become a common path?

As always, the answer lies in forms of obedience which reflect the eternal purity and justice of God within the limitations of a particular time, place and culture. We should, therefore, expect that at least some of the regulations highlighted in Leviticus will seem odd or irrelevant to our current concerns. In fact, much of this passage has contemporary relevance. The admonitions on gleaning (verses 9 and 10) are about economic justice and God's special concern for the poor. The bans on theft and false witness (verses 11 and 12) became part of what we know as the Decalogue, or Ten Commandments.

Verses 5-8, concerning sacrifice (cf. Leviticus 7.15-18), are much stranger to our ears. The concern is that meat offered in sacrifice should be fresh rather than foul – in other words, that we should offer only the best from daily life in the service of God. The practice described here may be redundant, but its spirit and intent live on.

✳ ***God of all, may our lives and our love of neighbour***
be a fitting sacrifice to you.

A distinctive people
Holiness is commonly assumed to be a matter of personal virtue in our increasingly individualistic modern world. To the ancient Israelites this notion would have made no sense at all. The whole point of ritual and devotional cleanliness was to create a holy nation – a people radically different in practice and purpose from surrounding nations.

Today some of the Levitical regulations and bans which ensured the purity of persons and property for the Holy Nation seem obscure and barbaric. But for the people of Israel, despised and outnumbered by cruel enemies, it was a matter of bare survival. Anything that made them more vulnerable was forbidden.

The prohibitions on child sacrifice (in the Ammonite worship of the god Molech) and on meddling in the realm of the dead (the implications of verse 6) make obvious sense. But later Levitical bans – on much foreign trade, and therefore, the wearing of clothes made of two materials (Leviticus 19.19), and on homosexuality (20.13) – are culturally specific. The former was held to result in economic vulnerability, the latter to weaken the numerical strength of the nation.

Christian people today are still called to live and promote holiness in the world. And while many of the specific Levitical commands are no longer necessary or right for us, the biblical challenge to distinctive, holy living in the spheres of society, the economy, politics and interpersonal relationships is as strong as ever. God's call, now as then, is to discover new ways of faithfulness for new, demanding times.

✳ *God of justice, make your ways known among us as we seek to become your holy people.*

Tuesday November 11   *Genesis 4.1-10* ✳
Beyond death-dealing
The tragic tale of Cain and Abel is one of the best known stories in the Bible. In Luke 11.51 it forms part of Jesus' diatribe against those teachers and doctors of the Law who perpetrated a religion of death rather than life.

The occupations of the two brothers are not arbitrary. They represent the two basic livelihoods of an early part of human history. Likewise the sacrifice of the first-fruits, which required no altar or cultic institution, was part of a cycle of offering and blessing whereby God was intimately connected with the very nature upon which human survival depended.

So Cain's anger was not petty pique but a cry for survival. His economic failure was not his fault. But in the religious culture of the day it was equated with lack of divine favour.

Scrambling for precious resources, seeking particular favour from God, the resolution of conflict by violence, the refusal of filial responsibility and (verse 7) the failure to acknowledge the dangerous consequences of power: all these are generic themes in the biblical story and in our human experience.

By contrast to the culture of death to which Cain submitted, the way of holiness is the way of life, co-operation and sharing for all. This is a way characterized by effective love, rather than by the creation of victims (verse 10) on an altar of conflict.

✳ *God of plenty,*
turn our world away from the paths of greed and
violence.

Wednesday November 12   1 John 3.9-18 *
Love is all you need
There is another way. That is the hopeful message of this powerful sermon addressed to early Christian communities facing division and suffering in the world.

The first epistle of John emphasizes that Jesus came in the flesh, that to know God is to practise love in human community, and that earthly faithfulness is the true mark of eternal life.

For the writer, holiness is a matter of distinctiveness. And real Christian distinctiveness is to be found, not in adherence to esoteric doctrines or extraordinary practices, but through loyalty to God in the depths of human ordinariness: good deeds, the pursuit of peace and truthfulness, never-failing care for our sisters and brothers. It is by faithful action that we become a people honouring the God who comes to us in the Word made flesh. As Stanley Hauweras has said, the church does not *have* a social ethic, the church (rightly responding to the divine call) *is* a social ethic.

✳ *God of hope, breathe into us your spirit of boundless*
giving.

Thursday November 13   Mark 7.14-23 *
True cleanliness
According to Thomas More 'tradition is a pool of imagination and not a basis for authority'. But in Jesus' day, some doctors of the Law used tradition like a sledgehammer to demand obedience. Christ caused uproar when he boldly accused them of abandoning the true spirit of God's command in favour of misguided human precepts (Mark 7.8). In this passage Jesus argues that the true fruit of holiness is the quality of life and response which issues from a person's inner being. It is not a matter of ritual purity determined by, for example, what we eat.

Today Christians are unlikely to judge spiritual maturity by Levitical standards of ritual cleanliness. But it is not uncommon for us to make doctrinal purity, or assent to the traditions of a particular denomination, the criterion for judging someone's loyalty to God. Surely this is as unhelpful as the legalism of those whom Jesus argued with? It is the heart which determines the moral and spiritual quality of our life, and it is the intentions of the heart which are subject to divine scrutiny.

✳ *God of mercy, spare us from false judgement*
and order our minds in accordance with your gracious
plan.

Friday November 14   *Matthew 23.25-28*
Perils of false piety
It is salutary for Christian people to recognize that Jesus' most savage indictments seem always to be reserved for the properly religious and the theologically educated.

Christ is quick to show mercy towards sinners, vulnerable people and those without pretence. He even commends the faithfulness of those who, like the good Samaritan and the centurion with a sick servant, belong to another faith or ethnic group. But he has no time for those who employ pious words and doctrinal eloquence to mask their own shortcomings and to condemn others.

Our world seems continually ripe for religious self-righteousness and exclusivity. Many are the Christian groups who claim a monopoly of truth and who seek to bar those they regard unfavourably from the route to salvation. Such behaviour is far from holy. Indeed it dishonours Jesus Christ, whose lordship derives from the one God whose love extends to all.

✳ *God of the outcast, may our expression of faith*
never be a stumbling block for those who need your love.

Saturday November 15   *1 Peter 2.13-25*
Following Christ together
The first letter of Peter was written to persecuted Christians throughout Asia Minor at a time when the Roman Empire threatened their faith and their communal life. Its central theme, therefore, is hope. By identifying with Christ's sufferings we shall eventually be delivered from oppression and restored to full life.

257

Once again, the path of holiness is one of distinctiveness. Christians are called to humility, service, love and support for rightly exercised authority.

Of course it is not always right for Christians to obey human institutions. When they become demonic, as in Revelation 13, they are to be firmly resisted. And the writer of this letter, perhaps conscious of imperial spies who might be reading it, presupposes as the basis for his argument the duty of leaders to uphold justice against injustice (verse 14). Similarly, developing Christian conscience and our understanding of core Gospel themes has now led all churches to oppose slavery (cf. verse 18).

Nevertheless, humble and effective public service are key areas where contemporary Christian discipleship can bear witness to the God who is in all and over all. Moreover, the Church as a collective body has continually to decide how it will respond to the actions of governors and rulers – especially when they abuse human rights and needs. The path of true holiness is rarely easy and often involves difficult choices, personally and corporately.

✳ *God of authority, strengthen us to stand up for right with wisdom, forbearance and humility.*

TO THINK ABOUT

● Do you perceive a shift in meaning and practice for God's holy people from Levitical times to Gospel times? Think of examples.
● What is the difference (and the connection) between personal and collective holiness?

FOR ACTION

1. Produce, or reconsider, a church mission statement which spells out how your congregation aims to be a distinctive, holy people in your community.
2. List the ways in which members of your church have an opportunity to exemplify the holy way of Christ in the world.
3. Consider offering prayerful and practical support for a Christian community – neighbouring or far away – which is seeking to witness to the love of Christ in the face of violence or injustice.

PRACTICAL FAITH
Epistle of James

Notes based on the New Revised Standard Version by
Michael Townsend

Michael J. Townsend is Chairman of the Leeds District of the Methodist Church (UK). He is the author of the Epworth Commentary on The Epistle of James and editor of Worshipping God Together (Epworth Press).

The Epistle of James was probably written by a Palestinian Jewish Christian around AD60. Some of its material may be derived from James the brother of Jesus. The author was writing to fellow Jewish Christians living in various parts of the Roman Empire. To help his readers to work out their faith in daily life, the author draws on resources of the teaching of Jesus, the Hebrew scriptures, contemporary thinkers and Jewish wisdom writings.

For further reading

Michael J Townsend, *The Epistle of James* Epworth Press 1994

J B Adamson, *James: The Man and His Message* Eerdmans 1989

6th Sunday before Christmas, November 16   *James 1.1-8*

Be single-minded

A test of how much we really want something is whether we are prepared to meet its cost. Today's reading stresses the importance of having a mature faith, able to cope with trials. This is described as 'wisdom' (verse 5). For James, this is the quality which enables believers to live their lives in the way God requires. If we know we are in need of such wisdom, we should ask for it, and we will receive it as a gift from God.

Yet, though God gives freely to those who ask, there is a condition. Some people are described as 'double-minded' (verse 8). This is a translation of a rare Greek word describing those whose fundamental allegiance is divided. They want to follow God's way, but at the same time they do not. That will not do. If we ask God to enable us to live as true disciples of Jesus we must be single-minded in following that through, and in accepting the consequences for our lifestyle. God cannot grant us this, of all things, unless we really mean it.

✳ *Grant us Lord, such a pure desire to walk in Christ's way, that we may receive from you the wisdom we need.*

Monday November 17   *James 1.9-11*
Equal before God

Most societies have a strong sense of class or caste. People are ranked and evaluated by their wealth or seeming importance. All too often such divisions creep into the life of the church. Yet in a quite fundamental sense the Christian message turns these conventional worldly judgments upside-down. The Christian community is one where rich and poor alike have the same calling by which to live or, as James puts it, in which to boast.

The thought is more startling than we at first realize. The believer who is lowly (as others see it) is a loved child of God. What could be of greater worth than that? Correspondingly, the wealthy Christian can rejoice in exactly the same salvation, recognizing that the wealth (which brings status as others see it) now counts for nothing. The implications of this for the life of fellowship within the church are truly revolutionary and Christians need continual reminders of it.

✳ *All that kills abundant living,*
    Let it from the earth be banned;
  Pride of status, race or schooling,
    Dogmas that affect your plan.
                                    Fred Kaan
                           (Methodist Publishing House)

Tuesday November 18   *James 1.12-19a*
The source of testing

Many people have a fatalistic attitude. When things go badly they assume that God is either punishing or testing them, and react with either resignation or anger. Today's reading offers a different perspective. Those who are being tested (a better translation than NRSV's 'tempted' in verse 13), should not say to themselves: 'It is God who is tempting me, so that I will fail this test'. Temptations come not from outside ourselves – and certainly not from God – but from within. There is something in us to which they appeal, and if there was not, they would have no force.

Not only does God not tempt us; it is from God that all good things come, and they come as gifts. The greatest of these is, of course, that God 'gave us birth by the word of truth' (verse 18), James' way of describing the new birth of Christian salvation. It is this which gives us power to resist temptation and to pass our tests.

✳ *Thank you God, for all your wonderful gifts.*

Wednesday November 19　　　　　　　　　　　　　*James 1.19b-27*

Moral improvement

Verses 23-24 echo the views of James' contemporaries, some of whom said that moral teachers were like mirrors in whom others could see themselves as they really were and thereby recognize the need for moral self-improvement. In James' illustration, those who carefully observe their features in a mirror, but then promptly forget what they look like, symbolize those who look into moral or spiritual teaching but fail to do anything about it. James is concerned that his readers should not only hear the message, but should also act upon it. Until hearing has been turned into action, the message has not been truly accepted.

As we look deeply into the Christian message, we must recognize the need for spiritual improvement. Reading the Bible, times of prayer, joining in fellowship groups and listening to sermons are not ends in themselves. Through them we should expect to grow in faith and in our understanding of what it means to be a Christian. The proof that we have done so will be seen in the way that faith is put to work in daily life.

✳ *Lord, help us to be doers of the word and not just hearers.*

Thursday November 20　　　　　　　　　　　　　*James 2.1-7*

No favouritism

Monday's reading stresses the equality of believers in the sight of God and each other. This is now given a vivid example.

Probably the Christian assembly into which these two people come is a meeting for decision-making or discipline, rather than for worship. The community is commanded not to treat them in a way which indicates that the wealthy person will be listened to with more respect than the poor person.

This might seem no more than common prudence; after all the

wealthy have no monopoly of wisdom or truthfulness. But James lifts it out of the realm of good advice into the realm of good news, insisting that Christians are those who believe in our 'glorious Lord Jesus Christ' (verse 1). What he has in mind is better represented by the REB: 'our Lord Jesus Christ who reigns in glory'. Favouritism is not only foolish, it is a denial of the reign of Christ whose Lordship is for all, rich and poor alike.

✳ *Life's poor distinctions vanish here;*
   Today the young, the old,
Our Saviour and his flock appear,
   One Shepherd and one fold.   James Montgomery
                                                    (1771-1854)

Friday November 21   *James 2.8-13*
Christian rules?

What place do rules or laws have in the Christian life? Keeping the rules (whether the Ten Commandments, the Sermon on the Mount or anything else) cannot be the means of salvation. The heart of Christian good news is that we are accepted and loved by God just as we are, not because of anything we have done. So where, if at all, do rules come in?

When James writes about fulfilling the 'royal law' (verse 8), he has in mind the way in which Jesus reinterpreted the Law of Moses. In the teaching of Jesus it is not a means of salvation, but it is a way of walking in the wisdom of God. This is particularly true of the 'love command' of Leviticus 19.18, quoted by James in verse 8 and by Jesus on five occasions. Our love for others will indeed be a measure of the reality of the faith we profess, perhaps the most important measure of all.

✳ *Give us, O Lord, hearts of love towards others,*
   that in serving them we may show our faith in you.

Saturday November 22   *James 2.14-26* ✱
Real faith

Faith, when it is real, demonstrates its reality in loving deeds. This practical Christianity is James' major contribution to how we understand our faith. In verses 15-16 he offers an example of a hollow profession of faith. It is strongly drawn so that we might recognize the absurdity of professing faith but not living it out. The argument is then developed through the story of Abraham, whose willingness to sacrifice his son Isaac is seen as the supreme example of faith and as radical obedience to God's command. To drive the point home, James then refers to Rahab, whose practical actions may be seen as a manifestation of her faith.

At every point, James insists that real faith is active and living, prepared to obey God's command even when the consequences cannot be foreseen. Today's reading may prod our consciences. If our faith has become something between ourselves and God, not involving our relationships with others, is it really Christian faith at all?

✳ *Lord, you placed me in the world*
to live in community.
Thus you taught me to love,
to share in life,
to struggle for bread and for justice,
your truth incarnate in my life.
So be it, Jesus.   Peggy M de Cuehlo, Uruguay
                From Your Will be Done (Christian Conference of Asia)

TO THINK ABOUT

● Re-read James 1.2-4. What trials come your way as a Christian? In what ways might they lead to growth in Christian maturity?

● In the light of James 2.1-4, how would you evaluate the way in which your own church fellowship handles differences of status, wealth and power within the congregation?

● Re-read James 2.8-13. In your view, what, if any, is the place of rules in the living of Christian life? Or was Augustine right when he said: 'Love God and do as you like'?

5th Sunday before Christmas, November 23   *James 3.1-12*

The dangerous tongue

A minister looked at the No Smoking notice on the wall of her church hall and commented: 'It would be more to the point if it said No Gossiping'. Many of us, while carefully avoiding, say violence or theft, do not mind a good gossip!

James' tirade against the misuse of the tongue springs from his role as a teacher. He knows something of the power of words and the effect they have, for good or ill.

We might think he exaggerates: perhaps he needs to! We

have an infinite capacity for self-deception. What we think of as rudeness on someone else's part, we call plain speaking when we do it ourselves. Careless speech can destroy lives and ruin people's reputations. Few things can as quickly destroy fellowship in a congregation and its ability to display the winsomeness of the gospel. Our speech indicates what is in our heart (see Matthew 15.18-20).

✳ *Lord, may the tongues which 'Holy' sang*
   keep free from all deceiving ...   *Liturgy of Malabar*

Monday November 24   *James 3.13-18*

Peacemakers

Again James encourages his readers to show by the way they live that they are motivated by divine wisdom rather than the evil which lurks in the human heart. The end result of wise living is, he says, that peace is the seed-bed of justice (verse 18, following the translation in NJB). This reverses what we think of as the usual order of things, where true peace can only flourish once justice and righteousness have been established (see Isaiah 32.17). James is echoing Jesus, referring not to those who seek peace – and especially not peace at any price – but to those who make peace (see Matthew 5.9). How can that be done, in the world in which we live, except by seeking out the root causes of conflicts and the injustices which lie behind many situations of violence, and seeking to put them right?

In making peace, whether between individuals or groups, we do indeed create the conditions in which righteousness and justice can flourish and come to harvest.

✳ *Give us courage, we pray, to stand up*
   for your truth.
   Make us apostles of your love, justice,
   hope, reconciliation and peace.   *Stanley Mogoba,*
              Southern Africa – From Oceans of Prayer (NCEC)

Tuesday November 25   *James 4.1-6*

Friends of God

When Christians become embroiled in conflicts and disputes, give in to their baser passions and even engage in violence, they prove that they have ceased to be friends of God. Such behaviour is 'friendship with the world' (verse 4).

The difficulty is that Christians are called to live out their discipleship in the world, not to withdraw from it. John's Gospel records Jesus praying for his disciples about this very thing (see John 17.15-16). In some respects the world has been affected by Kingdom values Christians have taught and lived down the centuries. In other respects the world is still organized in opposition to God's purposes and in ignorance of God's wisdom. Christians are called to be alert, sifting and evaluating all that comes to them, recognizing the need to reject whatever repudiates God's way of doing things. This calls for daily vigilance and is no easy task. We need faith and prayer to accomplish it successfully.

* *Give to us Lord,*
  hearts and minds to seek your way,
  grace to receive it
  and courage to embrace it.

Wednesday November 26   James 4.7-12

True repentance

Christians today are reticent about speaking of the devil, not least because the word conjures up unhelpful images. James undoubtedly believed in a personal devil; those who find such a belief difficult still need to recognize the reality of evil and the problems in dealing with it.

Our reading contains three commands. Firstly, evil is to be resisted, and this is accompanied by a confidence-giving assurance about the result. Secondly, we need to purify ourselves, morally rather than ritually, because evil brings contamination in its wake. Thirdly, there needs to be genuine repentance, symbolized by mourning and weeping. There are times, the writer suggests, when we need to subject our lives to serious scrutiny and put right what has gone wrong. We are given the assurance that when we do this, God will lift us from despair and grant us forgiveness because that is the nature of a God who is always constant towards us (see 1.17).

* *Almighty God, give us we pray, true penitence,*
  time for amendment of life,
  and the grace and comfort of your Holy Spirit.

Planning God's way

We all makes plans, for ourselves and for our families. There is nothing wrong with that, but the attitude of mind in which we do it is all-important.

In today's reading James addresses traders who have been overheard making their plans. Unfortunately, they have made them in the wrong way, speaking and acting as if they were in sole charge of their lives. They have failed to take into account the fact that, if they are Christians, God should reign over their lives. In the light of that, a little humility in making their plans would be appropriate. James does not want them to add 'If the Lord wishes' as a facile or pious formula, but wishes their lives to be conducted in accordance with God's will. Christian lives have an ultimate built-in accountability, and an important part of faithful living is the search for God's purposes within our daily planning and thinking. Our planning, therefore, needs to be careful and prayerful, open to the possibility that God might have other things in mind for us of which we have not yet even dreamed.

✳ *Lord, may all our hoping and planning*
be in accordance with your will and purpose for our lives.

Money and power

Today's reading includes the strongest denunciation of the misuse of wealth and power in the New Testament. The rich people addressed in this passage are not the same as those addressed in 4.13-17. Here there is no possibility of repentance, just condemnation for those who have used their wealth to defraud and oppress the poor. Such people, James says, will have God to reckon with.

It is a curious fact that few people are willing to describe themselves as rich! However much we have, we always seem to want more. Yet in relative terms, many people in developed nations are rich, at least by the standards of the developing world. Certainly there is a call to act justly and lovingly with our personal wealth, but the issues are bigger yet. Rich Christians in a poor world are caught up in mechanisms of international trade which oppress the poor and we need to recognize that. It calls for a commitment from Christians to work and campaign for a fairer and more just world (refer back to the notes for May 11-17).

✱ *O God, whose word is fruitless*
  when the mighty are not put down,
      the humble remain humiliated,
      the hungry are not filled,
      and the rich are:
  Make good your word,
  and begin with us.
  Open our hearts and unblock our ears
  to hear the voices of the poor
  and share their struggle;
  and send us away empty with longing
  for your promises to come true
  in Jesus Christ. Amen   Janet Morley
                         Tell out My Soul (Christian Aid 1990)

Saturday November 29   *James 5.13-19*

A healed community

Today's reading is often taken to be about healing. It is just as much about prayer.

Prayer is commended for those who are suffering (verse 13), those who are sick (verse 14) and for the whole Christian community (verse 16). The encouragement to prayer in these situations is reinforced by the example of Elijah. Nor can we say: 'God listened to Elijah because he was a great prophet, but we cannot expect the same result from our prayers', because Elijah was a human being like ourselves (verse 17).

We may have some difficulties with James' assumption that prayer for healing will automatically be answered (verse 15) because that is not everyone's experience. But we ought not to miss the strong emphasis on our ministry of prayer for one another. We are to pray and care for one another in both health and sickness, and that includes concern for each other's spiritual welfare (verse 19). Through all these activities the whole Christian community experiences true healing.

✱ *How can we fail to be restored,*
  When reached by love that never ends?   F Pratt Green
    (MPH)

TO THINK ABOUT
- Re-read James 3.1-12. Do you think James exaggerates the dangers of an unguarded tongue? How can we ensure that we do not sin in what we say?
- In the light of James 4.1-4, what does it mean in today's context to be a 'friend of God' or a 'friend of the world'?

FOR ACTION
Re-read James 5.1-6. Decide on either or both of (a) a way in which you can use your personal resources to make the world a fairer place (b) a way in which you can campaign for fairer structures in world trading.

ADVENT 1. Come and join the celebration

Notes based on the Hebrew Bible by
Malcolm Weisman

The Rev Malcolm Weisman is visiting Rabbi to small Jewish Communities throughout the British Isles, senior Jewish Chaplain to HM Forces and Jewish Chaplain to the University of Oxford. He has also lectured on Judaism to the Methodists for World Mission annual Conference.

As we enter Advent and turn our minds to Christmas, what can we learn from the Jewish Community about 'Celebration'? Malcolm Weisman writes:

As I reflect on the selected verses, I aim to stress their significance in two ways. First I stress the Jewish approach both from a spiritual and contemporary ritual point of view, laying emphasis where possible on the family aspect of our celebrations. Secondly, I seek the universal message of these verses which have a moral foundation common to both observant Christians and Jews. I hope I have succeeded.

Advent Sunday, November 30   *Isaiah 51.7-11 **
Why celebrate?

To Jews in particular, these verses are a source of great comfort. Though man's inhumanity to other human beings frequently plumbs the most obscene depths of despair, there is confidence that at the end of it all there is light, 'gladness and joy' will come and 'sorrow and sighing will flee away' as in verse 11. But optimism for the future always depends, as the prophet reminds us in verses 9-10, on our never forgetting our roots in the past. It is important, whether we be Christians or Jews, never to forget the eternal and always contemporary relevance of our tradition and history. On that basis, whatever the trials and traumas we have to endure in our national and/or personal lives, goodness and love really will triumph at the end of the day.

✳ *Alleluia!*
Praise Yahweh, my soul!

I will praise Yahweh all my life,
I will make music to my God as long as I live.
He keeps faith for ever,
gives justice to the oppressed,
gives food to the hungry;
Yahweh sets prisoners free. Psalm 146.1,2,6b and 7 (NJB)

Monday December 1   *Exodus 12.21-28*

The Passover and liberation

These verses are at the heart of the great Jewish festival of Passover, and are obviously central to Easter as well. The very name 'Passover' in English derives from the words in verse 23 which indicate that God will pass over those houses whose door posts are daubed with the blood of the slaughtered Paschal lambs, en route to the carrying out of the tenth plague – the death of the Egyptian first-born.

To this day, the events leading up to the Exodus from Egypt are recounted by Jews at the Passover supper that marks the commencement of the festival, the very selfsame last supper presided over by Jesus before his death.

The Jewish celebration of this festival has many themes. One of these is of universal significance. The Israelites were freed from slavery, not to do as they wished, but to be free under a Law of God to be handed to them in due course by Moses at Sinai. The festival therefore stresses that the only true freedom is found in a code of morals based on what we know as the 'Judaeo-Christian ethic'. Such a concept is not easy to grasp. That is why the Israelites wandered in the wilderness for forty years to get rid of their slave mentality. Only people accustomed to, or born in freedom, were to receive the Law at Sinai.

Modern parallels are obvious. Do new democracies in Eastern Europe, for example, really appreciate a non-communist system? Understanding moral freedom and practising it properly in our personal and national lives is not always that easy.

✱ *Alleluia!*
From the rising of the sun to its setting,
praised be the name of Yahweh!
Supreme over all nations is Yahweh ...
His throne is set on high,
but he stoops to look down on heaven and earth.
He raises the poor from the dust ...
to give them a place among princes. Psalm 113.1-8 (NJB)

The Passover and new beginnings

These verses are as relevant today to observant Jews as they were at the time they were composed. Such Jews during the whole of the nine-day Passover festival will not eat any food that has bread-like substance in it or has been in contact with such items. Indeed, the whole of a Jewish family home, during the weeks immediately before the festival, will be very precisely cleaned from top to bottom to ensure that no bread-like substances are to be found anywhere on the premises. Any such provisions must be removed from the home or have their ownership legally transferred from Jewish to non-Jewish ownership for the whole period of the Passover! This whole exercise must surely be the origin of 'spring cleaning'!

Symbolically, the festival of Passover denotes a new fresh year, a clean start to one's relationship with family, friends and the world generally. If you have not got your relationships in that respect right, what better than to start this when spring has truly arrived and hopefully the world is really beginning to look a better place. Optimism in all things is 'the name of the game' here.

✸ *May God show kindness and bless us,*
and make his face shine upon us.
Then the earth will acknowledge your ways,
and all nations your power to save.   Psalm 67.1-2 (NJB)

The festival of Tabernacles

To the Jew, these verses are certainly not a recounting of a curious ceremony now lost in the dim mists of primeval time. The divine ordination to the Israelites 'to live in booths during the feast of the seventh month' is observed to this day in the Hebrew month of *Tishre* by Jews the world over throughout the festival of Tabernacles. Weather permitting, observant Jewish families erect a temporary dwelling with at least three sides, and a very temporary open-to-the-stars roof, in their back gardens. In Israel if people live in a flat, they build them on their balconies. The one stipulation is that the see-through roof must be exposed to the elements, so a *Succah* (as the booth is called in Hebrew) cannot be erected under, for example an over-hanging tree or balcony. The purpose? Only a week before, the great period of penitence, the New year, culminating in *Yom Kippur*, the 25-hour fast of

Atonement, has just taken place. Some people might therefore feel that their penitential exercises are thankfully over for yet one more year. No, says God – your life on earth is impermanent; you are not the masters of this world. Spending some time in a booth in the autumn, when this festival takes place, when the weather – even in the Middle East – can be uncertain, helps humankind to remember its true humble place in the order of the universe.

Surely this is a message of universal relevance. It is best summed up by the Rabbi who on his death bed exhorted his disciples to repent the moment before they die. 'How do we know when we will die?' they ask. 'That is the point,' says the Rabbi. 'You do not, so you must behave the whole time!'

✳ *Living God, you have told us what you desire of us.*
So help us each day to do justly, to love mercy,
and to walk humbly with you.   *Based on Micah 6.8*

Thursday December 4   *1 Maccabees 4.41-59*

The festival of lights

For the benefit of readers who do not have access to the Apocrypha, here is today's text:

'Judas then ordered his men to keep the Citadel garrison engaged until he had purified the sanctuary. Next, he selected priests who were blameless and zealous for the Law to purify the sanctuary and remove the stones of the 'Pollution' to some unclean place.

They discussed what should be done about the altar of burnt offering which had been profaned, and very properly decided to pull it down, rather than later be embarrassed about it since it had been defiled by the gentiles. They therefore demolished it and deposited the stones in a suitable place on the hill of the Dwelling to await the appearance of a prophet who should give a ruling about them. They took unhewn stones, as the Law prescribed, and built a new altar on the lines of the old one. They restored the Holy Place and the interior of the Dwelling, and purified the courts. They made new sacred vessels, and brought the lamp-stand, the altar of incense, and the table into the Temple. They burned incense on the altar and lit the lamps on the lamp-stand, and these shone inside the Temple. They placed the loaves on the table and hung the curtains and completed all the tasks they had undertaken.

On the twenty-fifth of the ninth month, Chislev, in the year 148 they rose at dawn and offered a lawful sacrifice on the new altar of burnt offering which they had made. The altar was dedicated, to the sound of hymns, zithers, lyres and cymbals, at the same time of the year and on the same day on which the gentiles had originally profaned it. The whole people fell prostrate in adoration and then praised Heaven who had granted them success. For eight days they celebrated the dedication of the altar, joyfully offering burnt offerings, communion and thanksgiving sacrifices. They ornamented the front of the Temple with crowns and bosses of gold, renovated the gates and storerooms, providing the latter with doors. There was no end of rejoicing among the people, since the disgrace inflicted by the gentiles had been effaced. Judas, with his brothers and the whole assembly of Israel, made it a law that the days of the dedication of the altar should be celebrated yearly at the proper season, for eight days beginning on the twenty-fifth of the month of Chislev, with rejoicing and gladness' (1 Maccabees 4.41-59 – NJB).

The direct modern commemoration of the rededication of the Temple in Jerusalem described here is to be found in what the Jews call the 'Festival of Lights' or 'Renewal' – in Hebrew *Chanukah*. This is a joyful eight-day celebration of the Maccabees' victory over superior Syrian-Greek Forces, which enabled the Jews to consecrate the Temple to the service of God. The focal point was the re-lighting of the seven-branched candelabrum. Unfortunately only one cruse of rededicated oil – enough for one day – was available but miraculously it lasted for eight days. So on this day, Jews light one candle on an eight-branched lamp on the first night, increasing the candles one by one each night of the eight days, to mark this extra ordinary happening.

These events were actually achieved through a remarkable military campaign inspired by the great general, Judas Maccabeus. Yet the festival prayers hardly mention the military aspect. It is the spiritual renewal dimension that dominates the whole festival. Surely here is a message for all humankind, that the prophetic words that civilization will endure 'not by my might, not by my power but by my spirit' (Zechariah 4.6b – NJB) is the real guarantee of peaceful morality for the world.

✳ *God, create in me a clean heart,*
renew within me a resolute spirit,
do not thrust me away from your presence,
do not take away from me your spirit of holiness.
Psalm 51.10-11 (NJB)

Circumcision

In these verses is to be found what Judaism understands to be
the beginning of the special relationship between Jews and God.
Circumcision of all male children at the age of 8 days (see also
Genesis 21.4) is something practised by the great majority of
Jews to this day. By tradition, Abraham is the Father of the
Jewish people. With his son Isaac and grandson Jacob he
constitutes one of the three Patriarchs of the faith. But does that
mean that the Jews consider themselves a chosen people in the
sense of being superior to all others? No way! It merely means
that in the ancient world, Jews were the first to preach that basic
morality which surely is the foundation of modern civilization and
the Judaeo-Christian ethic.

Sometimes the Israelites propagated God's laws reluctantly.
Often they failed to live up to it themselves! But on the whole they
did not do too badly, especially with the prophets keeping an eye
on them! The message of these verses however is surely a
universal one. Circumcision of the heart and mind is just as
important as the ritual itself. They remind all believers in God,
through whatever tradition they follow, that civilization depends
on all people having a covenant with God. That is the only way to
a true appreciation of what is right and good in this world.

✳ *Guide my feet to walk in thy commandments*
And thy righteous ways,
And may thy mercies be turned upon me.   *Berakoth*

The Sabbath

God rested on the seventh day from all his activity in creating our
world. In Jewish tradition people do the same in recognition of
God's sovereignty over the universe. We do this to remind
ourselves that we are not 'top dog' in our existence. To this very
day, observant Jews mark this concept by ceasing from all
creative or secular activity on Saturday. So did early Christians till
the Sabbath was moved within their tradition to Sunday to mark
the resurrection. Thank goodness for a day off, without which
human life would be a drudge! The Sabbath should be a day of
joy, of relaxation with family and friends, a day of leisurely prayer
and reflection. It should also enable families to have time to get to
know each other. Certainly this is the case in the traditional

Jewish family when the secular world is forgotten, even to the extent of the telephone and television being ignored. Each meal on the Sabbath is a ritual occasion where the generation gap can be bridged by meaningful conversation.

This idea is surely universal in its significance. A Jewish philosopher once said, 'It is not so much the Jews that kept the Sabbath but the Sabbath that kept the Jews.' Surely that applies to Sunday in the Christian tradition as well. If only humankind could appreciate this approach!

✳ *For six days, if we are weary or bruised by the world,*
 if we think ourselves giants or cause others pain,
 there is never a moment to pause, and know what we
   should really be.
 On this, the Sabbath day, give us time.
 For six days we are torn between our private greed
 and the urgent needs of others,
 between the foolish noises in our ears
 and the silent prayer of our soul.
 On this, the Sabbath day, give us understanding and
   peace.

From Sabbath Prayers

TO THINK ABOUT

● Reflect on the roots of your faith which come from deep within the Jewish tradition. What are the most precious truths we hold in common?

● What challenges does the Jewish tradition make to the way Christians celebrate festivals and special days, especially Advent and Christmas?

FOR ACTION

Make a note of how you might answer a person of another faith who asks you about the significance of Christmas.

ADVENT 2. Light for our path

Notes based on the Revised English Bible by
Cluny Gillies

Cluny Gillies, a Methodist local preacher in Surrey (UK), has worked most of his life in professional book publishing. He is editor of IBRA's parallel series of Bible reading notes – Light for our Path – and the Preachers' Handbook.

Light shows us what we are, where we stand, and what the way forward looks like. It is used as a symbol of goodness, truth and sanity. It shows up the difference between good and evil. Its action reminds us of the way God sees into our inmost motives. If you shine white light into a prism, a rainbow emerges on the other side; so, surprisingly, white light turns out to be the source of the many bright colours that make life so vivid and enjoyable. Purity of vision works in the same way, as a basis for a richer understanding. These readings are about how the Bible acts as a guide to form the spirit and understanding that we need to help us take our own next step.

Bible Sunday, December 7   *2 Timothy 3.14 to 4.8 **

Light shows up essentials

In his poem *Prayer before birth* Louis MacNeice asks for an unborn child to have 'a white light at the back of my mind to guide me'. This passage assumes its reader already has a broad knowledge of the Jewish scriptures; when this was written the New Testament as we know it was not finally assembled, some of it perhaps not even written. How broadly do we know our Bible? Broadly means knowing different parts of it and holding them in balance with each other, building a knowledge base wide enough to provide stability, and to support persistent – but patient – discussion.

Timothy needed stability to withstand persecution from outside the church, and perversity inside it. Sometimes when people hit on new ideas, they believe that what they have found completely overturns all that has gone before, and the previous ideas sink out of sight simply because they are now unfashionable (later, they often resurface and eventually get a fairer valuation).

Timothy is asked to value what he has already been taught; and to identify the essentials that speak to his own time.

✳ **Lord, when we read the Bible**
help us to find the essentials of each passage,
and to apply them in the spirit of Jesus.

Monday December 8   *Psalm 119.105-112*

The many names of comfort

There was once a teenager who, when her family had shared sad news, would go and bury herself in a book. Some said she was indifferent; but that was not true at all. She went to the book for comfort *because* she was grieving. Here the psalmist says the law can revive and refresh. By the law he probably means all scripture: the rules, the stories, the prophecies and what they stand for. Have you any favourite passages? The more you look for, the more you will find.

Psalm 119 is elaborately structured: each section begins with a different Hebrew letter. That letter begins a word (here it is 'light'), so here the scriptures are praised for their light. But this is a labour of love: the complexity does not mean the feeling is any less genuine or strong. Verses 107 and 109 have a personal ring that dexterity alone could not give. The writer is telling how God's teaching has helped *him*.

✳ **Lord, help me to discover my way around your Bible,**
so that I will know where to find help.

Tuesday December 9   *Jeremiah 36.1-10* *

Brave witness

This could have happened yesterday. It is a scene constantly re-enacted in many countries (or companies) where Christians or others speak out against injustice: and, like Jeremiah, risk victimization or death for doing so. The prophecies were a carefully planned formal public recital of wrongs committed by the king and people over a period, written up and then held over for several months till the best moment came for maximum publicity. Jehoiakim is publicly contrasted with a previous and reforming king, Josiah. Later verses tell how Jehoiakim made a show of not being impressed; but all the same, he did remember to send round his police afterwards. Jeremiah knew what to expect, and had already vanished.

The Bible has many lists of injustices. Their setting may sometimes seem dated, but it is for us to recognize modern equivalents, and like Jeremiah to make sure that people know where wrongs exist. But prophets often pay a price: Jesus said some were murdered (Matthew 23.37).

✳ *Lord, we remember before you all who speak against evil and injustice. Defend them, let their words be heard, and help us to grow more brave, faithful and discerning, by cherishing their example.*

Human Rights Day, December 10   *Hebrews 4.12-13*

Cutting clean, cutting free

Today we use laser light in surgery and engineering, so we know better than ever how light can both illuminate and slice. As this is Human Rights Day, we should remember that the Bible in exposing injustice also cuts through into individual motives. What makes individuals power-hungry, manipulative or oppressive in the first place? What makes groups of others help them? What are the root causes of suspicion and enmity? Facing and trying to understand and challenge attitudes, in oneself and in others, can be like the surgeon's scalpel: wounding and painful, but in the end an aid to healing. If used unskilfully, though, it may do more harm than good.

Verse 12 says the word is active; it liberates, cutting people free, and setting things going. Knowing one's own hang-ups, or what enslaves a society, is a first step to freedom and action. Appreciating the fears of others helps us to approach them in a way they can accept, and lessens their isolation. The prayer below has always helped me because it means that since God sees into our deepest hearts, we are never ultimately lonely, and if there is anything inside ourselves that makes us afraid, he is there with us to share the burden, and is ready to help us cleanse our motives.

✳ *Almighty God, to whom all hearts are open, all desires known, and from whom no secrets are hid; cleanse the thoughts of our hearts by the inspiration of your Holy Spirit, that we may perfectly love you, and worthily magnify your holy name.*

From the Methodist Service Book

The ultimate

This Gospel associates light with goodness and glory; with Jesus
and his way of being, through which they shone (Mark 9.2-8).
Different translations of verse 5 use a variety of words: they say
that darkness (or evil) has never mastered, or overpowered, or
understood, or put out, the light. These are ways of proclaiming
that good is something far greater and stronger and more basic
than evil. Some people in John's time (and some today) believed
that evil and good were two equal and opposite sides struggling
for mastery (this belief is called dualism), but John's Gospel says
that is not so.

These verses also recall that people are free to reject or
misunderstand the gospel. We need to make sure they have no
excuse for doing so: and above all that we ourselves do not give
them any bad example that might support that excuse.

✶ *Lord, thank you for being all light and goodness.*
  Shine on me and drive out the darkness in me.
  Help me to let in your light and joy instead.

Open to all

Paul's experience of persecution and apparent failure may have
blinded some Christians to the truths he taught. Perhaps their
respect for success was stronger than their religious faith. Also,
new teachers had arrived, claiming to have a superior, hidden
knowledge of the gospel message, a secret only for the chosen
(and guess who did the choosing!). Paul is fighting against all
this. He says there is nothing convoluted or secret about
Christianity: it is not something that only special people can share
(in 1 Corinthians 13.8 he says knowledge itself is incomplete and
will vanish). On the contrary, Christianity is both clear and bright
(people who believe they have a great secret can be terribly
solemn and self-important).

Some cults (and some Christians) insist on absolute submission
in their converts. They may teach in a very controlling way, as if
there could only ever be one view. But Paul says 'it is not ourselves
that we proclaim.' His attitude is different, and his sufferings show
he is not in pursuit of comfort or money. Here there is a feeling that
his understanding is broad and lively, and theirs is narrow and
over-ingenious. Which type of teacher would you rather trust?

* *Lord, when I mention the gospel to others,*
  help me to put myself aside and trust you,
  so that you can work in your way.

Saturday December 13   1 John 1.1-10

Jesus is walking and talking

This carries Thursday's theme further and puts it in more concrete terms. Jesus is real: we touched him and walked with him; and he *was* the word – the command – of God in action. This reminds us that what we read has not fulfilled its purpose until it is made real in our behaviour. As Jesus was the walking, talking, active word of God, so must we be. And it also says that sharing Christ is a profoundly happy matter.

I was once in a group which discussed whether there should be one Christian political party. Most of us thought not, because there are so many honest differences, and the tactics of political campaigning were not thought very Christian, or constructive. This passage says that Christian relationships are characterized by light: by openness, humility, truth-telling, and repentance. The light shows up our mistakes; but it also cheers and cleanses us, and helps us see further. May we always trust God enough to choose that way.

* *Lord, we pray for politicians,*
  that they may be enabled to raise the level of debate,
  and for ourselves, that we may let through your light
  and make way for your kingdom.

TO THINK ABOUT

● How can Christians check the extent to which their political views and personal behaviour are coloured by their own background?

● What sort of things can they do to improve their vision?

FOR ACTION

Find two newspapers with opposing views. Choose the same story in both and carefully compare what they say (you may need to experiment with different kinds of story). If you find differences, consider them prayerfully, and see if there are any lessons for your own future awareness and behaviour.

ADVENT 3. Be ready to welcome Christ

Notes based on the Revised English Bible by
Jan Sutch Pickard

Jan Sutch Pickard is a writer and Editor of Connect, a Methodist magazine linking faith and action, and has lived in Nigeria, Notting Hill in London and New Mills in Derbyshire. She is a local preacher and member of the ecumenical Iona Community. At the time of writing, she has been designated as Vice President of the Methodist Conference 1996-7 (a duty which will have been discharged by the time these notes are used!).

A variety of people appear in the passages for this week: John the Baptist, a challenging voice in an unready world; Abraham, the perfect host; Sarah, laughing and afraid; Joseph, righteous and afraid; the people of Laodicea – lukewarm in their religious life. A wealth of images evoke the coming of Christ – like a thief in the night or a friend (or stranger) knocking on the door, counsel for the prosecution, or the one in need who receives a cup of water from our hands. The readings are not chronological. John challenges people to be ready for a Christ who is already a grown man; Joseph braces himself for the birth of baby Jesus. We move back and forth between the remote history of the Old Testament and prophecies of a later time. The message throughout is that God is moving among us, often unrecognized, unexpected. Are we ready to welcome Christ?

3rd Sunday in Advent, December 14   *Mark 1.1-8 **
Prepare the way

John the Baptist, a prophet living rough in the wilderness, in a place where few chose to go, was calling people to get ready for a great event, a coming, an advent. His hearers remembered a much older prophecy: 'Prepare the way for the Lord; clear a straight path for him.'

What kind of activity comes into your mind? Maybe people shovelling snow from the pavements somewhere in Northern Europe, or using a machete to clear a bush path in Africa. It could be a red carpet unrolled, while the sound of distant cheering gets nearer, or people in a shanty town putting down planks and stepping stones so that visitors can enter their homes dry-shod. These pictures of 'preparing the way' are about hard work and excited anticipation and welcome.

John called people to repentance – and that is hard work, too. They flocked to hear him. They listened eagerly to his words about 'the one who was to come'. Were they ready for the challenge of actually meeting Jesus, for the Holy Spirit working in their lives? Are we?

Hold in your mind a picture of people 'preparing the way'. Put yourself in that picture. Imagine it is Jesus coming towards you. Offer the 'Jesus prayer':

✳ *Jesus Christ, Son of the Living God,*
have mercy on me, a sinner.

Monday December 15   *2 Peter 3.8-14* *

The day of the Lord

What must the young Christians to whom it is written make of this letter? There is the terrifying description of 'the day of the Lord', a point in and beyond history when everything familiar will be destroyed or utterly changed, through purifying fire. Beyond the fire is the promise of 'a new heaven and a new earth'. This day will come when least expected 'like a thief', and yet those who believe in God need not only to be ready, 'at peace with him', but also to be looking forward to the day, working 'to hasten it on'.

Yet as soon as we start thinking about what we can do, we put it into the framework of human time: working days, timetables, weeks which start on Sunday, services exactly an hour long ... while 'the day of the Lord' exists in a different kind of time. Read verse 8 and reflect on it.

Read verse 9: what are we to make of the idea of God's patience? God is waiting for us to catch up. God is ready – are we?

✳ *Eternal God help us to keep time – your time;*
help us to respond to your patience, and to repent;
to recognize your different way of doing things
and to be ready for your day – whenever it may come.
   Amen

Through the fire

Unexpected visitors arrive. Is your house in a fit state to entertain them? I know that in ours there would probably be books and letters all over the dining table and a basket of ironing on the spare bed! But I hope that, in spite of the untidiness, they would feel warmly welcome. What, though, if we were having a family row, or did not want to open our home because we had something to hide? What about a different kind of unreadiness?

The prophecy describes God suddenly appearing in the Temple, where people believe they have been honouring him through worship. But their lives have given no honour to a God of justice. From sorcery to crimes against society – as specific as cheating a labourer of his wages – their lives have given the lie to their professions of faith. God's Spirit becomes the counsel for the prosecution. Respectable, religious people are in the dock, and the tough question is, 'Who can endure the day of his coming?'

Advent is traditionally a time when we think not just of hopeful, joyful expectation, but of judgment and repentance. For some, the encounter with the 'God of Justice' will be both a time of testing and of being painfully changed for the better, of being 'refined in the fire.'

Can you recall a 'time of trial' in your life? Did you have to re-examine your actions, your beliefs, your priorities? Did it feel like passing through fire? In what way were you changed? Did it bring you closer to God?

✳ *Spirit of God, refining fire, burn in our hearts;*
  destroy all that is unworthy and make us fit
  to bear your love for a world in need. Amen

A cup of cold water

Fill a glass with cold fresh water and use it to reflect on your reading.

'I was ready for that,' said the hiker, down off the fells, downing a pint at the pub.*(Sip water)*

The marathon runner said nothing, as she took the soft drink thrust into her hands, and drank it as she ran on; but clearly she needed it. *(Sip water)*

'Thank you,' whispered the survivor of an accident, with a cup of strong sweet tea in hands still shaking. *(Sip water)*

Think of others in need. the hunger and thirst of the refugee child lost on the road from Rwanda to Zaire, the old woman, victim of 'ethnic cleansing', sitting at the roadside in what was Yugoslavia? *(Sip water)*

When all is lost – home, family, self-respect, hope – what is the value of a cup of water? It is beyond price. It meets not only a real, urgent, physical need, but is also a recognition of the person who feels that need, a sign of worth, a symbol of love and care. *(Sip water)*

When have you been able to offer such a sign? It may have been literally a glass of water, or a cup of tea, or some other kind of hospitality. It may have been listening, or a word of appreciation or affirmation, or giving money or time.

* *Sip the water again, and **thank God for these opportunities and for the times when you have been offered something as precious as 'a cup of cold water'.***

Thursday December 18   Genesis 18.1-15

God, our Guest

This is a story of the expected and the unexpected, of common sense and mystery. Abraham and Sarah offered hospitality to strangers – but any other nomadic family would have done the same. Survival in the desert depends on people's willingness to share the shade and fresh water of an oasis, or maybe precious water supplies that have been carried for miles, or simply a cup of sweet, refreshing mint tea.

The same goes for the sharing of food – freshly baked bread and meat from the flock. Making sure that the feet of guests are washed is another way of caring within that culture – which we meet again in John's Gospel. So the welcome Abraham and Sarah offer is an expected one.

But these guests are more than they seem. They know that Sarah (who baked the bread but stayed out of sight) is childless. They know of the years of longing for a child. And in spite of her incredulous laughter they know that longing will be fulfilled and with it many other hopes ('is anything impossible for the Lord?').

The story begins 'The Lord appeared to Abraham' but God appears here in three persons. If you have seen the Orthodox monk Rublev's icon of 'the hospitality of Abraham' you will remember that, while it shows the guests around the table with the terebinth tree in the background, it is also a picture of the Trinity – three different aspects of God, inextricably linked like strands in a Celtic knot.

The story of Abraham and Sarah – of down-to-earth hospitality and of meeting God in strangers – is interwoven with our own: 'for many have entertained angels unawares'.

✴ *Remember a time when you opened your home, and were blessed by those who came to visit.*

Friday December 19   *Matthew 1.18-25*

God with us

Yesterday's story from Genesis prefigures several stories around the birth of Christ. Here Joseph, usually portrayed like Abraham as an old man, learns that Mary is going to have a baby. For Joseph, prospective husband and 'a man of principle' the whole thing is very confusing. Best to call the marriage off, to save shame and confusion for himself and Mary. This is no laughing matter. But he, too, encounters an angel. It is a terrifying experience. Notice how often, in the Gospel accounts of the Nativity, angels – messengers of God – have to preface their announcements, to Zechariah, the shepherds etc. with 'Do not be afraid'. Clearly these are not the small, sweet tinsel-over-one-ear angels of school nativity plays!

'It is through the Holy Spirit that she has conceived'. God's intervention enables an ordinary (and yet wonderful) human experience in extraordinary circumstances. The announcement that Isaac would be born met near-incredulity, as well as joy, giving two reasons for the child of Abraham and Sarah's old age to be called Isaac, meaning 'laughter'.

The child born into the marriage (brought back from breaking point) of Joseph and Mary is called Jesus, by his human family. He has another name which carries a meaning for all confused, frightened, incredulous, wondering humanity: 'Immanuel – God with us.'

✴ *Listen to our laughter, Lord,*
hard-edged or happy, helpless or close to tears;
help us to understand how serious your purpose
and how joyful your message.
Confront our fears and help us to see, through our tears,
that you are with us. Amen

A knock on the door

Is Christmas a time to be snug and smug? Today the postman may knock with a parcel; cards through the letter-box may bring greetings, with pictures of robins, kittens, holly wreaths, mail-coaches and cosy firesides – as well as religious subjects. Some will contain circular letters. Often the message is a comfortable one, of happy families, success in various areas of life.

The Christians in Laodicea had been congratulating themselves 'How rich I am ... I have everything I want.' But the message they receive is neither cosy nor congratulatory: 'Though you do not realize it you are pitiful ... poor, blind, and naked ... you are neither cold nor hot ... I will spit you out.' What kind of a greeting is this? And yet there is also an invitation – to look for what is of real worth: 'gold refined in the fire' – the fires of suffering – for 'all whom I love I reprove and discipline.'

It is with this invitation that Christ is knocking on their door – is knocking on our door – the invitation to open our hearts, to change, to live in God's way. This invitation includes the promise that God will be our guest: 'If anyone hears my voice and opens the door, I will come in and he and I will eat together.'

✳ *Come Lord, be our guest, find your way among us ...*
Earth, your former home, still is where we meet you;
Therefore we greet you, Christ, our God alone.

From 'Love from Below' (Wild Goose Publications, 1989)
copyright © 1989 WGRG, Iona Community,
Pearce Institute, Glasgow, G51 3UU, Scotland.
Used by permission

TO THINK ABOUT

Reflect on your experience of two very different kinds of blessing: a) of hospitality, given and received; b) of 'times of testing', challenges that you have met, ways you feel you have been 'refined in the fire'.

FOR ACTION

Is there some way that your Christmas celebrations can include hospitality and / or openness to strangers and outsiders? Find out what your church or community is doing.

LIGHT OF THE WORLD

Notes based on the Revised English Bible by
Bernard Thorogood

Starting his ministry in the South Pacific islands, Bernard Thorogood spent 18 years mainly in teaching students for ordination. Then followed ten years as General Secretary of the London Missionary Society which became the Council for World Mission. He was then called to be General Secretary of the United Reformed Church in the UK. In 1992, on retirement, he moved with his Australian wife to Sydney where he is a minister in the Uniting Church of Australia.

At every eucharist we remember the events of the passion of Jesus, and the cross stands centrally in most of our church buildings. Just once in the year we remember the birth, and celebrate it with joy. So it is good to recall all the detail of the birth stories in Matthew and Luke. But both the birth and the death are part of the whole – the whole event of Jesus, the Word become flesh. That life is also part of the whole – the entire caring, healing, saving presence of God in the world from its beginning to its ending. In these readings we are drawn to the light which is God's love, shining in a birth and spreading to the whole of humanity.

4th Sunday in Advent, December 21   *Luke 2.1-7* *
Spotlight on Bethlehem

How careful Luke was to write down the historical moment. He was not retelling a myth or a legend from the distant past. It was recent history. A great emperor had been on the throne and all the provinces did his bidding, for Roman law had force behind it.

The place also is named, with its tradition. It was not a great town but not insignificant either, for it held strongly to that name from the past, David the poet king. The tribal memories were strong; water from the well at Bethlehem was precious (2 Samuel 23.15-17). But Luke did not draw out the parallels from the scriptures; his eyes were fixed on the new light.

So the tired couple came to Bethlehem and found scant

hospitality and there the baby was born. It was at one moment of time and in one spot on the globe. However many generations turn it into greeting cards, and however many theologians meditate on the depth of meaning, we all come back to a date and a place. God is in the real world.

✳ *God, lover of the world,*
you have set us in this place and this day.
May this place be blessed
and this day be full of your life and love.

Monday December 22   *Luke 2.8-20* *

Messengers of the Light

What excitement there is in this passage. Ordinary people were stirred, mystified, overcome at the event in Bethlehem, and then they praised God for it all. For they knew that they had touched the wonder of the eternal.

We note that it was the song of the angels which brought this dazzling light into the minds of the shepherds; it was not something which they had dreamed up or thought out for themselves. All the people of Bethlehem were possible witnesses, but they did not stir from bed. No doubt there were wise and religious people among them, but they had no awareness that the greatest wonder was on their doorstep.

Someone had to be told. The message came to the shepherds and they were prepared to take it seriously. We have to be told. The great gift of God is not something which we reach by wisdom or logic; it has to be told to us. We are all indebted to those who told us of the goodness of God. So every Christmas we tell the story, and share it if we can with someone for whom it is news.

✳ *Wake us up, dazzling God,*
when our hearts and minds are asleep,
to see the amazing gift of love, Jesus, born to be king.
We praise you for what we have seen
and heard of your coming.

Tuesday December 23   *Titus 3.4-7* *

A new day dawns

In this little letter Paul was writing to his 'true-born son in the faith' whom he had left in Crete to take care of the infant church there. No doubt it was a tough assignment. Paul could not resist the old saying about the people of Crete (1.12); their bad reputation made their conversion even more remarkable.

In our short passage Paul rejoices in the power of the gospel, God's living word to change us. In Jesus the 'kindness and generosity of God our Saviour dawned upon the world' so that it was a new day. Christian writers have always loved the connection of the Son being born and the sun rising. It was truly a new day for our human family, and it came as a gift of God's love. We did not earn it, nor manufacture it, nor deduce it, nor imagine it. Jesus was born because God acted in love towards a world in need. Paul calls that 'generosity', or overflowing grace.

That is why Christmas is for gifts and giving.

* *Beyond all your gifts of beauty and delight, you give yourself,*
  great God of Bethlehem.
  May we give you ourselves, in response to your light,
  and live in your bright day.

Christmas Eve, December 24   *Hebrews 1.1-6 **

He is the shining one

In many and varied ways God spoke. In every human family where there was love between parents and children, in every act of self-sacrifice for others, in the astonishing beauty of every flower, in the endless stars, in the nimble fingers of weavers and carpenters, in the artists and thinkers of Greece and the farmers and writers of China – God spoke in every age and every place. The voice of God is in the creation. The image of God is in the whole family. Wherever there is goodness there is the imprint of God, whatever the name or the creed.

But now, as we read this page and as we prepare our homes for Christmas, God speaks in his Son. We can mistake the voice that comes in the universal life of the world; we may see only the violence and not the beauty of nature. But now the word is spoken as plainly as is possible, in a human life. It is as though the glow of light is focused so brightly that all may see it. He is the radiance, the shining one (verse 3).

In the verses about the angels, the writer is pointing to Jesus as in God and with God and one with God, far above all others.

* *Silent night, holy night!*
  Son of God, O how bright
  Love is smiling from thy face!

289

Christmas Day, December 25   *John 1.10-14 **

A day for wonder

It is a day for thanksgiving. Jesus has come into the world. It is a day for remembrance. Jesus came, as we all come, from a mother, whose pain and love cherished a new life. It is a day for wonder. God was there, God almighty, God eternal. And it is a family day. A family stands for ever at the heart of God's revelation.

* *The Father's wisdom willed it so,*
The Son's obedience knew no No,
Both wills were in one stature:
And as that wisdom hath decreed,
The Word was now made flesh indeed,
And took on Him our nature.
What comfort by Him do we win,
Who made Himself the price of sin,
To make us heirs of glory!
To see this Babe, all innocence,
A martyr born in our defence –
Can man forget this story?   *Ben Jonson 1573-1637*

Friday December 26   *Isaiah 49.8-13 **

A light to the nations

The theme of light as the saving gift of God was not a new one when the Gospel writers used it, for it comes many times in the Old Testament. Here the prophet at the time of the exile in Babylon preaches the amazing word that little Israel, so beaten and so insignificant in the world, is called to be a light to the nations.

The people are given a new chance and the fallen city of Jerusalem is to be restored, but this is not so that they can then build a wall around it and pretend that they are the only people to be blessed. The light which God gives to one people is for sharing.

We see this reaching fulfilment in the way the apostles shared the news of Jesus. From that closed room, where they hid in fear of the Jews, they moved out to the whole Roman world, so that people

Paper cut by students from the Nanjing Theological Seminary
Use by permission of China Christian Council, Nanjing Office.

from far off could enter into the freedom of the Spirit. We are able to rejoice in Christ only because others have shared the light with us.

✱ *May the light of Bethlehem be spread across the world*
and may we, in our turn, be bearers of the light.
Give us courage, Lord of the church.

Saturday December 27   *Isaiah 60.19-22*

Light for the journey

At this point in the book of Isaiah we meet a poet, a visionary, who saw beyond the present to the hope of blessing in the future. He knew that Israel would never become a great military power to threaten Egypt or Syria, but he believed totally that God had chosen this small nation to find greatness in its faith. So it would stand as a world focus.

Through this firm faith and obedience, it would have the light of God shining in it, so that even sun and moon become unnecessary (verse 19). This vision was picked up by John in Revelation 21.23 where we read of the new Jerusalem, a city which does not need the sun or moon to shine on it, for the glory of God gives it light, and its lamp is the Lamb.

In our world which is so often dark with cruelty, division and fear, can we ever see this city of light? I believe it is beyond our sight but not beyond our faith. God's work in creation and in salvation will be fulfilled, for God is the beginning and the ending of history. We are in the middle, somewhere on the way. We have enough light to travel by but full glory only comes at the end.

✱ *Shine today, God of light, on my path and in my heart.*

1st Sunday after Christmas, December 28   *John 8.12-20*

Light of the world

'I am the light of the world,' said Jesus. What did he mean and is it true? The light here is the knowledge of God and the nature of God shared with humanity. The darkness of the world is the constant failure of humankind to live in love and forgiveness and peace and honesty. Our daily news is full of darkness. The light is the God-ness of life, the God-way and the God-truth, which is the purpose of creation. Jesus brings that light in his life. Where he is, God's light is. That is the claim.

292

The question, 'Is it true?' has to be answered by each one of us. It is like the Caesarea Philippi question, 'Who do you say I am?' There are no proofs which will convince everyone, only witnesses who can say, 'Yes, it is true for me.' It is a matter of faith and trust and experience. Jesus is the light of the world for us because he alone makes plain the nature of God as self-sacrificing love. That is the heart of creation; it is how we find the way, truth and life. There are many today, like the Pharisees in these verses, who want some outside proof of such a claim. But the only way of knowing the light is to let it shine in our hearts and minds.

✳ *Eternal light, shine on us*
and on all the darkness of our world.

Monday December 29   *Ephesians 5.6-20*

Live in the light

There is both light and darkness in our lives, so are we all just grey? Are we for ever to be mediocre, uncertain people shifting this way and that as the wind blows? This passage written to new Christians is a call to recognize the light and the darkness for what they are and to make a decisive choice.

Can we live in the light? There are compromises all around us, for we are part of the nation's life and that is not all light. We may be caught up in business struggles which are not light at all. The word for us is that as we live in this grey world, we are to be points of light, never surrendering to the dark. The whole church of God is called to such a mission, to be the place of light. We can only be humble and say that the church has not always been like that and ask for forgiveness. The people in Ephesus were not so different and Paul called them to a life of daily prayer and praise, so that they might reflect the light of God in their city.

In verse 14 we find one of the earliest Christian hymns, to be sung at sunrise. In your hymnbook there are probably morning hymns with this same message.

✳ *Christ, whose glory fills the skies,*
Christ, the true, the only Light,
Sun of righteousness, arise,
*   Triumph o'er the shades of night.*
Day-spring from on high be near;
Day-star, in my heart appear.   *Charles Wesley 1707-88*

Shining in the darkest places

You shine like stars in a dark world. Yes, the world has been a dark place for many people through the centuries and it may be dark for you. We remember that when Jesus was on the cross, there was darkness over the land; he knew what it is like for the light to go out. It is still true that in the darkness the light shines.

At night the pavements along the Calcutta streets were home for thousands, wrapped in blankets, around little smoking fires or washing children in the gutter. Throughout the night friends from the cathedral and the Salvation Army were on patrol, with practical help for the hungry and the sick. Never cynical, never despairing, never impatient, they were like stars in the dark.

The darkest night of our century has been war. It has shattered life for millions, destroyed what is precious, wasted youth and defied God. But even there we have seen the stars. Love and loyalty in a concentration camp, steadfastness under the bombs.

So let your light shine. You – and we hear Jesus addressing us – are called to be light for this world.

✳ *In thought and word and action*
  may my life reflect your light, Lord Jesus.

City of light

The Bible begins with a garden and ends with a city. It is like human history, for we are now in an age of great cities. I write this in Australia, which is a vast land with the population concentrated in the cities around the coast. Cities began in China perhaps 5000 years ago, and developed in India, Egypt and Mexico soon after that. A city is a wonderful human organism, complex, technical, full of human energy, often ugly, sometimes handsome, a showplace for skill. But where is God? Is God in that little gothic church huddled beneath the tower blocks?

John in Revelation thought of the city of Rome and could not see God there. It seemed to have deposed God from the throne of life and put Caesar in God's place. He thought of Jerusalem but could see no glory of God there, for it was reduced to rubble by the fighting in AD70. He saw a new Jerusalem, God's gift and glory. In this city there is no temple, no Holy of Holies, for God is reflected in the entire life of the people. The light is God's presence. This, says John, is to be the end of the human adventure, with that full integration of our being and God's being which the Genesis garden was created to be.

✷ *At the end of the year, eternal God,*
we look back and we look forward.
Help us now to see ahead your leading light.
Lead us towards your city of light, for Christ's sake.

TO THINK ABOUT

- As you reflect on this Christmas season, what have been the highlights? Can you write them down and see the grace of God in them?
- The light of God comes in many ways through many lives. Are there people of other cultures and other faiths for whom you would give thanks?
- It is sometimes hard to see the true light of God when there are many competing voices around us. What helps us to know the true light from the false?

FOR ACTION

At the end of the year it is good to remember all the people who have helped us along the way and have made faith come alive for us. Is there someone on that list who would value a letter?

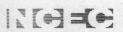

The editor and publisher express their thanks for permission to use many copyright items. Every effort has been made to trace copyright owners, but if any rights have been inadvertently overlooked, the necessary amendments will be made in subsequent editions.

Acknowledgments and abbreviations

We are grateful for permission to quote from the following versions of the Bible:

AV   Authorized Version

GNB   Good News Bible (The Bible Societies/Collins Publishers) – Old Testament © American Bible Society 1976; New Testament © American Bible Society 1966, 1971, 1976

NEB   The New English Bible (Oxford and Cambridge University Presses) © 1970

NIV   The Holy Bible, New International Version (Hodder & Stoughton) © 1973, 1978, 1984 by International Bible Society, Anglicisation © 1979,1984,1989

NJB   New Jerusalem Bible (Darton, Longman and Todd Ltd) © 1989

NRSV   New Revised Standard Version © 1989, Division of Christian Education of the National Council of Churches of Christ in the United States of America

REB   The Revised English Bible (Oxford and Cambridge University Presses) © 1989

* Readings from the Joint Liturgical Lectionary (JLG2)

Errata 1996

May 5 – paragraph 2, line 2 – *'marital infidelity'*.

May 7 – paragraph 3 – The end of Philippine Martial Law regime in *1985* ...'

September 23 paragraph 1 – 'N.B. Today it would take only four jumbo jets to remove all Christians from *Jerusalem.*'